LEARNING DIFFERENCE

LEARNING DIFFERENCE

Race and Schooling in the
Multiracial Metropolis

ANNEGRET DANIELA STAIGER

STANFORD UNIVERSITY PRESS
Stanford, California 2006

Stanford University Press
Stanford, California

Printed in the United States of America on acid-free, archival-quality paper

Library of Congress Cataloging-in-Publication Data

Staiger, Annegret Daniela.
    Learning difference : race and schooling in the multiracial metropolis / Annegret Daniela Staiger.
        p.   cm.
    Includes bibliographical references and index.
    ISBN-13: 978-0-8047-5315-9 (cloth : alk. paper)
    ISBN-13: 978-0-8047-5316-6 (pbk. : alk. paper)
    1. Race awareness in adolescence—California.   2. Identity (Psychology) in youth—California.
3. Ethnic attitudes—California.   I. Title.
    BF724.3.R3S73   2006
    305.235089′009794—dc22   2006009402

Typeset by G&S Typesetters in 10/13.5 Minion

CONTENTS

TABLE AND FIGURES

ACKNOWLEDGMENTS

Many people helped me through the long process of writing this book. My primary debt is to the students, teachers, counselors, and parents at Roosevelt High School in Newtown, who endured my questions and the nosiness that comes with being an ethnographer. I want to thank two students in particular, Nate and Karen. Nate, a latecomer to the exclusive club of the gifted, helped me recognize the contradictions of the program, and Karen opened herself up to me, confided her insights and troubles, and became a friend and ally.

The people who helped me to conceptualize this project in its early stages are Mayfair Yang, Don Brown, Connie McNeeley, and Sandy Robertson, my dissertation advisers at UC Santa Barbara. I cannot overstate the role of Mary Hancock as my dissertation chair. Her concrete suggestions, theoretical insights, and her empathetic advice were a luxury not all graduate students get to enjoy.

Several research grants and fellowships helped me to complete this project. A fellowship to the Minority Discourse Seminar from the Humanities Research Institute at the University of California, Irvine, in 1993–94 gave me the financial means to jump start my field research, and maybe more important, provided the opportunity to develop my project theoretically through close interaction with junior and senior scholars. I am particularly grateful for feedback from George Sanchez, Leo Chavez, Lisbeth Haas, and Melvin Oliver, and to Michael Omi and Neil Gotanda for introducing me to Critical Race Theory.

Many of my colleagues and friends at Clarkson University have given me generous support. Lew Hinchman has helped me to better recognize the political impact of my work; Dan Bradburd has generously shared his experience as an anthropologist, and Sheila Weiss has been a source of support and reminded me of the particular challenges women scholars from nonacademic families experience. Jerry Gravander, as dean of the School of Liberal Arts, supported this work by giving me a course release in Fall 2004 and a teaching schedule that allowed me to dedicate a large chunk of time to writing. My junior colleagues have always been friends and never competitors. I particularly thank Rick Welsh, who was a source of inspiration and available for last-minute editorial emergencies, and Laura Ettinger, who shared with me the experience of publishing a first book.

Several others helped me come to grips with my analytical hunches and apply them to my work. Faye Harrison generously read and commented on the chapter on giftedness; Joe Feagin reminded me about the long and pervasive history of White domination in the United States, and helped to make me aware of the misconceptions implicit in the term "black-white binary." Jim Holstein, editor of the journal *Social Problems*, helped me to extend the theoretical purchase of racial formation. John Hartigan commented on my work on masculinity and race, and Greg Dimitriadis advised me about publishing.

Last but not least, I want to thank my friends and family. First and foremost, I thank Christian Zlolniski, whose gentle criticism has become indispensable to me; also Anne Mamary, who made me aware of the parallels between racism and sexism; Soledad Vieitez, who shared with me many of the challenges of seeing a project through to completion; and Joan Weston, who showed me how rich ethnographic descriptions can increase the impact of academic writing.

My family could not escape the ups and downs of the research and writing process. Maybe more than what books and fellow academics could teach me, Bakari has had an impact on my growing understanding of race in the United States that cannot be overstated. His life experience has given him a recognition of suffering from which I continue to learn; our son, Meshach, with his unexplainably happy constitution and his Nike philosophy, "Just do it," has shown me that no one is too young to be an inspiration. Finally, I want to thank my family in Germany for patiently awaiting the moment when they can put a book on the coffee table whose author has the same name they do.

In finishing this book, I have come to realize that I often present a harsh picture of Roosevelt High School and its people. I want to remind the reader, however, that my intention is not to show people's fallibility, but rather to illustrate some of the ways in which people can become racialized in everyday life. Too often, this racialization carries over into our everyday interactions and helps to shield us from responsibility to fellow human beings.

One person I want to acknowledge in particular is the Roosevelt High School teacher who dedicated his life to the fight against racism and intolerance, and against the damages and pitfalls of what W.E.B. Du Bois called double consciousness. His everyday heroism touched me deeply, and his premature death was a huge loss. I hope that this book contributes to what he worked for so tirelessly as a teacher.

Annegret Daniela Staiger
Potsdam, New York
July 2006

LEARNING DIFFERENCE

1

INTRODUCTION [1]

> Black and Asian together, you know, it's like, united, like all mens [. . .], I mean like all ethnic mens, [. . .] we don't like Mexicans right now. You know, Mexican used to be in a lot of trouble with us.
>
> —*Joey and Mickey, Cambodian American students at Roosevelt High School*
>
> The image right here is, "If you're White, you're in the gifted program."[. . .] If you're in there, you can have a good education. If you are in regular, you're right where everybody's at. [. . .] I think they should have a good education for everybody. [. . .] I sort of got a second-rate education.
>
> —*José, Mexican American student*
>
> We all get along here. We don't have the racial problems that other schools have. [An hour earlier, a serious fight had broken out between Cambodians and African Americans against Latinos at the other end of the school yard.]
>
> —*Melissa and Kathy, two White students*

Roosevelt High School (RHS) was located on a busy, four-lane street and surrounded by a bustling commercial neighborhood.[2] The school was flanked by a public housing complex on one side and a gas station on the other. Across the street from Roosevelt High was an elementary school surrounded by a tall fence and with an asphalt playground without trees or grassy areas. The neighborhood was dotted with small Cambodian, Vietnamese, and Mexican restaurants, auto repair shops, Filipino groceries, taco and burger stands, check-cashing places, and numerous churches. In contrast to this colorful but poor urban immigrant community, Roosevelt High, with its wrought-iron front gate, its art deco tiles, and its landscaped campus, had the air of a more affluent period.

Newtown—the city in which RHS was located—is one of the most ethnically and racially diverse cities in the country. This diversity was concentrated in the neighborhoods from which Roosevelt High drew its students. Unlike many other U.S. schools in similar urban environments, it was an integrated school. According to the school district's official statistics, Roosevelt High had about equal percentages of African Americans, Whites, and Asians, and a smaller number of Latinos and Filipinos. But these official racial categories did not reflect the richness of RHS's cultural mosaic. In addition to a medley of European immigrants, who moved to the area at the turn of the century, it included Asian Americans whose ancestors were from China, Korea, and Japan, as well as more recent immigrants from Vietnam, Laos, Burma, Thailand, and Cambodia. Another large segment of the residents were Latinos whose parents or grandparents were born in Mexico, and others who were from Central and South America. Besides a sizable number of African American students, many of whom had moved to Newtown from the

South during World War II, Newtown also had a small but visible community of Pacific Islanders.

One of the most prominent topics in conversations among educators, Newtown's politicians, the local media, and Newtowners generally was youth, violence, and gangs. Since the mid-1980s, gang fights between and among Asians and Latinos had taken numerous lives, and conflicts between African American and Latino gangs, as well as between Latinos and Pacific Islanders, seemed to be daily news. White supremacist activities in and around the city had shaken some Newtowners' belief that violence was safely contained on the crowded, poorer eastside. The result was a siege mentality among many residents, and even adults often were afraid to walk on the street at night. With almost daily reports of youth violence, from race-based pencil stabbings to drive-by shootings, schools were a prime location for these conflicts.

Amidst such tensions, Roosevelt High was widely regarded as a haven of peace and racial tolerance. Roosevelt High celebrated its racial and ethnic diversity with an annual multicultural fair, where students sold homemade food, performed traditional dances, staged ethnic fashion shows, and engaged in numerous other activities that represented their culture. The school had also replaced the institution of Homecoming Queen—a source of racial conflict in the past—with "Cultural Ambassadors," whose task was to represent the variety of cultures on campus. Moreover, RHS sponsored events during the Black and Latino History Months, provided a course on multiculturalism, and had been a trendsetter for the school district by spearheading a weekend camp where students could explore diversity issues.

So RHS had a reputation for racial harmony; and it also had a reputation for academic excellence: it was recognized by the state as an outstanding school for its ambitious academic programs, and its graduates were regularly accepted by Ivy League colleges.

Yet despite this public image of multicultural harmony, racial integration, and academic success, Roosevelt High was also the site of deep racial fault lines. Mickey and Joey, the two Cambodian students quoted in the epigraph, articulated an identity of "Blacks and Asians together" as "ethnic mens" against their rivals, "Mexicans." For José, a Mexican American senior, race determined what kinds of courses and programs one was likely to be enrolled in. In contrast, for two White seniors, Melissa and Kathy—apparently unaware of the groundswell of tensions building among Latinos, African Americans, and Cambodians—race was "not a problem." They felt that everybody got along and that racial segregation and isolation were not as prevalent at RHS as in other schools. These commentaries, chosen because they represented student voices from different educational tiers, reflect their varied experiences.³

On the one hand, they illustrate how some students internalized racial categories, although by lumping "Blacks and Asians" together as "ethnic mens" against Latinos, they drew boundaries counterintuitive to common sense notions of race. Others challenged the idea that RHS was an integrated school and criticized RHS for not giving them equal access to educational opportunities. Still others agreed with the public image of the school as racially tolerant and peaceful, although their judgment was called into question by the racial conflict about to erupt with an intensity and scope not witnessed at Roosevelt High in several decades.

How could students attending the same school differ so much in their perception of the school? Why did they embrace racial identities as means to draw lines between friend and foe, when the school was supposedly a showcase of racial harmony?

LEARNING RACIAL DIFFERENCES IN SCHOOL

This book explores how race is formed and how it functions within an intensely multiethnic and multiracial urban high school. It is an ethnography of a school in metropolitan California, in a city where Whites have become a minority and where there is no longer a clear racial majority. Focusing on a school celebrated for its academic success and racial integration in an inner-city area, it is a story about the adolescents whose lives coalesce at this site, and about the political and institutional forces to which they are subjected. It shows how their lives are influenced by conflicts over busing and anti-immigrant politics in the city, by desegregation policies in the school, and by racial politics among their peers. They encounter racial struggles that victimize some, privilege others, and leave others relatively untouched. But it is also the story of how adolescents adopt, generate, and sometimes manipulate racial meanings to accomplish certain goals and navigate through the social minefield of the school.

Thus it is a study that links an analysis of racial structures of schooling with an analysis of how adolescents themselves actively shape racial meanings and structures to maneuver through this space. They do so by managing relationships with other racialized groups, both individually and collectively.⁴ Examining the interplay between institutional structures, representation, and social agency in the domains that constitute adolescent lives at school helps us to recognize both the dependence and the independence of the domains in which race is formed. It shows how racialization emerges and is maintained in the links between individuals and social structures. This helps us to comprehend the mechanics of race in the making.

In the post–civil rights era, and increasingly since the mid-1990s, the new concept of multiculturalism has gained broad acceptance as a means to acknowledge and celebrate diversity. However, celebrations of multiculturalism often go hand in hand with a discourse on color-blindness along the lines: since we are integrated, we don't need to talk about race any more.[5] This view is representative of the broader argument that the civil rights struggle and the policy changes it brought about abolished racism and that race has lost its significance.[6] In fact, a broad segment of the population believes that racial inequality is a matter of the past and has been successfully overcome.[7] Yet, rather than signaling the end of discrimination, color-blindness often works to implicitly endorse White privilege by denying the structural racism to which people of color are widely subjected.[8]

A number of studies have focused on how schools themselves are racializing institutions. Rather than using students' own cultural backgrounds or their particular "learning styles" to explain their behavior in school,[9] these studies have described the ways in which schools socialize their students into adopting specific racialized identities, whether through discipline regimes, course assignment, or intentional or unintentional institutional neglect.[10] This book goes further in examining the connections between students and schooling. Departing from the contrast between a school's public image and students' experiences, it examines the means and criteria by which a school produces this public image and compares it with students' experiences. It asks whose voice is represented and who benefits and loses through such a public representation, and it explores the structures that underlie these representations. In the process, this study illustrates the subtle but pervasive racializing effects of an apparently integrated and multicultural institution in the post–civil rights era.

The organizational structure of RHS and its labeling of students illustrates that color-blind labels such as "gifted" and "at risk" function as code words for race. I argue that organizational reforms meant to desegregate schools serve a public image of excellence and integration, but do so by effectively keeping students of different races apart. Besides producing unequal access to education, these reform structures contribute to a sense of second-class citizenship among those who are excluded, while bolstering Whites' "sincere fictions" about others and about themselves, particularly the belief that their educational privileges are based on merit alone.[11] The language of color-blind educational labels becomes the very means by which racial exclusion is perpetuated and through which a dialogue over inequalities is effectively silenced.[12]

Masked by this current of color-blindness is a new surge of race consciousness, evident for example in the White backlash against affirmative action as reverse discrimination victimizing Whites,[13] in the continuing resistance to busing,[14] or in the everyday language and interactions of people when they are not on guard, as illustrated by many of the protagonists of this study. Thus if color-blind labels racialize students and subject them to a pernicious justification of exclusion and difference, it is also through explicit racial discourse among students and teachers that racialization takes place.

We have learned from studies of race and schooling that students engage in a variety of strategies to deal with the status ascribed to them.[15] What we know less about is how adolescents engage in racializing practices and discourses in their interactions with each other, and how they do so collectively. There are some possible reasons for this absence. Studying identities has become a central focus for understanding race in recent years. Identity, after all, provides a rationale for action and thus can explain why people do what they do.[16] However—possibly out of a concern to not reproduce stereotypes—research on identity has often focused on individuals as if they were independently functioning entities within a broader social sphere.[17] Such a focus helps to challenge the notion of identity categories as monolithic blocks and provides a safeguard against wholesale racial generalizations. But identities are also informed by collectives and form collectives. Like-minded people joining hands can mobilize spontaneous or concerted action.[18] Such dynamics are most visible in social movements, or in large-scale conflicts, where people willingly sacrifice their individual needs and desires for the collective cause. But they occur on every level of association, from gangs to football teams, and from religious organizations to ethnic and national groups.

Forms of collective identification are illustrated in students' narratives about an event referred to by many at RHS as "the school riot." Their stories show how they invoke racialized identities to interpret events and motives, thus using race as a strategic means to position themselves and to interpret the existing power structures and hierarchies. Students use race as a tool with which it is "good to think,"[19] because it provides a shorthand for identifying motives, interest groups, and antagonists, and it generates fictions that easily catch on. In fact, in students' conflict-ridden relationships with each other, race and racial identity are used as a political means to draw boundaries, profess allegiances, and create alliances, where race functions as both a stigma and a form of social capital based on one's access to networks of people.[20] Adolescents' narratives revealed them to be political actors with an analytical acumen for assessing and forming power structures, recognizing and establishing hierarchies, and ascribing political motives to larger collective identities. All the while, though, these collective racial identities remained fluid and subject to political maneuvering and sometimes did not match racial categories used elsewhere.

The cultural fabric of Roosevelt High School and its multiple possible alliances, boundaries, and exclusions was complex. Within that context my study examines how students engaged in racializing practices and to what extent these differed from practices occurring in other contexts. I found that adolescents did not merely replicate how race was practiced in the media or other domains, but instead rearticulated new notions of racial identity, with which they sometimes acquired tangible benefits. The picture emerging from students' notions of race and racial identity points to a bipolar continuum with blackness on one end and whiteness on the other. Other racial identities are aligned along this continuum. But it also shows that racial configurations in one context do not necessarily map onto racial configurations in other contexts. This illustrates a degree of independence between the different domains of race-making and underscores our need to understand race as a multi-sited process.

RACE AND SCHOOLS IN THE MULTIRACIAL CITY

The demographic composition of American cities and schools has become increasingly multiethnic and multiracial.[21] The 2000 census revealed that among schoolchildren Whites had dropped to 60 percent nationwide, while the number of Latinos and Asians had grown steadily throughout the 1990s. This trend is most prevalent in metropolitan areas. In such a rapidly changing social landscape, identities shift, new alliances are forged, and positions of dominance and power are renegotiated. The arrival of new immigrants might intensify these processes. Newcomers might adopt existing racial categories, as nineteenth-century Irish immigrants did by learning to identify themselves as White and as recent second-generation West Indians did by learning to identify themselves as Black.[22] Increasingly, the argument has been made that Asian Americans are becoming honorary Whites and that both Latinos and Asians are seen and see themselves as White.[23]

Schools are sites where adolescents undergo a formative period of their identity formation and socialization.[24] The institution lays the foundations—or as scholars of social reproduction say, lays the tracks—for their future social and professional lives.[25] Schools are also sites where the state, through such means as curriculum design, obligatory attendance, testing, and issuing credentials, exerts a direct influence on young people and their parents. In their mandate to provide equal access to education for everyone, schools are a prime instrument for democracy and social progress. They are often described as great "social equalizers" and are one of the few institutions with the potential to bring people from different racial, ethnic, and class backgrounds into intimate and sustained contact with each other, although since the mid-1980s a trend toward segregation has returned.[26]

An integrated school such as Roosevelt High mixes youth from different parts of the city and with different racial and ethnic backgrounds who otherwise have little opportunity to interact. Such a desegregated school provides a "hyperspace" that transcends the residential and social segregation endemic in so many American cities and in society generally. Through this, desegregated schools are spaces of possibility that have the potential to undo racial inequality.[27] Such a vision was embraced in the Supreme Court's *Brown v. Board of Education* ruling, which provided a starting point for legally dismantling segregation. Schools themselves, then, are testing grounds for our society's dedication to the ideal of a nation "indivisible, with justice and liberty for all."

But if schools provide an important testing ground for the nation's commitment to social justice and racial equality, students and their relations with each other also provide a glimpse into the future of our society. Yet few studies exist that help us understand these increasingly multiracial institutions. More often, studies of race and schools have focused on youth of color, or on the relationship between Whites and students of color.[28] But as the United States and other countries become more multiracial and the Whites are becoming a minority in many urban areas, research needs to take account of those dynamics. Approaching identity as a relational construct requires us to take account of this demographic shift as it changes the fabric of racial identity and of racial formation more generally. It also requires a theoretical framework that goes beyond the Black-and-White or minority-majority conceptualizations of race relations and focuses instead on the emerging dynamics of a multiracial environment.[29] While dealing with these complexities, we also need to remain vigilant about the role of power and White privilege,[30] and about the extent to which entrenched structures of White domination and Black stigma set the stage for emerging racial formations.[31]

This ethnographic study of Roosevelt High promises to teach us important lessons. It shows us how adolescents are engulfed by racial and racist policies in the city and their school and how elusive racial equity is for many, even though their school's public image makes it appear otherwise. Racist outcomes are reproduced by educators and administrators who for the most part consider themselves to be racially progressive and liberal, and through policies that have grown out of school integration efforts. It illustrates how White privilege is reproduced and internalized, even where Whites have become a minority; but it also shows how White privilege has been challenged. In this multiracial space youth renegotiate racial identities, alliances, and hierarchies and thereby also actively participate in the making of their own racial identities. This is evident in their comments about their racial positions within the school and reflected in their analyses of a serious racial confrontation that occurred there; it is also evident in the ways they carve out spaces of racialized masculinities. Instead of being only the victims of racializing structures, they also creatively use and manipulate them.

LOOKING FOR RACE

Walking across the campus of Roosevelt High School during one of my first visits, it occurred to me that a good way to start my project would be to map the pattern of racial distributions in the school yard. Walking out into the school yard, I noticed teenagers clustered in groups on the lawns and crowded in front of the Mc-Donald's and Pizza Hut franchises. They sat on benches with their sweethearts, or moved busily from one group to another. What I saw was an ocean of faces; what I could not discern was any pattern of racial distribution that I had anticipated.

As I moved through the crowd, I passed a White boy squatting on one of the concrete pathways, eating his lunch. He was staring at a wall, which was about three feet in front of him, his back turned to the bustling school yard. I felt suddenly very uncomfortable clutching my notepad and pencil; I felt hopelessly out of place, visible, different, and conscious of my movements. Should I sit down on one of the benches? But maybe the benches were already claimed by someone and I would be regarded as an intruder. Would I be less noticeable in the denser crowd in the cafeteria? But it seemed impossible to find an empty seat there. No matter where I went, I felt thousands of eyes examining me, assessing me, recognizing that I, like the White boy facing the wall, was out of place.

Suddenly a White girl asked me curiously whether I was a researcher and what I was sketching. I felt my posture straightening; the pencil and notebook in my hand became my credentials; all of a sudden my mapping effort was legitimate. I felt welcomed, acknowledged. I had a role now, something that I could use to identify myself as a grown up, a researcher. I passed again by the White boy squatting on the path and found myself looking at him, now with pity and detachment, as I no longer identified with him.

This rapid shift from a self-conscious identification with a social outcast to a self-assured identity with a role to play puzzled me. How could I go through such intense yet opposite emotions in such a short period of time? Was this just the fear of entering a new and unfamiliar site, or was it that I identified with the boy facing the wall and with the welcoming girl who had asked me about my sketching because they were White, in a place where Whites were a minority? Why was I, then a woman in her early thirties, unable to distance myself from the youngsters I had set out to study? Why did I slip back into my own school persona, letting my own high school experience take over? In retrospect, this moment exemplifies for me the terror of the crowded space that is the school. It lost its frightening character as soon as I was identified as inhabiting a legitimate role and as soon as I had—at least imaginary—allies.

Many scholars of adolescence and schools have written about the importance of schools as sites of identity formation, as places where we undergo a thorough socialization of our racial and gender identities through institutional structures and peer cultures.[32] This process is not unproblematic. In fact, schools can be oppressive environments, as I was reminded during my initial walk across the campus. We are reminded about this too when we read descriptions of urban schools as dumping grounds for poor and minority children. Such schools, often crowded, dilapidated, and with inadequate resources, send a loud message to students about their status in society.[33] But we also are reminded of schools as oppressive environments when we hear of tragic incidents, such as the 1999 shooting at Columbine High School in Colorado, where two students killed many of their classmates to avenge years of ostracism and then turned the guns on themselves.[34]

Schools forge identities and rule hierarchically by organizing the relationships between adolescents and the institution. In school, adolescents become students who are supposed to learn and internalize a school identity. This is accomplished not only in the classroom, but also through the display of school colors, in athletics and in other activities that are designed to inculcate in students a sense of institutional allegiance.[35] Schools are also densely populated environments, where everyone is always in plain sight of peers, teachers, administrators, and other adults. Schools are places where vigilant surveillance and a system of norming and ranking generates a student identity that internalizes the school's discipline regime.[36] But adolescents are not only under pressure to identify with the school. They also are under pressure to identify with a peer group, because nonaffiliation and isolation can lead to ostracism, and even social death or physical harm.

In the course of the next eighteen months I would learn just how central race was in structuring adolescents' identities at RHS; it was reflected in the acuity with which students identified racialized space, groups, and motives. Observing and interviewing students and school adults, participating in their daily lives, and developing fledgling friendships with some of them taught me how students maneuvered through this space, sometimes using race as a vehicle.

Contrary to common sense notions of race as a category based on how people "look," it was only after I had learned the language of race as it existed at Roosevelt High, and only after I had learned from others the contours of racial boundaries relevant in this context, that I was able to see the racial geography of the space my-self. My experience of race in the United States up to this point had been limited to the campus of the University of California, in Santa Barbara, which was pre-dominantly White. That environment had not provided me with a racial "com-mon sense" useful at Roosevelt High School. Rather, the head-on collisions I would have with school personnel, as well as with some students, made me keenly aware of how inappropriate my racial common sense was in this setting, and that I needed to adjust or learn a new way of looking at things.

It was not because I went in color-blind that I did not see race. In fact, I went in deliberately looking for race. But I needed to learn the local meaning of race before I could see its spatial pattern. Thus, just as RHS transformed the adolescents that entered its gates, it also changed me. It forced me to confront my own whiteness and taught me to be on guard in a way I had not been before.

LEARNING ABOUT RACE — CONCEPTUAL TOOLS AND RESEARCH ISSUES

Before unpacking how race is formed at school, the basic concepts of race and identity need to be clarified. In our everyday language, we often speak of race and racial identity as if they were monolithic, universal, and unchanging phenomena. We speak as if race could be identified by how one "looks," an ascribed category, imposed on us by others on the basis of specific phenotypical characteristics such as skin color, hair, or facial features. While I could guess which racial identities were in use at Roosevelt High based on a generalized racial order in American so-ciety, this was not enough to understand the racial geography of the school. As an outsider, I first had to acquire the local lens for seeing race. My experience pro-vides one example of the localized production of racial constructions and their rel-ative instability and reveals the ongoing, multilayered, and often contradictory processes by which racial meanings and structures emerge.[37] Understanding the formation of race as an evolving and multilayered process requires us to under-stand race as a relational construct, which necessitates an outside or "other" from which to demarcate an inside or self.[38] It requires us to recognize race as formed both through structures and through meanings, and it requires us to look not for inventories of racial identities, but for the mechanisms by which people's identity is created.

Amanda Lewis describes schools as institutions where race is produced as a so-cial category "both through implicit and explicit lessons and through school prac-tices."[39] But these mechanisms are not limited to the classroom and the relation-ships between teachers and students. They are also rooted in urban politics, residential segregation, and school desegregation policies. Most important, they emerge in relations between people, and between groups of people, as they unfold in the school yard, the hallways, and the neighborhood.

Racial Formation

Racial formation theory provides a useful framework for understanding and studying the making of race. It argues that race is a fluid category that is continuously "created, inhabited, transformed, and destroyed" and understands race as the product of multiple construction sites—or "racial projects"—that occur simultaneously and on many different levels. Such racial projects, Michael Omi and Howard Winant say, are always historically anchored and together form an interrelated web that constitutes racial formation. Racial projects are therefore the "building blocks" of racial formation, specific to a particular historical and societal context.[40] Based on concrete and tangible structures, they inform ideas of race and thus contribute to the bigger and seemingly coherent picture of racial differences. Racial projects always consist of both structure and meaning and link the two: as structures emerge and influence meanings, meanings evolve and in turn shape social structures. Understanding racial projects as building blocks of racial formation recognizes race as the product of relations between people and groups of people, but also situates those relations within embedded structures, organizations, and discourses. By breaking down the complex phenomenon of race-making into specific, tangible racial projects, the theory of racial formation helps to identify the different construction sites of race and the links between them.

The concept of racial formation has commonly been used to explain macro-structural political and historical phenomena between the state and social movements.[41] While macro-structural phenomena such as residential segregation, differential wealth accumulation, and other forms of institutional racism have a pervasive impact on our lives, they are often experienced as indirect, intangible, or elusive. Instead, it is at the micro level, in our interactions with local institutions and people—individually and as groups—that racial structures become tangible and racial meanings are enacted.[42] At the micro level, racial projects operate through "common sense" and the way we "notice" race as our preconceived notions of a racialized social structure provide the basis for interpreting racial meanings.[43]

School, one of the central institutions of the modern state for shaping individual identities,[44] provides an ideal site for studying the link between the macro-structural perspective of the state expressed in its educational and racial policies and the micro-structural perspective of students and school adults' lives and interactions. The school site allows us to both witness and understand the experiences and interactions of people in the institutional and larger political context where they operate and to which they have to accommodate. But in addition to the constraints that these schools put on their students, they show us the diversity of representations, interpretations, and forms of agency that students and adults engage in, and which in turn feed back to the structural organization of schools.

One central problem of social theory is to explain the links between the micro level of personal experiences, ideas, and beliefs and the macro level of politics and social structures.[45] In this case study, racial formation theory provides a conceptual framework that shows the interdependence of both in the constant remaking and shifting of what race means and what race is: it oscillates between its manifestations in the state and its institutions on the one hand, and in the micro-level domains of representations and individual identities on the other.

Thus this book shows one way in which racial formation theory can contribute to empirically grounded, ethnographic studies of race. However, while racial formation theory helps to pose questions and provide conceptual tools for disentangling the processes by which race is formed, it is less applicable in arenas of social relations that are more removed from the direct access of the state. In the phenomena of school yard politics and masculinities, where the role of the state is indirect, the conceptual framework of racial formation is more difficult to apply. This area between micro-level personal experiences and macro-level projects of the state is the realm of collective identities, where common experiences are articulated and discourses formed.

Identity and Difference

The idea of identity formation as a boundary maintenance process[46] provides a theoretical basis for understanding this meso level[47] of social theorizing, the fertile ground where individuals develop collective identities and strategies in response to concrete racial projects. But identity formation may be better understood as identification. Learning differences involves one's ability to identify and differentiate. To identify oneself with a group or an identity means to differentiate oneself from something that is "other."[48]

Identity therefore always requires an outside that defines an inside, or a "we." At the basis of identity is the question of how to conceptualize the self. But rather than being already there with a stable core, or being created in isolation, identity emerges through relations and within discourse.[49] Just as relations with people provide the interactions through which we identify and differentiate ourselves, discourse provides the language and common sense with which we explain ourselves and the world. Both are the means by which we perform what we want to portray, and both also operate through the material conditions and relations that shape our everyday lives. But while identities can be self-determined, they can also be imposed from the outside, or "ascribed." This occurs when people are identified by others on the basis of criteria they might or might not want to adopt, and that often subject them to forms of discrimination. Racialized identities, by the very fact that they are based on phenotypical characteristics, are to a significant extent ascribed.

A focus on racial identity based on identification and difference explores race-making processes at the level of collective identities: as urban communities, as students tracked in particular educational programs, as friends of close-knit groups, as employees in the workplace, or as members of a racial group. Locating identity-making processes within collective frames of reference allows racial identification to be perceived not only as a question of personal experience, but also as a collective action, a reaction, and a perception of people who identify with each other.

By exploring racial identity as a critical facet of personhood, the collective aspect of identity-making has sometimes been overlooked in favor of a perspective that treats identity as a largely individualistic project. Such an approach, however, runs the risk of missing what is maybe the most critical dimension of identity-making: its embeddedness in relations with others. Identity as identification requires an ongoing assessment of who is inside and outside, and an ongoing dialogue with those with whom one identifies. However, contrary to the notion of race as a homogenizing force and homogeneous category, a focus on the collective aspects of identity-making also reveals the heterogeneities, contradictions, and negotiations that mark racialized identities, even if they emerge as a unifying front against a specified other. Last but not least, by recognizing that identities can be mobilizing forces that generate discourse and collective action, collective identities can also lead to transforming social processes and counter emerging or existing structures of racial exclusion.[50] Understanding race as an ongoing and multi-sited project requires us to untangle the different domains that coalesce in the institution and setting of the school: urban space and neighborhood politics, classrooms and educational programs, peer groups, masculine performances of dominance, and the larger discourses and policies of race operating at the state or national level. These different domains often reinforce each other; this is most evident in the accumulation of privileges associated with whiteness, where interlocking spheres produce a mirage of normality.[51] But they also can work at cross purposes. Dominant racialized identities in one context can be subordinated identities in another, as I will show in the analysis of the school yard hierarchy that challenged and even reversed the educational hierarchy. Specific racial projects thus create spheres with their own, individual power dynamic.

The study of racializing processes in a multiracial context also raises important questions about the location and formation of racial fault lines that go beyond the more familiar context of majority-versus-minority or White-versus-Black relations. Several racial groups in Newtown were not clearly identifiable as either minority or majority, and unexpected interracial alliances challenged more familiar conflicts. Thus Roosevelt High provides a view into a new era of racial formation.

Masculinity

If the social category of race is often compared to gender, its parallels to masculinity are even stronger. Both race and masculinity are linked to power and to the body. Bob Connell's contention that masculinity is "fundamentally linked to power, organized for domination, and resistant to change because of power relations"[52] can be equally applied to race. Both masculinity and race justify domination through difference, and both are based on differences that are thought of as embodied. Yet both embodied identities are abstractions that cannot be mapped neatly onto biological or individual boundaries. Finally, both masculinity and race have been theorized as performance.[53] Thus, rather than being essentialized categories in and of themselves, they are relational identities that depend for their enactment on an audience, and to be conceptualized they depend on a repertoire of discursive and bodily practices. But if race and masculinity bear similarities, what is the relationship between the two?

In this book, I look at manhood as an important staging arena of race. Performances of masculinity are used to demarcate identities, to draw boundaries between inside and outside, and to establish hierarchies.[54] This makes masculinity a prime arena in which to recognize power relations in the making. As we have learned from studies of masculinities, the ways by which men—and sometimes women—demonstrate that they are masculine, in control of situations, and "good at being a man" depend on their cultural milieu and social position.[55] Both create opportunities and pose certain demands, as they also impose restrictions on how manhood can be performed.[56] This means that specific racial formations and the different projects within such formations generate their own forms of masculinities.

If race shapes expressions of masculinity, masculinity also shapes racial structures and meanings. Masculinities, in their relational construction and collective identifications, and in their ability to portray or synthesize a collective consciousness, open a window onto the tangible aspects of collective identity in the making. The boundary-making processes that Frederik Barth has described for the development of ethnicity—which, he argues, are intensified in times of contact, not isolation[57]—are particularly visible in the competition over racialized masculinities that different groups of students carve out for themselves. Thus, how students create, live, and use masculinity, individually and collectively, is another racial project that links structure and meaning.

Schooling practices such as achievement-based ranking, sports, and discipline regimes,[58] as well as intense competition among peers, make schools function as both agents and settings that generate a "marketplace of masculinities."[59] The pressure on masculine performance as a form of dominance is intensified in urban schools, where structural forces such as poverty, segregation, tracking, and other institutional pressures provide few niches for more playful assertions of dominance, and where "respect" is a most precious resource of masculinity, carefully guarded and fervently defended.[60] Following the racial politics in the school yard to the micropolitics of cultivating relational masculinities in peer groups illustrates how racial identity provides a foundation for cultivating a specific code of masculinity and how competing masculinities actively contribute to the structure and meaning of racial identities.

DOING ETHNOGRAPHY AT RHS

While race is a collective issue, it is also an intensely personal one. When I began my fieldwork at RHS, I had not previously thought of myself as White. Coming to California as a graduate student from Germany several years earlier, I thought of "White Americans" as a research topic, not a description of my own identity. By the time I left RHS, this had changed: I had become aware of my whiteness and had learned that it opened some doors—some very comforting and convenient, others that I did not want to be opened—and closed others. I had also found that while my German accent did not make me an outsider with Whites, it made me a person of somewhat ambiguous whiteness for others, noticeable when my interlocutors offered to explain the U.S. racial order, and evident in their probing pauses.

I learned that my biracial child and occasional meal of black-eyed peas and yams gave me, in the eyes of some, an honorary "Black fictive kinship."[61] This became evident once when an African American student told me that she had seen me with my son. "So you're down with us," she said; "why didn't you tell us that?" I had not made public this aspect of my personal life in the school environment because it seemed not necessary and too transparent a means to try to gain acceptance with African American students. Having a biracial child does not automatically mean that I am a nonracist person, but it might have signaled a degree of familiarity, comfort, and exposure to African American culture.

I started conducting fieldwork at RHS as a relative newcomer to the American racial order. But I was even more of a newcomer to American high schools, which

I had never seen from the inside. So when I found out that schools wanted volunteers, I thought this would be a good way to get a first exposure. To my surprise, wherever I offered my help, no one knew quite what to do with me. If schools were so strapped for resources, why would nobody accept my offer to work for free? I came to realize later that school administrators did not readily trust someone who was neither a parent nor a future teacher. After explaining to one principal that I wanted to become a volunteer because I planned to do research in schools, he told me that he did not like people who came with "ulterior motives." His fear of outsiders gaining entry into the institution was precipitated by a public meeting at his school, in which students had criticized him for not addressing racist practices, an event that might have contributed eventually to his demotion. His fear was representative of many schools and their administrators, who, terrified by negative publicity, kept a vigilant eye on anyone who could spoil their public image.

Between waiting to become a volunteer and later waiting to get the school district's permission to conduct research, I participated in activities all over the city to get a better understanding of American youth and schools. I attended city and community events of many sorts: a human relations camp for youth sponsored by the city; a manhood/womanhood training workshop for African American youth organized by a former member of the Black Panther Party; school board meetings; and neighborhood meetings against busing. I found my way to numerous city-sponsored youth conferences where I listened to discussions of how to improve race relations; I attended church services, picked up trash with Latinas and their children in police-sponsored neighborhood clean-ups, and ate hot dogs with them afterward; I worked for gang prevention services, and I tutored Southeast Asian teenagers at a local cultural center. Later on, with my financial support dwindling rapidly, I worked as a substitute teacher in the area, and a few times also at RHS itself. This allowed me to compare Roosevelt with other schools and opened up the perspective of teachers.

By the time I received permission to conduct research, I had come to know the city and some of its neighborhoods from a number of angles. During the next eighteen months, I would go to the school every day, or every other day. The principal of RHS, Mr. Brown, was welcoming and supportive and gave me much leeway to move around the school and attend classes and other school activities. In the first few months, I visited a wide range of classrooms and hung out in the school yard, attended sports games, cultural performances, and the school's interracial parent committee, and had lunch in one of the burger joints in the adjacent mall frequented by many RHS students. Gradually I came to know the school campus, its people, and its spaces—its classrooms, offices, and detention halls—as well as its hierarchy of educational programs.

After several months of attending a cross section of classes and activities, I selected four different groups of friends to study who were representative of the racial composition of the different educational programs. These friendship groups usually hung out together in the school yard and sometimes met outside of school. I accompanied at least one student from each peer group through an entire school day and spent many hours in their classes. During those times, I observed their daily routine, engaged in classroom teamwork, joined their friendship groups during breaks, and watched their interaction with their classmates and with their teachers and other school adults. I also conducted open-ended interviews, lasting from half an hour to two hours, with five to eight members of these peer groups, which I taped and later transcribed. In total I interviewed about sixty-five students: forty-five males and twenty females. With sixteen of them I conducted follow-ups, which usually took place one-on-one, but sometimes friends or other people joined us. The interviews were loosely structured, containing a set of standard questions about their socioeconomic background, their residence, their family life, and the educational program they were enrolled in. I also asked about stereotypes associated with their own and other racial groups.

I was often surprised by the frankness with which young women and men shared their views with me. It seemed that they not only enjoyed the interviews as a break from the regular school day, but also enjoyed taking on the "expert" role for a change, and talking themselves rather than being talked to. It is their insights and astute observations that helped me understand the complexity of racial formation.

In addition to the more formal interviews, I talked to a wide cross section of students and school adults to gain broader information with which to evaluate the material provided by the peer groups and to gain a better sense of more widely circulating racial discourses. These additional conversations were with students recommended to me by teachers and administrators for their leadership qualities or for their outspokenness and students I came to know during classes or school-sponsored events. When possible, I spoke with larger groups of students, such as student government, student clubs, entire classes, and peer groups. I also conducted interviews with five key administrators and ten teachers and engaged in numerous casual conversations with students, teachers, administrators, counselors, security personnel, and other school staff throughout the course of my participant observation.

While I carefully recorded all of these planned observations and scheduled interviews daily, it was often the haphazard events, unexpected reactions, silences and evasions, and occasional hostilities that provided glimpses of race in the making.

CHAPTER OVERVIEW

Chapter Two describes the urban context of Roosevelt High School and the larger racial geography of the city: how Newtown became one of the most diverse cities in the country, yet remained as racially segregated as many other American cities. In addition to racial fault lines drawn on the basis of whiteness, wealth, and residence, there were others emerging between Latinos and Cambodians based on gang conflict, and between Latinos and Whites based on the divisive political anti-immigrant rhetoric of Proposition 187. This proposition, strongly supported by former California governor Pete Wilson in his reelection campaign, was based on the idea that undocumented immigrants were a drain on the California economy. It proposed that undocumented immigrants be denied social services such as pre-natal care, health care, and education. In this urban environment, racial tensions were widespread, and schools were often at the center of such tensions: from arguments over busing, unequal access to resources, multicultural education, and bilingual classes to gangs and declining property values. All the more surprising was that a school like Roosevelt High, located in the heart of the urban center, was able to steer clear of many of these conflicts.

As I explain in Chapter Three, Roosevelt High's public image was impressive, but also misleading. Comparing two different educational reform programs, one geared to the gifted and the other to at-risk students, I describe how the school and the district's desegregation strategy played a central role in producing racial identities and racial inequalities. Examining how these programs were organized, how they presented a picture of integration and excellence to the wider public, and what kind of interactions they engendered among students and teachers, I show how they contributed to a widespread notion among students that being White was synonymous with being gifted, and being non-White was synonymous with being non-gifted. Thus, educational reform invented to overcome racial inequality became a tool for perpetuating racial inequality.

In Chapter Four, I look at the ways in which students themselves negotiated and created racial identities and constructed racial hierarchies. Examining what had become referred to as the "race riot" at RHS, I examine the emergence of racial coalitions, exclusions, and dominations. I compare the events during the riot with students' insights about the event and their observations about race relations more broadly. This comparison shows that within the structural landscape of race in which they were placed, students also actively produced their own systems of racial order, which reversed the educational hierarchy of race. In this order, White students become the marked, and Black students become the unmarked, while

Latinos and Cambodians positioned themselves along a continuum between Black and White.

Given the prominent role students assigned to males in their interpretation of the events of "the riot" and its causes, I take a closer look in Chapter Five at race and masculinity. Both forms of identities are organized around dominance and power. I ask how racial categories become masculinized, and how interracial alliances, dominations, and subordinations are worked out through masculinities. An intimate portrait of four peer groups shows how each cultivated an ethos of masculinity that created a space in which to establish dominance over others it considered critical. This reveals the creative agency adolescents develop to overcome positions of racial subordination in other contexts, and how masculine ethos can provide a niche in which to reinvent one's own place in the racial power structures. But one's place in the racial hierarchy also imposes limitations on what roles one can assume.

This book, then, provides insight into the mechanics of race-making in the multiracial metropolis in one institution, a school. Untangling the different threads of race-making at this site makes visible the interactions between the racial orders that emerge in different contexts. Racial meanings and structures intersect and evolve through the interplay between institutions, individuals, and groups, who are at once influenced by and influence and shape racial structures and meanings. Race operates as an axis of power: a dynamic force—readily available to the institution and those it serves—to organize people, distribute resources, mobilize action, create inclusion and exclusion, manipulate political outcomes, and provide a platform on which to perform masculinity.

The story of race-making as it unfolds at this urban site provides insights into the competing power relations that can unfold and coalesce in a multiracial space. But this story about the formation of racial identities in a multiracial institution is also a cautionary tale about how White privilege is perpetuated, even where Whites have become a minority, and even in the name of desegregation. And finally, by showing how racial differences and identities are made, it shows that these differences are not always antagonistic, but also can provide the basis for interracial alliances at odds with race relations at the level of the community, the city, or the state.

NEWTOWN, ITS COMMUNITIES,
AND ROOSEVELT HIGH SCHOOL

POLITICAL MOBILIZATION AGAINST BUSING

In November 1994, a letter from a westside resident published in a small neighborhood newspaper sounded an alarm about deteriorating schools in the neighborhood:

> At the elementary level, and because of shere [sic] numbers, teaching has to be slowed down to accommodate Limited English Proficient [LEP] children. [. . .] In addition to concerns about LEP children in regular classrooms, there is also significant concern about gang participation, violence, and the abusive negative behavior exhibited by many inner-city children towards our children. [. . .] Why do foreign illegal immigrants have more rights than Americans because of the color of their skin?

Surprised by the language in the letter, I decided to attend the meeting that a group of westside parents had organized at a local residence. Searching for the right street and address in the quiet residential area, I noticed the careful landscaping that surrounded the well-kept, single-family residences in the neighborhood. Mrs. Ramirez, the host, who had also organized the meeting, cordially invited me into the comfortable living room of her spacious ranch house. Several people were already there and were engaged in lively discussions.

Most of the people in the living room were all White, except for two Mexican American women. Most were parents who had children in Newtown schools. They were enraged about a report that Newtown students ranked only in the twentieth percentile statewide. This contrasted sharply with a neighboring city, which did not have busing and where students performed in the eightieth and ninetieth percentiles. What is more, comparable property there was valued twice as high as it was in this Newtown neighborhood. The main culprit, according to these parents, was the school district's busing system and the district's burden of illegal immigrants.

As the meeting progressed, speakers addressed a medley of issues about what they described as racial problems in and around the Newtown school district. The first invited speaker, a retired engineering professor, spoke about "the waste of bilingual education." Even worse, he charged, instead of letting teachers, parents, and principals make decisions about the content of the curriculum, the United States now let the Mexican government decide what students should learn. His audience applauded enthusiastically. Another woman voiced a concern others had mentioned earlier. She said she was tired of giving up all the "brain programs"—such as the magnet programs for gifted students—to the eastside, while the westside had to cope with all the problems of the eastside students, who were bused into their neighborhoods. One parent complained that because of a majority of Latinos in westside high schools, White girls had no chance anymore to become cheerleaders. Another woman was outraged that an eastside student, who had been found with a knife in school, was allowed to return to class after only three days of suspension.

Mrs. Ramirez, whom I later saw regularly at school board meetings and in parent activist groups, described herself as a Mexican American who was fed up with fellow Latinos who blamed the system rather than working their way up. She urged everyone in the room to express their frustration by attending local school board meetings and by speaking out against the "grave injustices." An aide to the district's councilman emphatically endorsed her call and said: "For too long, this voice has been silenced, because it was considered prejudiced, but now is the time to change that." He did not stray far from his boss, the councilman, who was quoted in the local newspaper as saying: "Any gang graffiti I see in West Newtown is, almost without exception, in close proximity to one of the middle schools with bused-in students." The meeting eventually lost focus and deteriorated into a broad onslaught against anything that was wrong with Newtown, including its colleges, where, one of the visitors charged, communist activities reminiscent of the 1960s had reemerged.

The meeting not only revealed the westsiders' deep racial and class-based resentment against eastsiders in regard to schools; it also signaled the westsiders' political and racialized mobilization on a platform of having become the victims of busing and of "foreign illegal immigrants" who were privileged because of "the color of their skin."

The political controversies over Newtown's school district policies exemplify a central dilemma of many urban school districts and the communities they serve. Following the landmark 1954 Supreme Court decision in *Brown v. Board of Education* and subsequent desegregation rulings, many school districts in the country were forced to establish racially balanced schools. Half a century after *Brown* and after decades of White flight, continued residential segregation, a retreat of the courts from desegregation rulings, and a growing population of Latinos, African Americans, and Asians, many schools continue to have a high degree of racial segregation.[1]

Meanwhile, many White and wealthier constituents continue to charge that busing threatens their rights and violates their interests and puts undue economic burden on them,[2] as was evident in the neighborhood meeting, where low school scores and busing were blamed for low property values. One core dilemma behind the conflict over busing remains the ongoing residential segregation and unequal distribution of wealth, which fuels the fight over limited resources.

This chapter examines the conflict between the city's eastside and westside by tracing Newtown's shifting spatial and political geography of race and its impact on schools and school policies. Using accounts from local newspapers and census statistics in addition to ethnographic observations, this chapter provides the background on how Newtown and its communities came to be defined spatially and racially. It uncovers the shifting strategies of residential segregation that created a racial divide between the eastside and the westside, but it also shows how racial fault lines in the city multiplied in the crowded eastside, where successive groups of immigrants were forced to share limited space and resources.

How this racialized space and its communities came to be reflects the shifting nature of the processes of racial formation in Newtown's history. Newtown's spatial racialization would require districtwide busing and other forms of desegregation, as it also set the stage for the social relations that developed in schools among students and teachers. Understanding urban space as an important arena in which racial struggles become manifest reveals an important link between the pressures and forces influencing urban school politics and race-making in schools.

NEWTOWN: EASTSIDE VERSUS WESTSIDE

Newtown was a city of several hundred thousand inhabitants. According to census figures, by 1990 about half of its population was White, about one-quarter was Latino, and about one-eighth was African American and Asian American. By 2000 the percentage of Whites had dropped to less than one-third of the city's popula-

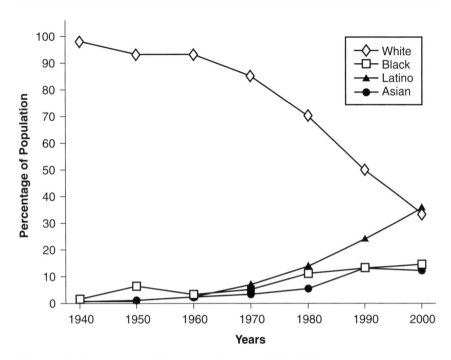

Figure 2.1 Demographic Changes in Newtown, 1940–2000.

tion, and the number of Latinos had grown to constitute more than one-third of Newtown's residents (see Figure 2.1).

Newtowners divided their city into eastside and westside. The eastside was characterized by intense crowding, poverty, and desolation. Dilapidated multi-family apartment buildings, often surrounded by barbed-wire fencing and secured with window bars, dominated the scene. Industrial wasteland, barricaded shops, and garbage-filled abandoned lots were located next to Mexican, Cambodian, and Filipino grocery shops and restaurants with colorful hand-painted advertisements and decorations. Against a backdrop of urban neglect and economic despair, storefront churches, check-cashing franchises, everyday garage sales, popsicle vendors on bicycles, grocery and produce trucks functioning as stores on wheels, and a lively movement of people in the streets created the image of a vibrant immigrant economy.

In contrast, the westside, inhabited by predominantly White, middle- and up-per-middle-class residents, was more characteristic of American suburbs. Here streets were wide and clean, and comfortably spaced single-family homes sat on plots of well-manicured lawns and landscaped front yards. In contrast to the busy streets and sidewalks bustling with people on the eastside, pedestrians were no-where to be found on the westside, except for the occasional resident walking her pet. Parks and golf courses produced an almost pastoral image, and modern shop-ping malls radiated a sense of prosperity and comfort.

Beginning in the mid-1980s, Newtown experienced an economic recession linked to larger structural changes in the region. Far-reaching fiscal reforms of the late 1970s—particularly Proposition 13, which had frozen property taxes at a very low rate—had reduced the funds available for urban infrastructure and services. Schools and youth were particularly hard hit. In the mid-1990s, these conditions escalated and city and schools faced serious problems. Unemployment was high, and crime rates soared, particularly juvenile delinquency and racially motivated school violence.

The racial climate in Newtown in 1994 was also profoundly affected by the con-troversial Proposition 187. The memories of the Los Angeles riot in 1992 were still fresh, the O. J. Simpson trial had been the hottest news topic for months, and dis-cussions of school vouchers dominated the debate over finding a remedy for the malaise of urban schools. It was also the year in which the controversial best-seller *The Bell Curve* tried to lend scientific support to the century-old myth of Blacks being intellectually inferior to other racial groups.

The economic decline of the city fueled the search for a scapegoat. Conflicts in-tensified along racial and ethnic lines. Schools, accountable to state legislation, lo-cal school boards, and different parent interest groups, became the contested grounds on which racial battles over dwindling resources were fought. In this racially charged climate, Roosevelt High School was widely celebrated as a re-markable example of integration and, as one counselor noted to me, "one of the best schools west of the Mississippi."

School politics took center stage in the struggle between the Latino, Asian, and Black eastside and the predominantly White westside. Almost half of the students in the district lived in the Roosevelt High School attendance area, an area located on the eastside but comprising less than one-fifth of the urban space. While east-side schools were crowded, most on the westside would have remained half-empty if not for the eastside children arriving in yellow school buses every morning. As the vignette earlier made clear, children from the eastside who were bused to the westside were often not welcomed by westsiders. One westside councilman was quoted in the newspaper as saying that "public safety in [our] community has de-teriorated, and [we] attribute much of that to the problems busing has brought into the community."

But despite busing one-fifth of all students from one side to the other, the schools in the city were not fully integrated by 1992. Almost half of the public schools were less than 20 percent White, and almost a quarter of the schools were less than 10 percent White. In contrast, many schools on the westside were more than 50 percent White.

A HISTORICAL SKETCH OF NEWTOWN

Newtown had been predominantly White until World War II. As one of the city's early African American residents remembers, there was little organized discrimination against the small group of African Americans who lived in Newtown in the 1930s. With their growing numbers in the following years, however, deed restrictions and other forms of residential segregation came into effect, creating a designated Black ghetto on the eastside. Expected to work in menial jobs, African Americans who had successful businesses had to fight allegations that they attracted criminal elements or sold liquor to under-age customers. As a result, they continuously battled threats that their businesses would be closed down. African American residents remember that when they ventured outside this ghetto they were often refused service and sometimes arrested on charges of rape or kidnapping. One resident remembered a time when the city offered convicted offenders a suspension of their sentence if they promised to move out of the county.

The first large influx of African Americans from the South occurred during World War II, when the city's war economy started to boom. Many African American families, excluded from parts of Newtown, moved into federally owned but segregated housing on the eastside. Nicknamed "Gorilla Housing," the city tore this housing complex down during the so-called urban renewal after the war—a euphemism for a period that witnessed the systematic destruction of urban African American communities all over the United States in the name of fighting urban blight[3]—and so effectively displaced many African American families from Newtown.

Residential segregation intensified during the postwar years. This was particularly evident in the new subdivisions with their modern tract homes, which had been made affordable through low mortgages and subsidized federal loans. However, deed restrictions prevented Blacks, Latinos, Asians, and Jews from becoming buyers. The latter, living in areas that were often redlined by banks, were unable to access similar loans, and gradually saw their property values decline. The postwar housing and loan policies and the new subdivisions that emerged through these policies not only gave Whites an unfair advantage in owning a house, but also produced urban entities that were able to retain city-sponsored services at discount prices, while being fiscally sheltered from the city.[4]

Despite the existence of federal desegregation legislation since 1948, residential segregation continued for many more decades in Newtown. According to a local African American newspaper, non-White residents moving into White neighborhoods often experienced terror and vandalism in addition to discrimination by real estate agents. Today the racialized conflict between the westside and the eastside is a stark reminder of this legacy and continues to set the stage for the political struggles in the city.

Residential segregation also affected Latinos. In the 1930s, Mexican communities emerged and began to coexist with Japanese and African American residents in one of the main thoroughfares on the eastside. Like African Americans, Mexicans were watched closely by police and restricted to "their" part of town. Adults and children alike had to undergo "Americanization programs," where Anglos decided that Mexicans should not only be taught English, but also adopt Anglo tastes, in order to become an acculturated labor force.[5]

The city early on was home to an active and tightly knit Mexican community of several thousand people, and Mexican cultural organizations staged celebrations in the local parks and the auditorium. But clashes with the Anglo population in nearby cities reminded Mexicans of their fragile political position in the city.

Despite the fact that Mexicans were effectively shut out of much of the local housing market, California's demand for cheap labor, in tandem with the rampant poverty in rural Mexico, produced a growing Mexican American community. Later, immigrants from war-torn Central American countries would increasingly make up a substantial percentage of Latinos in California. Panethnic Latino organizations emerged, and Latino activists became a noticeable voice in city politics.

Asian Americans also had become a large and diverse part of the Newtown population. Many of the Chinese, Japanese, Korean, and Filipino Americans in Newtown were third- and fourth-generation immigrants; in addition, Southeast Asians from Cambodia, Vietnam, Laos, and Thailand arrived in the 1970s and 1980s as refugees of the Vietnam War. Many of the Southeast Asian students at Roosevelt High were members of the "1.5 generation," meaning that they were born in Southeast Asia shortly before or during their escape from their war-torn countries. According to official statistics, the number of Cambodians was comparable to that of Filipino Americans, but Cambodians had a much higher visibility. Although this might have been because Filipinos were considered by many Newtowners to be more integrated, some city officials interpreted it as a sign that the actual number of Cambodians was two to three times what the census figures claimed. Southeast Asians generally, and Cambodians specifically, constituted some of the largest groups among Asian Americans at Roosevelt High School and played a significant role in the racial dynamics of the school.

The immigration of Cambodian refugees began in the mid- and late 1970s and continued through the late 1980s. The first Cambodian immigrants were well-educated urban elites who had recognized the imminent threat of the new regime and had the means to escape. By 1981 the population of Cambodians in Newtown had grown to 4,000. After the Pol Pot regime enacted executions on a mass scale, rural Cambodians also escaped in large numbers to refugee camps in Thailand and the Philippines. More Cambodians arrived in Newtown, and by the mid-1990s they constituted a substantial number of the city's Asian American population.

Many Cambodians who escaped the genocide of the Khmer Rouge suffered from post-traumatic stress syndrome. "Memories" of terror, blood baths, and torture were present even among students who were too young to remember. A fourteen-year-old girl, a tutor for elementary school children at a tutoring center, told me that she regularly saw headless ghosts in the tree behind her house. She explained that these were spirits of people who had been killed in Cambodia. After listening to her story, the two children she had been tutoring contributed their own horror stories about how their siblings or other relatives had been killed in front of their parents' eyes.

The war destroyed families, separating wives from husbands and parents from children. While many were eventually reunited, others were not. Lack of English-language skills among adults, their predominantly rural backgrounds, and psychological trauma made integration into American society difficult.[6] In order to supplement federal or state aid, many resorted to informal job networks where exploitation was rampant. In the general political climate of Proposition 187, newspapers reported regularly about the desolate living conditions of many Cambodians, often at the same time describing their dependence on welfare and their supposed unwillingness or inability to integrate into American culture.

Cambodian parents often depended on their English-speaking children to translate and manage crucial household matters. These circumstances undermined the traditional role of respect for elders and widened the gap between adults and their children, the latter often finding their parents hopelessly out of touch with life in the United States. Buddhist temples in Newtown helped the displaced Cambodians maintain a sense of community and retain practices and traditions that provided a counterpoint to life at the bottom of American society. Christian churches were also active in Cambodian communities, with Mormons being among the most aggressive proselytizers. One Cambodian student explained that his mother, who raised him and his little brothers by herself, had joined the Mormon Church because it offered her family badly needed support. She never abandoned Buddhism, though, and ultimately left the Mormon Church; her son decided to become a Buddhist monk for a year.

While their experience as recent refugees, poor and from war-torn countries, differed dramatically from the experiences of their third- and fourth-generation classmates from China, Japan, and Korea, it also differed from the experience of Mexican Americans and Central Americans in Newtown, who usually could not claim refugee status. As refugees of mass executions and reeducation camps under the Pol Pot regime, Cambodians received federal assistance and government support. Although the war from which they had fled and the political turmoil it had fostered were to a significant extent prompted by American interventions, the United States played the role of a savior by extending a helping hand (though sometimes with a clenched fist) and providing the possibility for a new life. Sometimes the city's support for Cambodians came at the expense of Mexican or other Latino immigrants. This was particularly evident when a Cambodian cultural center was built on the former site of a Mexican cultural center, or when the White director of the Cambodian cultural center ran against the single Latino candidate for a seat on the local school board.

While Cambodians generally were received with more welcoming arms than economic refugees from Mexico or political refugees from war-torn Latin America, the news media often compared them to African Americans because of their supposedly high number of teenage pregnancies, large percentage of female-headed households, and high rate of unemployment. Increasingly, resentment had been voiced in the local newspapers and elsewhere about local and state governments, which allegedly kept Cambodians dependent instead of teaching them American values of hard work and success.[7]

Cambodians in Newtown were concentrated in a small section of the eastside. There, in order to alleviate the housing crunch, the city had passed zoning ordinances in the early 1980s that allowed the construction of multi-unit apartment complexes on single-unit plots. The new zoning laws caused overcrowding and led to a severe lack of green space and insufficient parking. Windows of neighboring buildings were often only a few feet apart. Despite mounting protest from neighborhood groups, which feared that the new zoning codes were a recipe for a new ghetto, construction of these apartments moved rapidly. In the years that followed, crime rates for theft and aggravated assault grew twice as fast as in the city overall, while the proportion of residents living in poverty also increased dramatically. These new zoning codes, in conjunction with racial segregation from earlier eras, made the Roosevelt High School attendance area the neighborhood with the highest population density.

The spatial practices of changed zoning laws as the new de facto residential segregation eventually produced a profound polarization between the eastside and the westside, with the westside housing a suburban, predominantly White, middle-class population, while the eastside accommodated the large influx of new immigrants in an already decaying rental market and an economy that was rapidly disintegrating. With the economic decline and increasing crime rate of the late 1980s and 1990s, westsiders regarded the eastside as the "source of all evil"—as one westside resident was quoted in the local newspaper—that should best "rot in its own filth."

SEGREGATION, BUSING, AND THE DYNAMICS OF RACIAL FORMATION

Residential segregation and its legacy left a deep imprint on the racial geography of the city. With most African American, Latino, and later Cambodian newcomers relegated to the eastside, the eastside has remained the most segregated part of Newtown, where crowding, a decaying infrastructure, and urban neglect provide a stark contrast to the recently gentrified downtown and the middle-class residences on the westside. In fact, the newly redeveloped downtown area ended so abruptly that no more than one block separated high-end retailers from ghetto walls.

Busing had become a major issue dividing the eastside from the westside. Designed to rid the neighborhood of racial inequalities in access to education, busing itself was the result of a decade-long struggle to overcome the damage of segregated schools and segregated neighborhoods. Looking at the history of race and space in Newtown and its ebb and flow[8] reveals distinct stages. In the early twentieth century, when Newtown had only a very small community of people of color, there was no formal racial exclusion. Formal segregation became prominent only in the 1940s and 1950s, when more African Americans moved to the city. With the growing influx of Latinos, African Americans, and in the 1970s and 1980s Southeast Asians, combined with the new antidiscrimination laws in housing, zoning laws became the means by which ghetto walls were maintained. It was these segregated neighborhoods that produced segregated schools, which in turn gave rise to busing as a means to ameliorate the damages of segregation.

In this context, the busing and antibusing movements can be regarded as different but related projects or building blocks of racial formation. Busing was designed to distribute resources along racial lines as a means to overcome the racial inequality caused by decades of residential segregation. At the same time, busing eastside children to westside schools forged a new cultural meaning of whiteness among westside residents, who regarded themselves as the economic and educational victims of a forced influx of undesirable eastsiders. While westsiders racialized eastsiders as "foreign illegal immigrants" who had more rights "because of the color of their skin," westsiders framed themselves increasingly, though implicitly, as Whites, a movement that is reflected also in the larger national debate about "reverse discrimination."

Thus both the busing and the antibusing movements illustrate the dynamic nature of racial projects, where one emerges in response to another, which in turn generates a new form of racial mobilization and thus contributes to the ongoing process of racial formation.

YOUTH AND SCHOOLS IN NEWTOWN

Racial conflicts between African Americans, Latinos, and Asian Americans in schools had alarmed school and city officials. The reports of increasing violence culminated in a spectacle at one eastside high school, where a fight between Latinos and African Americans had broken out. A large front-page picture in the local newspaper showed a police helicopter landing on the school grounds, with about thirty police officers in riot gear taking over the school campus. The principal of the school—whose reputation had been badly damaged by the sensationalized newspaper coverage—was later forced to step down. Another well-publicized conflict in Newtown was what the news media called the "race war" between Latino and Southeast Asian gangs. In addition, conflicts between Latino and Black gangs had become more frequent; and White supremacists had launched an attack on Black churches and vowed to engage in a race war before they were intercepted by police.

Newtown city officials and schools responded with a frenzy of activity. Local colleges and universities sponsored regional youth meetings, where "student leaders," often hand-selected by administrators, were invited to work with teachers, social workers, administrators, and community representatives to develop solutions. City leaders brought together all youth-related organizations to find solutions to the crisis, and sometimes provided adolescents a chance to participate in related events.

The city-sponsored Gang Eradication Committee, for example, developed the idea of youth forums as mediation instruments for high schools. The police department offered Neighborhood Watch Programs and organized an initiative whereby selected students would convey information among fellow students, the school, and the police department itself. In addition, the police established a hotline for students to call if they suspected someone of bringing a gun to school.

ROOSEVELT HIGH SCHOOL

Roosevelt High School had long enjoyed its reputation as a high school without racial tensions. But it was not a school without a troubled past. Discrimination against minority students at RHS had been reported between the 1930s and the 1950s. But it was in the 1960s and 1970s, propelled by the Vietnam era, the civil rights movement, and the federal mandate to integrate, that relations between White and Black students had become explosive.

After an outbreak of racial tensions in 1967, Roosevelt High set up a race relations committee; parents and students met weekly to discuss school and community issues. This was meant to ease confrontation and facilitate communication between White and Black students and parents. In 1968, according to a local newspaper report, another long-lasting conflict emerged between Black and White students, after members of a sports team protested the mistreatment of a Black student who had broken up a fight. Police were called in and remained present until the end of the year.

The same local newspaper reported that tensions flared up again, a year later, after a leaflet circulated in the school agitating White students to unite against Blacks. This pamphlet and the hate meetings that it attempted to instigate led to fights between Black and White students. Police were called in, and White students were escorted home, while Black students were locked inside the school yard and not permitted to leave until all of the White students had left.

A community meeting of several hundred Black parents and students was held the same day at a local park. Black students recounted how they had been attacked by White students and fought back. Some brought up the idea of a Black boycott, not only at Roosevelt High School but citywide. Black parents organized to confront the school's administration and faculty and to demand an investigation of the event and the origin of the racist leaflet. They demanded fair treatment of their children by the Board of Education and resented the police presence on campus. They also requested greater involvement in school matters, more accountability by the school, and the right for students to form a Black student union and to engage in other forms of assembly. This was a critical demand because the school at that time had the ability to break up any group of Black students by calling it a conspiracy.

Following reports in the city's alternative newspaper, the polarization and confrontation between the Black and the White community had become clear. While White parents trusted the police to restore peace on the school grounds, Black parents felt their children were threatened by the police. According to this source, the Board of Education served primarily as a political extension of the White community.

After a number of relatively quiet years, racial conflict erupted again in the spring of 1972, taking many school administrators by surprise. The local newspaper quoted an administrator who would later assume a top position in the school district: "We were shocked. We thought that we had established a very good rapport with students and that we were building positive community relations." Roosevelt High School students requested a Black student union, which the administration denied. However, administrators did allow the formation of the Black History and Culture Club and began sponsoring race relations workshops in order to improve the climate on campus. In an early move toward multiculturalism, Roosevelt High named student Cultural Ambassadors, and in 1976 the school district decided to begin a magnet program for gifted students at Roosevelt High to integrate what had become the most racially segregated high school in Newtown.

SCHOOL FORTIFICATIONS

Schools have been described as near "total institutions."[9] As such, they are similar to prisons, hospitals, and the military, where inmates, patients, and soldiers eat, play, and sleep. Although schools are not as all-encompassing as prisons or mental hospitals, they share many characteristics of the latter. Students are under constant surveillance and subject to disciplinary practices, from dress codes to behavior and academic performance. Individual identities are repressed in order to instill a prescribed school identity, which involves academic pursuits as well as extra-curricular activities such as school sports and clubs. Through the constant reminder and presence of the school's institutional identity, students' identities are molded into an identification with the school.

If schools resemble prisons in function, they also more and more resemble prisons in form. The architectural layout of the school underscored its mission as a total institution. A large iron gate locked the main entrance of the school for most of the day. Only between 7:15 and 7:30 in the morning was the front entrance open, with its electronic billboard in the school colors of gold and brown and the school's towering image of a grizzly bear, the school mascot. At that time, under the close surveillance of the principal, staff, and police cars, several thousand students arriving by foot, car, and bus passed through the gate, while others were loaded onto buses parked in the street and driven to other schools. Then the gate was locked and not opened again until 2:40 in the afternoon, when the events were repeated in reverse. In addition, gates had been installed on the streets surrounding the school. These also remained closed during school hours to prevent through-traffic. A staffed watchtower at the side entrance provided additional surveillance and security.

Passing through the main entrance, one entered the quad, the main plaza around which the various school buildings were arranged. In the center of the quad were two flagpoles, one flying the American and the other the California state flag. The more pervasive symbols of identity, however, were the school colors, which were displayed on every aspect of physical and mental space: school walls, classrooms, floors, gyms, football fields and benches, sports arenas, flower beds, school awards and yearbooks, and school folders. Every Friday, many students and adults showed their school spirit by wearing gold and brown caps and sweatshirts with the school logo and school mascot embroidered on them. It seemed that only the twelve-foot fence around the school could contain the endless repetition of brown and gold.[10]

Once inside the building, a pungent scent of cleaning detergent mixed with a century of human perspiration greeted the visitor. The scent was particularly nauseating in the cafeteria, where thousands of breakfast and lunch meals were served that satisfied strict nutritional guidelines, although rarely aesthetic sensibilities or taste buds. Almost half of the students at RHS qualified for free or reduced-price lunch through Aid to Families with Dependent Children, but many rejected the dreadful food and flocked in large numbers to the pizza and burger franchises in the quad.

Students were required to be on time. Those who arrived after the first morning bell had to pass the guarded watchtower at the corner of the school and enter through a small but well-staffed side entrance. There school security checked for current student IDs, issued late passes, and sent the latecomers to a holding tank in the library, where they were retained for the first fifteen minutes of class. Latecomers had to clean up the quad area after lunch and serve a one-hour detention at the end of the day. Circumventing the checkpoint by climbing the tall fence was a welcome challenge in an all too predictable school day, but provided little chance of escaping the holding tank. Teachers had strict instructions to keep their doors locked for the first fifteen minutes of class, and staff issued detentions to anyone who was seen wandering about the school yard without an official pass. Or at least that was the rule.

After the first class period, students were granted a seven-minute "passing period" to get to their next class. This was barely enough time to hurry from one end of the sprawling campus to another. Little time was left for checking in with friends. Behind the quad and the old school buildings were a series of extensions: sports facilities, bungalows, science buildings, and JROTC, where gun-slinging drills reinforced the image of a fortified garrison.

While the spatial layout of the campus controlled the movement of students into and out of the school, dress and discipline codes established rules of conduct. Students were required to dress appropriately: no Los Angeles Raiders football paraphernalia was allowed, no belt buckles with initials, no baggy pants, no caps or anything else that could be identified as gang attire. Girls were not allowed to wear strapless tops or skirts too high above the knees. Violators were photographed and sent home to change, and their pictures were sent to the police for gang identification. Dogs had been recently added to the school police to intensify the search of students and lockers for guns and drugs.

Such surveillance and control did not remain unchallenged by students, who invented new ways and symbols to undermine the administration's control. While Raiders jackets were prohibited because they signaled an alliance with gangs, many—particularly Asian students—wore blue Dallas Cowboys jackets to signal their allegiance to another gang that students claimed was the dominant gang on the campus. The gold-colored school walls provided an ideal canvas for gang and taggers' graffiti. In turn, graffiti provided full-time employment for a school painter, whose main job was to restore the school's color scheme of gold and brown over the graffiti scribblings. Of course, the fresh walls just provided another clean canvas for a new cycle of claiming territory, leaving messages, and signaling standoffs and threats between rival groups, before the space was eventually claimed again by the school.

A first round of claiming usually consisted of a gang name or initials, and a list of gang members' names. If a rival gang crossed out the gang name and the names of the gang members, it was usually interpreted as a threat of imminent attack. Concerned about the safety of its students, the administration dealt quickly with such graffiti. I was impressed by the rapidity with which the wall space was claimed consecutively by the school painter and rival gangs after Senior Night at an amusement park. The school painter had just finished repainting a large part of the exterior walls the night before, but by 6:00 the next morning, most of the wall space was again covered with the gang initials of the Asian Posse.

Bathrooms were another, more secluded space where adolescents communicated with each other, and presumably with the school. The school painter told me that once he found a smeared, brownish scribbling on the wall. With disgust in his voice, he said, he realized that a girl had used her tampon to write graffiti.

The quad area, surrounded by the first set of buildings, was the primary arena in which to see and be seen. Here rallies were staged, food was sold, and students met with their friends in specific areas. Although there were no sharply defined racial territories, students were well aware who claimed which areas. Black students congregated in front of the administration building at the opposite end of the main entrance and close to the rally stage. White and magnet students met around the rally stage. Asian students were known to gather primarily in front of the library and near the cafeteria. Latinos, the smallest group, gathered primarily under "the tree" outside the main quad area. This, however, was only the most visible group. Several other Latinos hung out around the cafeteria, and many more, particularly

more recent immigrants, gathered at the far end of the school campus near the soccer field.

CONCLUSION

Newtown was a city deeply divided. Decades of residential segregation had produced a sharp distinction between a densely populated urban area on the eastside,
where recent immigrants lived next to African Americans, Latinos, and Asians,
and the westside, which had emerged as a community of predominantly White
and wealthier residents. Busing and other desegregation efforts were introduced
to overcome the inequality between the two sides of Newtown. But westsiders resented those efforts and increasingly engaged in a discourse of White victimization
as a rallying cry for their cause.

Roosevelt High, more than any other high school in the city, reflected the rapidly changing and growing ethnic and racial diversity in Newtown, and with it,
witnessed the shifting power relations. Having been the center of racial conflict in
the late 1960s and early 1970s, Roosevelt High began to develop initiatives designed to alleviate the tensions and established a magnet program to keep White
students at the school. By the mid-1990s, against the backdrop of deep racial divisions and fissures in the social fabric of the city, Roosevelt High stood as a fortress
of peace. Yet the strong sense of cohesiveness and equality expressed in its emphasis on school symbols betrayed an underlying educational hierarchy closely correlated with race.

3 "GIFTED WHITES" AND "AT-RISK BLACKS"

The Educational Organization
of Racial Differences

It was trickery and magic that told Negroes they were desegregated—Hooray!
Hooray!—and at the same time it told whites "Here are your loopholes."

—*Malcolm X and Alex Haley (1999, p. 247)*

Roosevelt High School was home to about a number of different educational programs, called academies. The most prestigious one was GROW, a magnet program
for gifted students, followed by the Academy for Agriculture, Business and Industry (ABI). About a dozen other academies with different emphases followed, with
the Business and Technology (BusTech) Academy being widely considered the
lowest ranking. Each academy enrolled several hundred students and offered a different curriculum based on students' academic needs and career interests. Academies were also designed to break up the large number of students into smaller,
more manageable groups that fostered a sense of belonging and continuity.

When I first started fieldwork at Roosevelt High, I introduced myself to the
counselors in the different educational programs. Explaining my research, I asked
routinely for the racial composition of the academies for which they were responsible. The counselors usually reached for a folder that was lying on the desk or went
to a filing cabinet and produced a printout of a spreadsheet with these statistics, often handing me a copy of it to keep. It was a different story when I asked about
GROW, the magnet program for gifted students.[1] The same counselor who had
just handed me a copy of the breakdown for several academies became suddenly
suspicious. She asked why that should be of interest to anyone. Taken aback by her
abrupt response, I did not press further. I then went to the principal to see whether
he would be more forthcoming. He told me that he did not have those data or the
time to collect them, and then sent me off to his secretary. His secretary told me
she was busy, and I should come back the next week. When I did come back the
following week, she looked at me with a pained expression and told me the school
just did not have "the manpower to collect these data."

Perplexed by this unexpected response, I now had become really curious. However, with every new attempt and every new rejection my relationship with the school's personnel deteriorated, jeopardizing the ethnographic project I had just begun. So I decided to turn to the school district office instead. There, however, the assistant superintendent informed me that they kept racial statistics only at the school level, not at the program level.

Frustrated by the runaround and worried about what appeared to be growing hostility among teachers and administrators toward me, I decided to wait until after I had finished my fieldwork to probe any further. When I came back a year after official completion, I went directly to the director of the gifted program to ask him for the data. He answered brusquely: "We don't have statistics about the racial breakdown of the GROW program. Why would we collect that? [...] Maybe other programs have these statistics because they use it for their selection criteria. We don't." Only after a sympathetic teacher suggested that I contact RHS's data manager directly did my search finally succeed. The numbers reflected what I had seen in the GROW classroom all the while. More than half of the students in GROW were White, although Whites constituted only one-fifth of the school's total student body.

The reluctance and sometimes outright hostility with which the counselors, principal, secretary, the director of the gifted magnet, and even the school district office responded to my request, and the wild goose chase on which they sent me, took me by surprise. What could have been so dangerous, uncomfortable, or revealing that so many people within Roosevelt High refused this simple request, a request that seemed unproblematic for any other of their programs? And if it was true that racial statistics about the gifted program were not available, why were they available for all the other programs?

Roosevelt High School had been celebrated for its harmonious race relations and its high academic standards in the school's yearbook and on the district's web page. What my research revealed in the end was a different story. Contrary to this public image, the school orchestrated the creation of racial categories and facilitated the perpetuation of racial inequalities. To describe this process, I compare GROW, the magnet program for students labeled "gifted," with the Business and Technology Academy (BusTech), a program for students labeled "at risk." The goal of both programs was to mend racial inequalities in education. But both systemically reconstituted racial categories and expectations: a large proportion of White students were labeled and treated as "gifted," while a sizable segment of Black students were labeled "at risk" and treated as if they were inept or inferior. This chapter shows how racial meanings and structures were resurrected by the very initiatives designed to overcome racial inequality, and how students internalized, adapted, and sometimes resisted and rejected these forces.

Colors of the Educational Pyramid

All of RHS's academies were officially labeled college-preparatory. But many teachers and students ranked the academies on a rigid hierarchy, with GROW at the top and BusTech at the bottom. This educational hierarchy was closely correlated with race. In GROW, more than half of the students were White; in the mid-level programs, a majority of students were Latino and Southeast Asian; and in the bottom tier, half of the students were African American. In other words, the educational hierarchy was most polarized between Whites and Blacks: White students were as overrepresented in the top programs as they were underrepresented at the bottom, while Black students were as underrepresented at the top as they were overrepresented in the bottom programs.

Correlations between race and educational track in American schools have been reported on frequently.[2] Nationwide, Asian Americans are overrepresented in the higher tracks, while Latinos are overrepresented in the lower tracks. But this was not the case at Roosevelt High School, where Asian Americans, most of them Southeast Asian, lagged behind the national average on academic performance and test scores. Latinos' position was equally unusual, in that they were slightly overrepresented in the higher tracks.[3]

Racial Formation through Racial Projects

To unravel the processes by which racial categories were evolving or being reinvented at RHS, I return to racial formation theory. This theoretical framework regards race as a dynamic process that occurs through

> a linkage between structure and representation. Racial *projects* do the ideological "work" of making these links. [. . .] Racial projects connect what race *means* in a particular discursive practice and the ways in which both social structures and everyday experiences are racially *organized*, based upon that meaning.[4]

While racial projects can be identified at the macro level of racial politics and policies, they also work at the micro level of everyday experiences and across historical contexts, just as society as a whole consists of multiple racial projects whose mutual interaction constitutes the larger picture of racial formation.

GROW and BusTech, I will show, can be treated as racial projects that do the ideological "work" of linking the organization and structure of resources with a racial interpretation. Without referring to race directly, both projects manage to reorganize and redistribute resources along racial lines and reproduce a set of racial labels and expectations: GROW via the concept of "giftedness," and BusTech via the label "at risk." Both projects form part of a larger process of racial formation that links intellectual ability with race.[5]

GROW and BusTech are both products of school reforms—directly as desegregation remedies or indirectly as intervention for disadvantaged students—and influenced by federal and statewide educational policies. Both were supposed to provide a nurturing environment for students with academic potential. The racial projects that these programs constituted and the ideological work they accomplished, however, led to diametrically opposed results. Instead of closing the racial gap in students' school performance, both programs exacerbated it: GROW by cementing privileges for a group of predominantly White students via the label "gifted," and BusTech by cementing disadvantages for a group of predominantly Black students via the label "at risk."

PART I: WHITENESS AS GIFTEDNESS

Racial projects are always situated in a specific historical context.[6] The magnet program GROW had its origin in the civil rights struggles of the 1950s and 1960s: the social movement for desegregation that was won—in theory if not in practice—with *Brown v. Board of Education*. The long legal struggle to put *Brown* into practice and the often hostile reactions desegregation efforts encountered from Whites made school boards and policymakers look for more palatable alternatives.

History of Newtown Unified School District

By the mid-1960s, when desegregation efforts were discussed in Newtown, the school district comprised about 70,000 students, of whom more than 80 percent were White. African Americans and Latinos each constituted less than 10 percent. But while Latinos were spread out across several schools, African Americans were heavily concentrated in five of the district's eighty schools, where they made up more than 50 percent of the student body. At the secondary-school level, Roosevelt High School alone, which was one of five large high schools in the district, served 80 percent of the district's African Americans and 30 percent of the district's Latinos.[7]

The growing Black and Latino population in the 1960s and their residential concentration in a small area of the city had produced highly segregated schools. Newtown was therefore faced with a mandate to integrate its schools. During the late 1960s, a multiracial citizen committee decided to adopt magnet programs as a means of achieving "voluntary" desegregation: rather than forcing students to be bused to other schools, magnet programs would attract students to specific curricular programs and thereby ensure greater racial diversity.[8] Studies of gifted magnets elsewhere had proven to be very attractive to White parents.[9] By adopting this voluntary desegregation tool, the committee avoided the racial tensions that desegregation through state-ordered busing had caused in neighboring school districts. As the school with the highest concentration of non-White students, Roosevelt High was the one most urgently in need of desegregation, and by the mid-1970s the gifted magnet GROW had been established.

By 1980 the percentage of the district's African Americans enrolled at RHS had dropped from 75 percent in 1970 to less than 30 percent, and the number of Latinos had dropped from 45 percent to 20 percent. By 1992 the percentage of Whites at RHS had become comparable to the percentage of Whites in the district (see Figure 3.2). Thus, within fifteen years of its inception, GROW had helped to stabilize the percentage of White students at the school at a rate comparable to the representation of Whites in the district overall. As a tool for desegregation and racial balancing, the gifted magnet had achieved its goal.

Giftedness in Newtown and Its Intersection with Race

Like many other school districts, Newtown used IQ scores and standardized tests to determine whether a student was gifted. As even scholars who support gifted programs have pointed out, however, this practice is not unproblematic, because IQ tests tend to be racially and culturally biased.[10] Further, before students in the Newtown school district could be tested for giftedness, they needed to have a referral from a parent or teacher.

But many of the African American parents were not well informed about school matters and were often suspicious of schools generally.[11] They were not necessarily aware of the school's gifted program or of the educational advantages associated with it. Similarly, Latino and Asian parents who did not speak English were unlikely to have access to this cultural capital.[12] And for their part, teachers are sometimes poor judges of students' educational abilities,[13] a problem that is exacerbated if their cultural backgrounds differ from their students'. In Newtown's classrooms, teachers and counselors were predominantly White.[14] With parents ill-informed about gifted programs, and with teachers less perceptive of exceptional talent in African American, Latino, and Asian children, these children's chances to be tested were low.

Another structural inequality in the identification process was the fact that students who were identified as gifted retained this label throughout their school career, and with it, preferential access to enriched and accelerated programs. This privilege remained in effect even when a student's performance deteriorated. For example, acceptance into the gifted magnet at RHS was based on grade-point averages and entrance test scores. However, the gifted label automatically took priority over these two criteria. As the outgoing director of the gifted magnet explained, "Complications arise if a gifted student wants to get into the gifted program but does not meet the entrance requirements. So, [out of 185 admitted] every year there are thirty to forty students [admitted] because of their label but who do not actually perform so well."

So, roughly 15–20 percent of the students admitted to GROW were admitted over students who performed better academically, but were not identified as gifted. Thus, while identification procedures provided an uneven playing field for non-White students and those with less cultural capital, the entitlement associated with the gifted label and the retaining of the label throughout one's school career intensified the inequities in access to gifted education and cemented the link between whiteness and giftedness.

To explain how the label "gifted" became a convenient magnet for White students, it is crucial to understand also how giftedness has historically been correlated with whiteness. Tracking practices generally have been linked to class, ethnicity, and race.[15] In Newtown, a district still predominantly White in 1970, only a negligible number of non-White students (less than 5 percent) were in gifted programs districtwide. Thus, when GROW was established in the mid-1970s, giftedness district-wide was an almost exclusively White category. Even the high representation of Asian Americans was hardly noticeable because their population overall was very small.

But by 1980, only half of the district's students were White, while Latinos, African Americans, and Asian Americans constituted the other half. By 2001, Whites constituted less than one-fifth of the student population in the district. Over the same period (1970–2001), the percentage of African Americans and Latinos in gifted programs increased from half a percent to 3 percent. The proportion of Asian Americans increased from 6 to 10 percent. In contrast, the percentage of White students in gifted programs increased from 4 to almost 14 percent. During the rapid decline of White students in the district from more than 80 percent in 1970 to less than 20 percent in 2001, their percentage in the gifted programs climbed dramatically (see Figure 3.1).

Roosevelt High School and Its Gifted Magnet

To the public, racial integration at Roosevelt High School had been successful. But it became so only through a magnet program that had effectively produced within-school segregation. This paradoxical outcome was concealed from the public. The

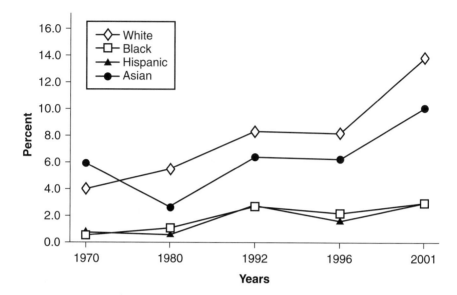

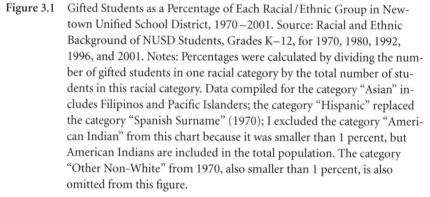

Figure 3.1 Gifted Students as a Percentage of Each Racial/Ethnic Group in New-town Unified School District, 1970–2001. Source: Racial and Ethnic Background of NUSD Students, Grades K–12, for 1970, 1980, 1992, 1996, and 2001. Notes: Percentages were calculated by dividing the number of gifted students in one racial category by the total number of students in this racial category. Data compiled for the category "Asian" includes Filipinos and Pacific Islanders; the category "Hispanic" replaced the category "Spanish Surname" (1970); I excluded the category "American Indian" from this chart because it was smaller than 1 percent, but American Indians are included in the total population. The category "Other Non-White" from 1970, also smaller than 1 percent, is also omitted from this figure.

school and district websites emphasized the school's successful integration and overall academic excellence to a general audience, while websites dedicated to prospective gifted students and their parents emphasized the exclusive nature of the gifted magnet.

The district's website described Roosevelt High School as one of "the top ten schools in the U.S. in the number of students taking and passing AP college tests." It boasted that at RHS students passed 600 AP exams every year, in comparison with a nationwide school average of 57 exams passed per year. But the gifted magnet's web page told a slightly different story to parents interested in the gifted program. There it was stated that "academic excellence is proven each year as GROW

TABLE 3.1
Selected Student Characteristics by High School, 1994–95

Student characteristics	California (total)	Newtown Unified School District	Keppler High School	Roosevelt High School	City High School	Whitney High School
Limited English Proficient (LEP)(%)	16	22	24	15	23	0
Receiving AFDC (%)	16	27	35	49	28	0
Average SAT score	902	784	729	921	881	1233
Percentage taking SAT	41	30	25	43	25	100

SOURCE: California Department of Education (1995b), High School Performance Report, 1994–95, Research, Evaluation and Technology Division.

NOTE: All of the school names are pseudonyms.

students take more than 700 Advanced Placement tests with a pass rate averaging between 70 and 80 percent."

Comparing the two statements shows that, of 600 Advanced Placement (AP) exams students passed every year at Roosevelt High, between 490 and 570 were passed by GROW students alone. Only 30–110 were passed by non-GROW students. Given that RHS, with over 4,000 students, was unusually large, this number was not dramatically different from the national average of 57 exams passed per school.

SAT scores, often used as a college admission requirement, were another subject for dual representation. The figures in Table 3.1 show that 43 percent of the students at Roosevelt High took the SAT. This was almost twice the percentage of students taking the SAT at two comparable and neighboring schools, Keppler (25 percent) and City High (25 percent). The scores of Roosevelt High's students were closer to the suburban Whitney High, a school without any students receiving Aid to Families with Dependent Children (AFDC), and with very few students classified as having limited English proficiency (LEP). This again appeared to confirm Roosevelt High School's academic excellence. However, if one assumes that all students in the gifted program—18 percent of the school population—were going on to college and therefore taking the SAT, this number can be subtracted from the 43 percent of Roosevelt High students taking the SAT. The remaining 25 percent was the same percentage of students taking the SAT at Keppler and City High, significantly lower than the average for California.

In sum, the features of academic excellence the websites had used to describe Roosevelt High as an outstanding school were in large part due to the gifted magnet, the disproportionately White enclave in this "minority" school, while students

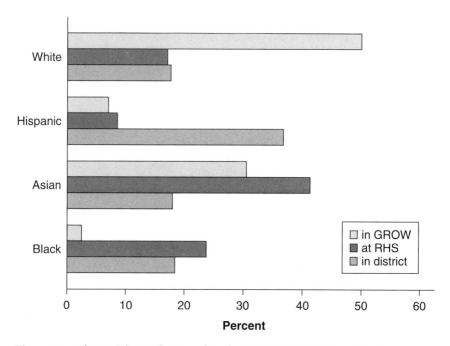

Figure 3.2   The Racial Distribution of Students in GROW, RHS, and Newtown
Unified School District.

outside the magnet program performed at the same low level as students in comparable schools elsewhere.

The most guarded statistic in the school, however, was the racial distribution of students within the magnet, as noted earlier. The numbers in Figure 3.2 confirm the racial imbalance I observed in the classroom throughout my fieldwork. White students, who accounted for less than one-fifth of the total student population, made up more than half of the students in GROW; Hispanic and Asian American students were slightly underrepresented, different from the state and national representation of Latinos and Asian Americans in gifted programs. In contrast, African American students, accounting for about one-quarter of the total student population, made up less than one-twentieth of the GROW enrollment.

These representations of GROW at the district and school levels revealed the balancing act of two contradictory messages: one highlighting the success of the school's desegregation strategies as inclusive and beneficial to a general audience, the other highlighting GROW's exclusive status to a specific audience. Thus the contradictions between the original mission of desegregation—to offer improved education for all—and the actual within-school segregation were made invisible; the whiteness of giftedness had been eclipsed from the public view, but was emphasized to a selective GROW audience. When this image was threatened, as when I asked for the racial breakdown of GROW, information suddenly was unavailable. Such an interpretation is consistent with research that shows the political resistance to desegregation and the inordinate pressure that politically powerful—usually White and wealthier—parents exert on schools.[16] It is also likely that school officials were trying to avoid the inevitable criticism they would be subjected to if it became public that the beneficiaries of desegregation were primarily White students.

Securing Physical Segregation

The magnet program's web page and information brochure handed out to parents of prospective students explicitly stated that it would ensure the physical integration of GROW students with non-GROW students, an issue particularly relevant to the gifted magnet as a desegregation instrument. It stated:

> GROW students are not isolated from other students on the Roosevelt High campus. Some of the classes (notably Physical Education, Drivers Education, and some electives) are mixed classes with both GROW and non-GROW students. This increases the number of students that GROW students interact with, and friendships often form between GROW and non-GROW students. The classes themselves are spread throughout the campus. There is no GROW building on campus.

While the paragraph directly addressed the issue of within-school segregation, it also assured parents of prospective GROW students that integration took place in such classes as physical education and driver education. Thus, while promising integration on one level, the subtext of this paragraph was that integration took place in nonacademic courses and thus did not interfere with the academic opportunities of GROW students when they shared the classroom with non-GROW students. As I found throughout my fieldwork, many of the electives that gifted students had to take as non-GROW classes were Advanced Placement, Honors, or other accelerated classes that consisted predominantly or entirely of gifted students.

Finally, until 1995 a separate bell schedule was in effect. While magnet students were taught in blocks of eighty minutes, regular students were taught in fifty-five-minute periods. This resulted in different passing periods and breaks, which kept both groups of students further apart. Moreover, the two schedules made it difficult for nonmagnet students to enroll in AP classes, although AP classes were theoretically open to any qualified student. Only after pressure from the high school accreditation team to teach on a unified schedule did RHS finally comply in the mid-1990s. Yet gifted students still had one additional hour of instruction and classrooms with five to seven fewer students than regular classes.

Thus Newtown's decision to establish a partial-site magnet program for gifted students at Roosevelt High School managed to balance student numbers across the schools, but it had done so by using a criterion in which Whites were historically overrepresented, and then used this criterion to justify segregating students within the school. Through the tools of desegregation, it had effectively organized the meritocratic label "gifted" to coincide with the racial category "White."

Whiteness as Giftedness in Discourse and Interaction

The contradictions in the institutional organization were hidden through careful orchestration of public information. But how was this duality expressed within the school, inside and outside the gifted magnet? How did teachers, administrators, and students, gifted and non-gifted, White and non-White, enact whiteness as giftedness? To understand this aspect of this racial project, it is helpful to consider the concept of common sense. Omi and Winant argue that racial meaning and structure are embedded in the way common sense organizes and underlies everyday interactions and discourses: "Everybody learns some combination, some version of the rules of racial classification and of her own racial identity, often without obvious teaching or conscious inculcation. [. . .] Race becomes 'common sense'—a way of comprehending, explaining, and acting in the world."[17]

The emerging literature of critical white studies has theorized whiteness as privilege and as made invisible in its normalizing function.[18] As the dominant racial category, White identity is different from others: it is the norm against which others are judged, often rendering whiteness largely invisible against a background of non-White others, and with it the privileges and unearned benefits whiteness entails.[19] Thus Whites have often been found more likely to refer to their own identity in ethnic rather than in racial terms.[20] However, despite its normative and often invisible quality, whiteness does not mean that there is a homogeneous White identity, as evidenced by such expressions as "White trash."[21] The following interactions and narratives illustrate how the magnet program as a racial project produced a multivalent notion of whiteness/giftedness. Given the invisibility of whiteness in conjunction with the discourse of "color-blindness" that marks the post–civil rights era, it comes as no surprise that teachers in the gifted magnet and their students made few explicit statements about race. The means by which teachers and students identified giftedness as being synonymous with whiteness was often hidden or indirect. One way teachers and administrators created this conflation was through the ubiquitous narrative of "having to be protective" of their students. In contrast to their teachers, who presented this as a race-neutral statement, GROW students were aware that those from whom they supposedly needed protection were the non-Whites outside the gifted magnet. Nevertheless, most of these students did not question the privileges that their whiteness enabled, but thought of getting a first-rate education as something to which their giftedness entitled them.

TEACHERS AND ADMINISTRATORS:
A DISCOURSE OF PROTECTION

The discourse of protection was so entrenched in everyday interactions between magnet teachers and students that they rarely bothered to define the source of the danger, or from whom or what gifted students had to be protected.

I first became aware of the concept of protection when I tried to locate Joe, one of few African Americans in GROW, through the counselor's office. The GROW counselor told me that he could not give me Joe's whereabouts. He said: "I am very protective of my students" and asked instead that I leave a note for Joe so he could contact me on his own. I was puzzled by the counselor's sudden concern, because he had given me this information for White, Latino, and Asian American students many times before, without expressing any concerns, as had the GROW director. When I saw Joe again much later, at his graduation, he told me he had wondered why I never asked him for an interview and that he had never received a note from his counselor.

A second instance of a GROW teacher portraying gifted students as "in need of protection" occurred one day when I joined teachers in the lunchroom. I sat down next to Ms. Murray, a GROW English teacher, who was engaged in a conversation with three colleagues about an incident in which one of her gifted students was threatened by a regular student in the hallway. But it was worse, she said: "Staff assistants are supposed to protect students and teachers. But they often do not even show up when they are called. I mean, the staff assistants, they hide." As it happened, most of the staff assistants were African Americans. At this point in the conversation one African American staff assistant cheerfully entered the room and sat down at the table. The conversation ended abruptly, but not without Ms. Murray's final comment: "Someone ought to alert the parents about that situation. Or just tell the kids that they should tell their parents. I talked with the GROW director about that. At least they should be warned that no one is policing the hallway."

The discourse of protection also came to the fore when Roger, a tall, White

GROW student with a strong and broad build decided to enroll in a Business English course. This class ranked in the lowest academic tier and enrolled mostly African American students. Mrs. Darren, the teacher, told me that a White magnet student had been placed in her class and that his counselor became very upset when he found out. As Mrs. Darren described it, he "almost fainted." Mrs. Darren explained that the counselor had assumed that the student was enrolled in the class because of an error in the student registration and immediately tried to get him out. But, Mrs. Darren said, the student wanted to stay and apparently enjoyed the class very much because he found that the students knew better how to think in this class than in his GROW classes. It turned out that the student was one of my key informants. In a meeting with Roger one day after his Business English class, he explained to me: "[This class] is something different. It's something that I wanted to do, actually, because, GROW students are sheltered, they are boring too, and I always wanted to have classes like this. [. . .] GROW is this ivory tower, but life is not an ivory tower." He confirmed Mrs. Darren's account about his counselor and told me that before the counselor permitted him to stay in the class he had had to convince him that he had deliberately signed up for it, that his classmates did not threaten him, and that, in fact, he was not in need of any protection.

The common sense notion underlying this discourse of protection used by the teachers and the counselor was that of a generalized as well as a racialized threat. In the case of Joe, I as researcher was cast as a potential threat to gifted students, or specifically, to an African American gifted student. But should the counselor not have welcomed the opportunity to showcase one of the few African American gifted students? The selective concern with protecting some gifted students—that is, one of the few African Americans—from an interview with me but not others was reminiscent of the difficulties I had obtaining racial statistics for the gifted magnet. Considering that several African American students criticized GROW for treating them with less consideration than their White classmates, I wondered whether the "protection" the GROW counselor had in mind was the "protection" of the magnet's public image of integration and racial impartiality, rather than Joe's privacy. While I do not have conclusive evidence about this particular case, such an interpretation is suggested by the larger picture of GROW's dual representation.

In Ms. Murray's conversation with her GROW colleagues about the incident in the hallway, and in the case of Roger, who decided to escape "protection" by enrolling in a predominantly African American BusTech class, the threat emanated from the non-gifted, who were cast as endangering the safety of gifted students. Whiteness was not explicit but implicit, because those doing the alleged harassing were not White. In these examples, the non-White students in the hallways and the Black classmates in the English class produced the contours of whiteness. In a structure similar to a Wittgensteinian "double cross," the outlines of blackness or non-whiteness/non-giftedness brought into view the contours of the previously invisible whiteness/giftedness, without the latter needing to be named.[22] Latinos and Asian Americans were absent in this discourse of protection, leaving it unclear whether they were cast as "honorary Whites,"[23] an exception to their race, or whether they were aligned with Blacks and predators.

In the context of RHS—where it would have been inappropriate for teachers to talk about White students needing protection—protection of gifted students allowed them to communicate a selective concern for gifted students that at once whitened those inside against a backdrop of non-whiteness and non-giftedness on the outside. The common sense notion of protection thus served as a rationalization for limiting unwanted access and contact, for maintaining privilege, and ultimately for segregation, all the while maintaining a color-blind language.

GROW teachers' use of protection was reminiscent also of an earlier discourse about the gifted that was used to mobilize recognition and support for this emerging, privileged social category in the 1950s.[24] It was indicative of other racial projects in the post–civil rights era that adopted a minority discourse to portray Whites as victims: California's Proposition 209, which cast affirmative action as reverse racism; Proposition 187, which portrayed undocumented immigrants as causing undue strain on the social budget; and the antibusing movements nationwide. Teachers and administrators "rearticulated" the meaning of whiteness. In this rearticulation, "protection" as well as "giftedness" itself became code words that indicated race, but without confronting "popular democratic or egalitarian ideals."[25]

Similarly, White supremacists use a rhetoric of victimization to abdicate responsibility for any repercussions of their own discriminatory practices.[26] Although the gifted magnet is far removed from self-identified White supremacists and securely lodged in the mainstream, it appears that by using the detour of giftedness as an endangered and victimized status in need of protection—rather than referring to whiteness explicitly—teachers at RHS were "deflecting" from their own discriminatory practices of privileging a selected group of students, which might have raised the ire of those excluded from this privilege.

Thus the common sense underlying the notion of gifted students in need of protection reflects a peculiar ideological junction: it is situated on the one hand within a generalized discourse of reverse discrimination in the California of the mid-1990s, which casts Whites as victims of civil rights legislation and, on the other, within desegregation and a discourse of racial equality itself. This constellation of contradictory discourses made the earlier concept of the "gifted as victim" a convenient and effective concept with which to conceal the prominent whiteness of the gifted.

GROW teachers' apparently race-neutral language of protection was complemented by an attitude toward gifted students that naturalized their predominant whiteness. "Naturalized whiteness," writes Pamela Perry, "is securely grounded in and validated by the normal way of things in the present."[27] Such a naturalization of whiteness was evident in teachers' casual comments about their gifted students. For example, after observing a ninth-grade English class in the gifted magnet, I asked the teacher to describe her students. She said: "There are many Filipino students in this program. But they are pushed in here by their parents, not because they are gifted. Asians generally leave their children little space. White parents leave their kids more space. For African Americans, sports is a big issue. And Mexicans, particularly first-generation Mexican kids, have no interest in education. Their parents don't even know what's going on." Similarly, in an interview with the director of the gifted magnet about the relative lack of Latino and African American students, he said: "Among African Americans the idea rubs off that as a minority you will get into college on an affirmative action program, so they fall behind."

Both the teacher and the GROW director described giftedness in a context where Whites were a majority. Whites were the unmarked, whose giftedness was naturalized. In contrast, Blacks, Latinos, and Asians were the marked. Their giftedness was questioned when they were in GROW, and their lack of giftedness was naturalized when they were not: Asians were in the gifted programs because their parents pushed them, not because they were gifted; and Latinos and Blacks were not in GROW because of their cultural preferences or because they relied on affirmative action to get into college.

But more common than explicit references of naturalizing White giftedness were what Perry describes as the nondiscursive practices of "collective consensus, reinforcement, and approval" of whiteness.[28] This was evident when teachers described themselves as their students' coaches—an idea echoed by the GROW director—whose intention was for their students not only to pass, but to "become winners." One math teacher had covered his classroom with inspirational posters that compared math to a sport and to winning a contest. Another GROW teacher gave her student a supportive hug after she could not solve a math problem. GROW teachers generally respected and trusted their students and gave them considerably more freedom than regular teachers gave to their students. For example, when the GROW French teacher had left her class without supervision for an entire period, she proudly explained to me that she could trust her students. Another magnet teacher described her students as "more precocious in many ways, not just academically and intellectually, but also otherwise. I wonder whether it has to do with their home environment."

Such practices in GROW classes were most noticeable because they were absent in the regular classes, where teachers were more likely to see themselves as disciplinarians; instead of posters encouraging students to become winners, walls were covered with discipline rules; instead of getting supportive hugs when they failed to do an assignment, students were more likely to be reprimanded. Often the classroom atmosphere was not one of trust and respect but crowd control, and students were not regarded as "precocious" but more likely as "immature" and as potential troublemakers.

Not all teachers shared such a bifurcated perception of students. There were also teachers who were critical of GROW and the protective attitude of their GROW colleagues toward their students. There was Mrs. Darren, who had mockingly told me of the GROW counselor's shock in finding out that a gifted student was in her lower-tier English class. There was the African American teacher who had argued: "If you have a magnet program for the gifted in the inner city, intended to attract White people, but you don't make room for the inclusion of Black and Latino people, your assumption is that the academically smart people come only from the White population." There was the White psychology teacher who openly disapproved of what he described as pampering gifted students into dependency. And finally, there were the two White teachers who criticized the magnet program for using giftedness as a pretext to give White students a superior education. Such counter-discourses underscored the pervasive notion of giftedness as whiteness.

VOICES FROM STUDENTS INSIDE GROW

GROW students frequently discussed the meaning of "protection" and of "being sheltered." In contrast to their teachers and counselors, who used it to conceal their view of whiteness as giftedness, students made the connections explicit. Although they fell short of reflecting on their own whiteness, they clearly realized that those from whom they were sheltered were non-GROW and non-White students. This emerged during an open-ended group interview with four White and one biracial student. All of them were in GROW, except Bruce and Ted, who were forced to leave GROW for disciplinary reasons.

J: He used a new term that he called "jockin" or whatever.

B: That's not new. I've [. . .] been jocked for two years by Ashley Putnam [. . .]

J: But see, I have never heard that term.

T: It's cause you are sheltered in GROW.

J: We are sheltered in GROW, but it is not that big a deal.

B: I swear to God, I swear to God, it is pretty bad, cause . . .

J: Well, it's not . . . our fault.

A: I think we are sheltered, 'cause I was thinking, the people I hear all the new expressions from aren't, they aren't in GROW.

J: I don't feel like I want to be sheltered. But then, I don't hang out with the people that I am learning those things from. And if I feel comfortable hanging out with people that are in GROW, then that's my life. I don't . . .

B: [interrupts] That's really big, that's really big 'cause that's how I was. 'Cause, when I transferred from GROW out to regular, I didn't talk to anybody for six months, I thought everybody was, like, a gun-slinging ghetto baby talking shit. 'Cause I was White, I wouldn't talk to anybody there.

The debate was not about whether they were sheltered; they all agreed that they were. Nor was the question from whom they were sheltered—they all knew that it was their non-GROW, non-White schoolmates, and in this discussion, African American students and their language. What they did debate, however, was whether this protection was "a big deal." Here again, the discourse of protection in the form of "being sheltered" implied that the non-gifted were racial others, who here were clearly identifiable as Blacks and Black language. The strongest critic of protection and the most explicit about the non-whiteness of the non-gifted was Bruce, who was forced to leave GROW for disciplinary reasons. After that, in his daily interactions with his classmates, he was confronted with the handicapping consequences of his former protection.

Another illustration of how giftedness was linked to whiteness emerged around the question of how Bruce and Ted could have been forced to leave GROW:

J: The thing is that GROW is an educational thing, and I don't understand why they kick people out, with disciplinary actions [. . .]

A: It should be done for grades, yeah, unless you are getting in fights in all your classes.

B: Right, the idea is that you are there because that is what you need to know. Because you are above the regular classes. [. . .] So why shouldn't they leave you there?

J: And if you got into GROW, why should they just kick you out? [. . .] 'Cause if you got into it being smart, why should you . . .

A: They expect us, because we are smart, we should be, like, tiny little Yuppies.

These friends wondered why and how their giftedness and the educational resources to which it entitled them could be withheld, not on the basis of failing grades—which several of them readily admitted they had received—but on the basis of discipline problems. This apparent contradiction suggested that disciplinary issues were antithetical to giftedness: if White meant good, and giftedness meant "goodness personified,"[29] then less-than-virtuous behavior disrupted the frame of whiteness/giftedness. Those who didn't follow the rules were kicked out of the gifted program and thrown into the ocean of non-White and non-gifted predators.

Although Whites at Roosevelt High School were a minority, in GROW they were the absolute majority. For GROW students that meant that the contours of White identity were most clearly linked to giftedness, which provided a seemingly race-neutral and positive identity. Within GROW, whiteness was the naturalized norm that did not need to be rationalized.

But in the second tier of academic programs, Whites were no longer an absolute majority. Thus, when confronted with the more than 3,400 non-gifted students outside the magnet, White students' marginal status made it more important for them to negotiate their whiteness in different ways.

Perry suggests that Whites' construction of their own whiteness varies depending on their environment: While Whites tend to engage in more passive constructions of whiteness when in the majority, a process she describes as naturalizing whiteness, "it may be that when naturalization processes are not possible because of close interracial associations, then rationalization processes must come into play to preserve White hegemony."[30] At the basis of this rationalization of whiteness, she argues, is the notion that White identity is anchored in reason and rationality and that non-White identities are steeped in culture and tradition.

In the racially more exposed environment outside GROW, some White students were explicit about their own race and their presumed intellectual superiority. As one of these students put it: "If you're Caucasian, you are either in GROW or in the second tier, but you won't be in the bottom programs." Other White students in this predominantly non-White, non-gifted environment, voiced the strongest critique of GROW as a racially exclusive institution that reproduced class and racial privileges.

But how did non-White GROW students think about themselves in relation to this notion of giftedness/whiteness? Latinos were not noticeably underrepresented in GROW in comparison with their numbers in the school overall. Many of the

Latinos in the magnet program did not speak Spanish; if they did, many spoke English with no accent; and some did not have a Spanish surname. They often were second- or third-generation Mexican immigrants and had parents who were college-educated. This combination of class status and lack of identifying racializing markers helped them blend in easily with White students.

Richard, a senior in GROW who was also the Latino Cultural Ambassador for the school, was a third-generation Mexican American. He said about his identity: "To be accurate, I would have to say that I am Latino or Chicano, but I call myself American. Most of my friends are White. This has to do with my parents, how they brought me up. Since I am from the upper class in terms of income, my friends tend to be predominantly White, and this continued in GROW." Although Latinos are classified in the U.S. census as an ethnic group, whether they themselves consider being Latino a racial rather than an ethnic identity is a source of debate.[31] Richard described himself as technically Latino, but self-identified as American/White, underscoring a racial juxtaposition between being Latino/Chicano or American/White. At the same time, Richard chose to use an optional identity.[32]

Sarah, similarly, opted for whiteness when she answered my question about her racial background, although race and culture for her seemed interchangeable: "My parents are Mexicans, but I don't really know much culturally about it. I am familiar with the holidays and stuff, but it's not really my thing." For Richard and Sarah, both their Mexican and their White identities were optional. Jorge was more explicit about his White identity and, self-critically, articulated how whiteness was equated with being successful: while active in Latino politics at the school and demanding that his name be pronounced the Spanish way, he also described himself as hanging out with the predominantly White "rower crowd," which, he added, represented another aspect of his identity, "considering how expensive it is to row" he said, "one of being upper class—and White." Jorge explained, "In order to succeed, you really have to conform to White standards, and that just seems like a natural process of assimilation. This is the group that, when we come here we're shown that we wanna be like rich White people. This, of course, will get you to the finish line the fastest."

If being identified as gifted can be construed as success, then this strategy of conforming seemed to have worked well for them. Whether they assumed a whitened identity as a rational choice, a haphazard outcome, or a consequence of class status, they chose it over their Mexican or Latino identity. They regarded being friends with well-to-do people as critical for defining who they were. An important variable in their opting for whiteness was thus their class status. On a seamless class/race continuum, the gradient moved from wealthy and White to not wealthy and not White.

Insofar as these students rationalized their giftedness as whiteness, Perry's concept of rationalizing whiteness can also be applied here. By being at least technically Latinos, they needed to rationalize why they considered themselves White. At the same time, by positioning themselves as White, they embraced the rationalizing aspects of whiteness, which were epitomized by their giftedness, while clearly distancing themselves from the nonrational tradition- and culture-steeped Mexican or Latino identity, implied in Sarah's reference to Mexican "holidays and stuff."

The comments of those who left GROW, either on their own or because they were forced to, also illustrate the magnet-specific discourse of giftedness as synonymous with whiteness. Bruce was the most explicit about saying that "being sheltered" was "a big deal" and about the non-whiteness of the students outside GROW, but there were other ex-GROW students who shared his views. Vicky, who left GROW of her own accord, described her experience as "too protected; lots of GROW students are really immature, and people treat them as if they're better. If they come late, they just say they're in GROW and teachers let them go. GROW students just live in their wealthy White neighborhoods, but don't really see what's going on." And finally, there was Dan, who—forced to leave due to a serious illness—criticized the magnet students as privileged and the program as "racially exclusive." In their critique of the gifted magnet's racial exclusion, these students confirmed the prevailing discourse that constructed giftedness as whiteness and vice versa.

VOICES FROM STUDENTS OUTSIDE THE GIFTED MAGNET

Students outside the magnet program were not all aware that there was a gifted magnet at their school, and those who were aware of it did not all resent it. For example, during interviews about racial images, none of the Asian American (predominantly Cambodian) students volunteered any references to GROW at all. Some White students in the regular programs were equally unconcerned about GROW. Yet when I interviewed African Americans and Latinos about their image of different racial groups, one of the most commonly invoked topics was that GROW was "a program for White students only."

José, a senior, during his last days at school described himself as "a Mexican born in America." He was from a working-class family and took turns with his older sisters watching over his younger siblings while his mother worked. José was outspoken and had taken on a leading role in the school's Latino Club. During the interview about images of different racial groups he expressed criticism about "excuses all the minorities are using" that "the White man keeps [them] down." He said: "I don't buy it. The only person who keeps me down is myself." When I asked him which program he was enrolled in he explained:

> I was in the regular program. This school, when I came here, they had academies, but they don't give you an option where you want to be. So sometimes you still don't know what's going on, don't really know the difference. [. . .] The gifted program is traditionally for rich kids, who happen to be mostly White, kids that usually go to schools in the suburbs or to a private school. There are some Asian American, some Black kids in the gifted program. But the image right here is, 'if you're White, you're in the gifted program.' [. . .] If you're in there, you can have a good education. If you are in regular, you're right where everybody's at. [. . .] I think they should have a good education for everybody. [. . .] I sort of got a second-rate education, not the best.

José's skepticism about "minority excuses" was regularly voiced by other Latino students at RHS, perhaps because they felt it necessary to clear themselves of the stereotype of Latinos as lazy. Notwithstanding this caveat, José was firm in his assessment that he was not given a fair chance because he did not know about GROW, which was "traditionally for White kids." This he thought had less to do with ability and merit than with wealth and knowing the value of giftedness.

Discussing whether he thought he himself could have been in GROW, he continued:

> I think I could have [been in GROW]. Maybe I wouldn't have scored a 4.0. [But] I think I could have done like everybody else. [. . .] I don't think being a [gifted student] really has to do with IQ. [. . .] 'Cause, you look at the gifted kids, you look at their parents, most of them are doctors, teachers, they have a high-skilled profession. [. . .] They gonna show them how to read [. . . and] all the things they know as soon as possible. [. . .] So, those kids that are supposed to be gifted just learned how to read at an early age. I don't think they have superior brains. That's how I think.

For José, the association of whiteness with giftedness was a reality he faced daily. But he refused the notion of "superior brains" or meritocracy, and instead saw giftedness as the product of class privilege, which often went hand in hand with whiteness. The common sense assumption he appealed to was that "everybody should be given a fair chance." Yet this clashed with his personal experience of how educational choice and access were practiced at RHS.

JuanJo was another first-generation Mexican American. He was in tenth grade, in one of the lower-tier academies. His father had recently died, and after living with his aunt for a while, he had returned to live with his mother. Like José, he was from a working-class family, but his family life was more unpredictable than José's. He did not participate in official school organizations. Like José, he described GROW as giving Whites preferential access. When our conversation turned to his own experience at RHS, he responded:

J: The White man, the White people that come here, they get better classes. I don't know why. They're getting to GROW or the next tier, and, if a Latino gets in, he won't see no more Latinos.

ADS [ANNEGRET D. STAIGER]: Why do you think that is?

J: Most classes, they're easy for us. That's why we become lazy, and we don't work hard. It's boring. Most of us are getting C's and D's.

ADS: Why don't you work harder, towards an A and try to get into GROW or the second tier?

J: I wouldn't see no Hispanics there. I wouldn't relate to nobody out there.

ADS: But once you would be there, wouldn't more Latinos feel like wanting to be there?

J: Yeah, but most of them don't get in. If they wanna be in it, they won't get in. One of the Black girls in my English class wanted to take an AP English class, and they wouldn't give it to her. She gets straight A's and they wouldn't give it to her.

JuanJo regarded Whites as having preferential access to GROW and thought it would be difficult for Latinos to deal with the racial isolation in GROW. But his fatalistic explanations also sounded like excuses: that Latinos were under-challenged and, referring to the experiences of one African American student, even with good grades would likely not be accepted. With his low grades, JuanJo certainly was not a prime candidate for GROW. Yet his explanation of his low grades echoed the words of Dave, another Latino. Dave had moved to Newtown specifically to enroll in GROW. Once he was in GROW, his grades soared, he said, because his classes were so much more interesting. Unlike JuanJo, however, Dave had college-educated parents with advanced degrees.

But since Latinos were technically only slightly underrepresented in GROW, why was there such a widespread sense among Latinos that they were excluded from it on the basis of their race? In contrast to the discussion earlier about Latino GROW students, who were middle to upper class and had college-educated parents, the working-class Latinos outside GROW did not regard whitening as an option. José, JuanJo, and others, then, did not identify with Latinos in GROW.

Rather, they perceived themselves as blue-collar, first-generation, poor immigrants who had no choice but be excluded from whiteness and thus underrepresented in GROW.

It was less surprising that African Americans expressed a sense of GROW as a program for Whites only. Gary was an African American freshman in the second-tier program. When I asked him about his image of Whites, he described them as "intelligent, [they] are treated better than other students." When our conversation turned to his own school experience in the second-tier program, he answered:

G: I was turned down from GROW, and I know that I had higher math scores than most people.

ADS: And they still got in? [. . .]

G: I need to keep applying and applying, until spaces are open.

ADS: So you would rather be in GROW!

G: Too many goobers in GROW, too many people that go on my nerves, people that don't see it my way. I can't communicate with them. [. . .] I can't talk to them [interrupted]. It's not integrated at all. [. . .] More, more ah . . . Whites, it's not mixed at all, [there are too many] people that just can't try to relate. They do try to relate, but it's just so horrible.

Gary was explicit about the widespread notion of Whites as supposedly more intelligent and of being treated preferentially. But unlike JuanJo, Gary claimed to have had the math scores to get into GROW—although not the gifted label—and felt unfairly excluded. Like JuanJo, though, he said the costs of White prominence and the racial isolation in GROW were too great. These comments could also be read as a protective, face-saving device for dealing with his rejection.

Eduardo, also first-generation Mexican American and a senior, was tall and heavy-set. He had been a star player on the school's varsity football team, where he spent much time with African Americans. But Eduardo also had exposure to gifted students through his AP course in Spanish, which consisted predominantly of magnet students. During our interview, I asked him which program he was enrolled in. He explained:

It was during my freshman year. I got accepted to a special program, the gifted program, but I was dropped too. I was accepted and dropped before I came. [GROW] students think that they are the best part of the whole school, I guess. [. . .] I have gifted students in some of my classes. Some of them are not as bright as the regular students. [. . .] But they are still in the gifted magnet. [laughs]. They still get through. I don't know, but one of my teachers told me that the gifted magnet was kind of originally brought up so they can bring White people into the school, cause this is a minor . . . , it's an inner-city school, and there are not many White neighborhoods around here. And they decided to set up a gifted program to make it more attractive to them. [. . .] So in there, it's mostly Asian and White, and that's why it is that way. [. . .] A lot of the regular students they really hate the students in the gifted magnet. Because of the way they act. [. . .] They act so much superior to the rest of the students. That's how they are treated too, that's how the teachers treat them, the counselors treat them, and that's how they believe they are. [. . .] They feel they are better than the rest of the school.

Eduardo, like José, was explicit about the privilege of gifted students and the prominence of White students in the magnet. His experiences with GROW, though, were more personal. In retrospect, he said, not being accepted to GROW had allowed him to concentrate on his football career. But he criticized the presumed intellectual superiority of gifted students and the preferential treatment their teachers gave them. According to him, GROW students were not as gifted as their teachers made them out to be. Eduardo understood the politics behind GROW and resisted the school's construction of giftedness as synonymous with being White.

In contrast to the unsolicited comments about GROW discussed so far, the following observations were solicited during a follow-up visit to RHS, where I asked students to write down their experiences with the gifted magnet. J.R., an African American senior from a mid-level academy, expressed his disappointment with his education and the school's hypocrisy:

I was withdrawn from my intermediate algebra class because I wasn't a magnet student. A person, no matter what academy they are in, should be able to have the same classes as any other student. It's weird how in school and in life we are taught not to discriminate or to segregate, but yet we are going through this every day at school.

J.R.'s response expresses his view of the gifted magnet's racial exclusion. He does not complain about selective admissions, or about not having the cultural capital to get into GROW, but about having to give up his place in an advanced math course—not a gifted course—to a gifted student. He exposes the contradiction between what he is supposed to learn in school and what he experiences the school doing to him. His comments suggest that the cost of the gifted magnet might be greatest for those who are academically ambitious. The experience of exclusion fosters a sense of distrust and resignation toward the school, an institution that also claims to teach them civic virtues and fairness.

As these cases illustrate, while the notion of whiteness as giftedness was ubiquitous, its interpretation varied with the position of the actors. GROW teachers'
color-blind discourse of protection reflected their equation of giftedness with
whiteness and their construal of the non-gifted as non-White. This discourse,
though, was not without contestations among teachers, particularly teachers of the
non-gifted. Magnet students recognized that their teachers' discourse of protection was a racial codeword that signified the non-whiteness of those from whom
they supposedly needed protection, although they were less explicit about their
own whiteness. The one most explicit about the whiteness of protection was the
former GROW student who had to confront his "protected"—that is, racially exclusive—status in GROW after he was forced to transfer into regular classes. Latino GROW students stressed a whitened identity, which they were able to claim
because of their class background. Because White students outside GROW were in
the minority, their awareness of whiteness was higher. They were the ones who expressed a belief that Whites at RHS were supposed to be in GROW, and it was
White students in the bottom program who expressed the strongest resentment
about their "misplaced" position.

Another meaning of whiteness as giftedness emerged from the testimony of Latino and African American students. While they were explicit in saying that Whites
received privileged access to GROW, they resisted the implicit assumption of
White giftedness and non-White non-giftedness. They noted the inconsistencies
between what they were taught to be quintessential American values of equality
and fairness on one hand, and their own experience of inequality and unfairness
on the other. Although most of the non-GROW students discussed above were
academically ambitious and had personal experiences with GROW, they seem to
have been the most harmed by what they perceived as their exclusion from the
gifted magnet.

Racial Formation of Whiteness as Giftedness

The concept of racial formation generally, and of the racial project specifically, has
provided a lens through which to see the making of race, and particularly the equation of whiteness with giftedness, as it emerges from one point of production, the
gifted magnet. Like a prism that refracts light, the concept of a racial project can be
broken into structure and representation and reflects the various and conflicting
interests of its constituents.

By treating the gifted magnet at RHS as a racial project, this study reveals the
processes by which a desegregation program functioned to produce a system that
conflated being White with being gifted. It illustrates how a school could portray
itself as a showcase of integration and academic excellence while perpetuating a

system of racial inequality. The magnet program for gifted students made the racial category "White" disappear in its public discourse behind an alleged system of meritocracy, but not without producing a widespread conflation of whiteness as giftedness. Whereas the goal of desegregation was to raise the educational opportunities for non-White students, the beneficiaries of integration at Roosevelt High School were disproportionately White students in the gifted program. Integration and academic excellence was advertised in the school's public discourse, but White exclusivity via giftedness was assured to the predominantly White audience of prospective magnet students.

While whiteness as giftedness was effectively concealed in the image of RHS as a successful integrated school, it was constructed in everyday interactions among GROW personnel through a pervasive discourse of gifted students as in need of "protection," a color-blind codeword that cloaked whiteness/giftedness with a victim status, but not without being transparent to students. Students inside and outside GROW, White and non-White, produced a variety of responses to the prevailing discourse of whiteness as giftedness.

For White students inside the gifted magnet, the discourse of whiteness/giftedness normalized and naturalized their racial privilege and provided what have been called "sincere fictions" about themselves that justified their privileged status.[33] Similarly, Latino GROW students rationalized their giftedness by emphasizing a whitened identity. White students outside GROW used the notion of whiteness as giftedness as a point of reference for judging their own position in the racial hierarchy: being naturally in the top tier, or not belonging in the bottom tier. Latinos' and Black students' understanding of the discourse of whiteness as giftedness was a critique of the gifted magnet as exclusive, unfair, and implying non-White inferiority, while Asian Americans—inside and outside GROW—were comparatively silent on this issue. Reflecting Omi and Winant's contention that racial formation is an uneven and contradictory process, whiteness as giftedness, then, was not a monolithic reality, but one that varied with the different actors' location within this racial project.

The sense of exclusion, unfairness, and implied inferiority expressed by a segment of the non-gifted and non-White exacerbates the conditions of "negative stereotype threat," which is the difficulty of performing to one's potential when facing stereotypes of inferiority attributed to one's own group.[34] This effect is compounded by the trend to abolish affirmative action in higher education. Thus, while one might disagree about whether gifted programs per se are justified in a democratic society, gifted programs as partial-site gifted magnets, as exemplified by this case study, are clearly counterproductive to the goals of desegregation.

PART II: THE BUSTECH ACADEMY:
"AN ACADEMY FOR MORONS"

The Business and Technology Academy provided a stark contrast to GROW. Described by its administrators as a challenging academic program, BusTech was part of a school-to-work reform program that offered not only a specialized curriculum and college preparation, but also job opportunities after graduation. Although such programs were highly regarded within the school reform literature, BusTech's image among many students and teachers was that it was the lowest ranking and least demanding program of all.

Like GROW, the BusTech Academy also can be regarded as a racial project that organizes and represents people and categories on the basis of race. It organized resources along racial lines through the racially neutral label "at risk," its curriculum, and its institutional accountability, while the representational or cultural aspects of BusTech as a racial project came into being through BusTech students' interaction with each other and other students, and with teachers and administrators. But it differed from the gifted magnet in important ways. BusTech did not need to lure a specific racial clientele to its neighborhood and school: African American students were already there. It also did not have to prove to parents that their children were receiving special treatment, because parents of BusTech students often were grateful that their "at-risk" children were being given a chance to make it through high school successfully. Belonging to a statewide reform effort of Partnership Academies, BusTech was more accountable to educational institutions at the state level than to parents and local school boards. However, like GROW, it was the interface between the educational structures on one hand, and student and teacher interaction on the other, that produced the disturbing image of BusTech as a holding tank for failures, and its wider implication of associating blackness with intellectual inferiority.

Representation of BusTech by Students and Teachers

How negative the image of BusTech and its students was became clear to me during one of my few substitute teaching assignments. The following is a vignette from my fieldnotes.

> The first period was a class of eighteen students; about eight were African American, five Asian American, and five Latino or White. This was the first time I had seen any White students in a BusTech class. As part of the daily routine, one of the students read aloud the daily School Bulletin, which promoted BusTech as "an exciting program, with many fieldtrips" to the new freshmen. Hearing this, some

students in the class started laughing, and others made sarcastic remarks. Curious about their response, I asked what they were laughing about. Al, a chubby White guy wearing a gray, military-style coat, said he thought BusTech was a "moron academy." But Deborah, an African American girl, denied his charge and vehemently defended the program. Al remained unimpressed and reminded her that everybody viewed them as if they were "retards" and found a reason to look down on them. He explained how he used to be in the second-tier academy, ABI, but then was placed in BusTech because he had been sick for a long time. More students joined in to support Al, complaining that the promised fieldtrips were rare and that BusTech did not prepare them for college at all. Others expressed their frustration with this situation and said they had tried to bring these issues to the attention of their counselor, Mrs. Washington, but without success. Apparently encouraged by my response, they suggested I ask Mrs. Washington to come to their class and talk about the program. So I called her.

Mrs. Washington was willing to discuss the issue on the phone, but not willing to come to class. She said these kids needed strong teachers and that many of the BusTech students ended up there because they were ditching school and had discipline problems. She asked whether they had improved, as if that was a precondition for her to come and listen to their concerns. I was disappointed that she was so unresponsive.

Meanwhile, the student team "Let's All Get Along" (LAGA) had come to the classroom and was waiting for me to get off the phone. LAGA was a group of students that had been organized by the administration to promote interracial harmony after the riot.[35] LAGA consisted of five students, including an African American who had been involved in the recent riots; Richard, the Hispanic Ambassador mentioned earlier; and a White girl from GROW. Lining up in front of the class, they reminded their fellow students how important it was not to bring drugs, guns, fights, or violence into the school.

On their way out, somebody asked Richard what he thought about the BusTech Academy. Seemingly unaware that he was in a BusTech class, he answered that it was for students who were likely to drop out, and that the school therefore placed few demands on them so that they would be able to graduate. After the team left, someone commented: "See what we meant?"

During a conversation I had with the counselor, Mrs. Washington, later that week, she said she was glad that her son had decided to stay in ABI rather than switch to BusTech. Even if he got better grades in BusTech, she said, he would not learn much there. As some students told me later, this was the same comment she had made to them about BusTech, which they found very insulting.

These episodes and comments reflected a negative reputation of the BusTech

Academy and its students among different segments of the school. In questioning students about the relative ranking of educational programs, BusTech was consistently ranked as one of the lowest or the lowest. In contrast, the school and the district described it as a promising academy for smart students that "provided a bridge for socially disadvantaged students into middle-class jobs and lives."[36]

The History of California Partnership Academies and BusTech

The establishment of the gifted magnet was based on an agenda of desegregation. White students were needed to integrate inner-city schools. In contrast, California Partnership Academies (CAPAs)—of which BusTech was one—were developed out of concern that students from vocational tracks were ill-prepared for service jobs. Pioneered in the 1980s, the goal of CAPAs was to provide vocational training and social mobility to the "forgotten half": "the young people who build our homes, drive our buses, repair our automobiles, fix our televisions, maintain and serve our offices, schools, and hospitals, and keep the production lines of our mills and factories moving." CAPAs were intended to satisfy the demand for increasingly complex skills by the labor market, while also providing students with the skills to become economically self-sufficient. Symbolic of what seemed like a growing demand in the new American economy for highly skilled workers, the first Partnership Academies were a Computer Academy and an Electronics Academy in Silicon Valley high schools. CAPA architects were less explicit about the fact that the targets of this program were racial minorities. They stated: "We have repeatedly been forced to confront a troubling picture of declining knowledge and skills among America's young people, particularly those who do not attend college. These youths [. . .] come increasingly from the poor and minority populations [who] too often do not value education or even speak English."[37]

That minority and immigrant students were the target of these programs, and that their alleged disinterest in education and inability to speak English were among the problems the program identified, was absent from the 1995/96 CAPA Handbook for Teachers and Mentors. Its only reference to race was that African American students were overrepresented in CAPA by a factor of two, whereas White students were underrepresented by a factor of 0.6 (18 percent versus 9 percent for African Americans, and 28 percent versus 42 percent for Whites).[38] Similarly, BusTech's information brochures made no reference to race. Yet an administrator for the school district confirmed that considerations of racial inequality in education had been a crucial aspect in developing the program, a statement supported also by the director of BusTech, who acknowledged that a majority of students in the program were African American.

Avoiding race in public discourse has become a significant political strategy over the past several decades and is as much the result of the post–civil rights era as it is of a shift in institutional structures. By framing educational inequality in psychological and economic terms, educators and policymakers could portray themselves as helping an "at risk" student population gain entrance to the work world. This strategy solved several problems with one stroke. First, it responded to the stated economic crisis and addressed the needs of vocational students. Second, it provided an incentive for schools to support such programs by promising improved performance, retaining a larger number of potential dropouts, and improving attendance. Last but not least, the "at-risk" label was race-neutral and therefore not likely to reopen old wounds about desegregation.

ORGANIZING CATEGORIES AND PEOPLE: "AT-RISK" STUDENTS

Like "gifted," "at risk" is a label with the potential to be a self-fulfilling prophecy, although with a quite different outcome. The discourse of risk, now widely used in institutions of social welfare and education, is borrowed from the commercial insurance industry and can be considered a social technology that imports elements of economic soundness, indemnification, and likelihood of failure into the social and educational assessment of youth.[39] As such, it has been described as a rhetorical device to detect, contain, and improve those coming from families that are socially or racially disenfranchised and as framing problems of interaction between youth and institution as deficiencies of the child rather than deficiencies of the institution.[40] Facing the growing importance of the language of risk in youth-related institutions and urban reform programs, Beth Blue Swadener warns that this language contributes to an opposition between helper and helped that precludes true collaboration and makes one wonder "who the implied or intended audience may be [. . .] and to what end?"[41]

The audience for the at-risk discourse was not parents or communities. In fact, BusTech did not have a website of its own and was not mentioned on the school or district website. But within the educational institution, Partnership Academies were the subject of a large information industry, consisting of handbooks for teachers and mentors, reports, newsletters, executive summaries, reform literature, and evaluative research. This literature used the term "at risk" to describe the targeted population, and identified a student as "at risk" if he or she had three of the following problems: (1) irregular attendance, (2) underachievement (3) low motivation, and (4) economic disadvantage. "These," the handbook stated explicitly, "are indicators of motivational deficiencies, not ability."[42]

How these criteria were interpreted and applied, however, depended on the specific school. The program director for BusTech described the targeted students in the following way:

> They should be better called "discouraged learners," students who do well on standardized tests, but who do not perform well in class, or who have discipline problems. They are generally students who have attendance problems, self-image problems, students who do not feel confident about themselves. Often they come from difficult socio-economic conditions or they have a home situation that is difficult, maybe they have emotional stuff going on or they come from a family where no one has ever gone to college, maybe they come from abusing family situations, or maybe they have to stay home to watch a sibling, so that the mother can go to work. They often have attitude problems; they act as if they have a chip on their shoulder. They are at risk of not graduating and of becoming noncontributing members of society, such as teenage mothers.

The term "at risk" did not appear in the BusTech information pamphlet handed out to students and parents. Instead, the pamphlet described BusTech as a "school-to-work" program for "college-bound" students, as a program providing connections to local businesses through paid internships, apprenticeships, and the promise of future jobs, and as having a curriculum that integrated business and technology courses relevant to the local economy. Local business representatives would serve as student mentors and provide a liaison to the "world of work." According to the literature, teachers in the academy were specially trained, and additional student aides would be available for tutoring, as would computer equipment and instruction, textbooks, and scholarships. Fieldtrips, popular among students because they broke up the dull school routine, were promised to various sites in Newtown. The classes were said to be small, as was the program as a whole, so that students could benefit from a more "family-like atmosphere."

In contrast to the discourse used in these communications with parents and students, the communication with other administrators explicitly used the "at risk" label. "At risk" served as a shorthand for a host of symptoms; it was deliberately broad, flexible, and adaptable to local needs.

How are people organized racially through the seemingly color-blind label "at risk"? As demonstrated by the gifted program, an institution or policy does not need to invoke race in order to become a racial project. The historical context of BusTech, its organization of people and categories, and the wider discourse about "at-risk" students showed that the history and the politics of CAPA were substantially different from those of GROW and that race had played a limited role in the educational discourse about CAPAs. The concentration of African Americans in the program was a crucial reminder of the racial realities of BusTech. But to what extent did BusTech's organization racialize students? To answer this question, I now turn to the criteria established to measure the educational quality of BusTech.

Markers of Educational Quality

To ensure continued funding, BusTech had to compile a statistical report about students' performance, including GPA, credits completed, attendance, and drop-out rates. According to the report, BusTech performed satisfactorily to secure future funding. But these data did not provide indicators for whether the academy prepared students successfully for work or college. Instead, all the criteria used to evaluate BusTech were also important for a school's "report card"—that publicly available document used to rank schools. For example, high drop-out rates are a blemish on a school's performance record, indicating that a school does not succeed in its mission of providing its charges with a high school degree. Similarly, a low average daily attendance rate suggests many students are in the streets instead of the schools. In addition, it limits the amount of money the school can claim from the state. Therefore, such criteria matter to both the independently financed BusTech Program and the school as a whole.

But how objective were these quality indicators? For example, to ensure that students come to class, attendance can be weighted more heavily than performance or can become the primary requirement for a good grade. Grades can also be inflated to reward even minimal effort. During an annual award ceremony I witnessed, I learned that students received prizes for straight A's, perfect attendance, and significant improvement, but also for good citizenship and for maintaining a C average. It is possible that BusTech administrators faced a dilemma: whether to give students an incentive to stay in school by boosting their self-confidence, thus generating statistics that met the requirements for renewed funding; or whether to provide a demanding curriculum that provided necessary skills for college and career, but was more likely to encounter resistance from students or produce lower performance statistics, which in turn would jeopardize the funding of BusTech.

If the information that was collected gave cause to caution, the kind of information that was not collected was alarming. For example, since the program was described as a program for the "college-bound," it might have been interesting to know how many students had taken the Scholastic Aptitude Test (SAT), a statistic schools often use to indicate the number of students likely to go to college. But such numbers were not requested in the summary evaluation. Similarly, data were collected about students' intentions to go to college or start work, but there was no follow-up study to see how well BusTech graduates had carried out those plans, a lack that has been acknowledged for CAPAs generally and has since been addressed.[43]

Finally, although BusTech promised business-related activities and enhanced job prospects to its students, it was able to fulfill these promises only partially. Many of the fieldtrips to local industries were canceled; only a handful of internships were offered to students during the course of a year; the promised summer employment turned out to be a small number of low-paid, dead-end jobs, such as warehouse and clerical assistant; and there were few jobs in local industry awaiting graduates of the BusTech program. Despite these shortcomings, about which students had complained numerous times, there was no parental movement demanding accountability.

Teachers' Perceptions: "Incapable of Success"

Teachers' and administrators' comments about BusTech were often less than flattering, despite the administration's official support and high ranking of the program. Many teachers, most having never taught in BusTech, described the students as "unruly" and "unmotivated" and their teachers as "unable to control them." I had witnessed this sometimes in BusTech classes as I did in others, but it certainly was not always the case. Judging by my experience as a participant observer and occasional substitute teacher in BusTech, it appeared that some teachers had preconceived expectations of BusTech students, as illustrated by the following entry in my fieldnotes:

> Mrs. Anderson warned me about Mr. McAuley. She told me that he did not have "a grip on his students" and added that she thought it was difficult for him to compete with a previous English teacher who had been immensely popular. Her remarks disturbed me. I had visited his classroom regularly, and although I agreed with her that some of his classes were hard to manage, his persistent enthusiasm, concern, and constant patience amazed me. His students did not always treat him respectfully, but it was obvious that they generally valued him. I had also attended Mrs. Anderson's class, an Advanced Placement class in French, which consisted primarily of GROW students. During that period, she took half of the students to the language lab and left the other half alone. Without adult supervision other than myself, who had no formal authority, this group of students from the gifted program spent the entire class period in conversations about boyfriends.

BusTech teachers did not commonly display this level of confidence in their students. I learned this one day in a substitute assignment, when I ended class a few minutes early. While I was involved in a conversation with some students, three of the neighboring teachers came to my classroom and reprimanded me for allowing students to leave early, which they said had disturbed everybody else. I was baffled, because I had not seen anybody leaving the room and had not heard any of the noise to which they referred. My sudden fall from grace in the eyes of these teachers came as a surprise; a few days earlier, when I had substituted for one of them, they had been very collegial.

Some teachers even considered the BusTech environment to be "dangerous," particularly for gifted students. Recall Roger, who was allowed to stay in a BusTech class only after convincing his GROW counselor that he was safe there. The director of BusTech was very aware of the program's negative reputation and even acknowledged it in the yearly report, where he stated: "Some teachers and administrative staff do not encourage our students and do not believe that they are capable of success."

The negative image that emerged from the various stakeholders contradicted the public statements referring to BusTech as an academy that "provided a bridge for socially disadvantaged students into middle-class jobs and lives."[44]

Students' Responses

How did BusTech students respond to this ambivalent treatment? As noted earlier, their responses ranged from enthusiasm about the program to deep resentment.

Resistance theories have suggested that many acts that are read as failure by the school are rooted in students' experience of subordination. Rather than failure, students experience them as empowerment.[45] But resisting school culture can also reproduce patterns of subordination. Looking at English working-class students, Paul Willis argued that adolescents' resistance helped recreate the conditions for their future working-class lives, although they experienced those acts, subjectively, as empowering. In this way, paradoxically, acts of resistance also constitute a form of "self-damnation."[46] In the U.S. context, some have argued that involuntary minorities—those who did not come to the United States of their own free will—experienced repression and developed cultures that are in opposition to the school and mainstream culture.[47] According to these authors, many African American students deliberately avoid doing well in school, because they regard school as part of the system that racially oppresses them. Others who do well in school engage in various acts of "camouflage" out of fear of being ostracized by their peers for "acting white." Because these students experience the racial stigma of intellectual inferiority on so many fronts, policing each other against "acting white" becomes a means of maintaining the bonds of "Black fictive kinship" and thus allows African Americans to reclaim their humanness.[48]

While the concept of "acting white" has become widely disseminated, Ogbu and Fordham's thesis has been equally widely criticized for blaming students and their culture rather than the "savagely unequal" schools and educational opportunities African American and Latino students are likely to encounter.[49] Others have criticized them for overlooking the variety in minority students' experiences.[50] But, aided by a pervasive and racialized "at-risk" ideology, the theory of the "burden of acting white" also has suffered from being understood simplistically and has often been uncritically adopted without the benefit of thorough debates.[51] Since the mid-1990s, several studies have reexamined and tested this hypothesis. They have provided ambiguous evidence, but also a fine-tuning of the theoretical framework. While "acting white" does not seem to occur among elementary school children, it does occur in some high schools. It was more likely for African Americans to have notions about "acting white" in schools where Black students were underrepresented in advanced courses and overrepresented in lower-tier courses. Echoing the conditions at Roosevelt High, Tyson and her colleagues found that this bred a degree of animosity toward their privileged, mostly White, and wealthier peers. Rather than relegating "acting white" to a preexisting autonomous African American culture, as the "acting white hypothesis" was often interpreted, this research redirects the focus of investigation to the institutional structures to which students responded. Complementing this argument, McNamara and Lewis have found that the role of peer groups is a decisive factor in whether Black students develop a culture oppositional to school; where achievement is high among African American students generally, or when there is diversity within peer groups, students do not experience the burden of "acting white" as a dominant factor.[52]

The case of BusTech at Roosevelt High provides an interesting comparison to these studies and the debate about "acting white." The "risk factor" of racial segregation was borne out by the racial stratification in the school's multitiered programs, but although many students had expressed strong resentments against GROW, the segregation was not equally apparent to everyone. Similarly, there were conflicting notions about whether BusTech was the demanding program administrators presented it to be, or whether it was just another remedial dead-end track. BusTech students were given substantial additional resources and, at least officially, confirmation of their intellectual abilities. But clearly, they also had to deal with negative stereotypes associated with their program.

So far I have shown the extent to which the school generated a racially identifiable multi-tiered system and the animosity this produced among Black and Latino students. Next I look more closely at students' interactions with each other and with school personnel, which reflect the peer cultures and identities engendered by this program and the school overall. In particular, I examine three forms of interaction I observed frequently in BusTech classes: signifying as a form of sabotage and role reversal; "acting white" as a boundary violation; and conformity as a strategy for coping with expectations of failure.

Signifying

Signifying is a particular verbal art form in African American culture, about which the African American literary critic Henry Louis Gates writes, "Learning how to signify is often part of our adolescent education."[53] In signifying, "The signifier reports or repeats what someone else has said about the listener; the 'report' is couched in plausible language designed to compel belief and arouse feelings of anger and hostility. There is also the implication that if the listener fails to do anything about it—what has to be done is usually quite clear—his status will be seriously compromised."[54]

Such an example of signifying occurred when Ben targeted Mr. McAuley's expression of emotion and vulnerability. In a discussion of the lives of slaves and the struggle of the abolitionists, Mr. McAuley introduced Frederick Douglass's famous letter to his master. Describing how Douglass's house was burned down by Whites, Mr. McAuley told his class how deeply touched he felt by the letter. "I shed some tears. Some people would say, 'Ah you're so soft!' But . . ." At that time Ben used the vulnerability Mr. McAuley had shown and interrupted him: "Don't act like a bitch." Mr. McAuley was startled and asked Ben whether that was directed at him. The girl next to him asked Mr. McAuley if Ben now had to pay a quarter, which was the fine for cursing in class. Without losing his composure, Mr. McAuley said no, that this time he would not get off so easily, and then continued to read the letter. Everybody in the class was miraculously quiet.

If one interprets this comment as a form of signifying, Ben forced Mr. McAuley either to punish him (which he did by reporting the incident to his mother) or to lose status himself, neither one particularly attractive to a teacher who wanted to foster trust and compassion among his students. On one hand, Mr. McAuley was concerned with maintaining discipline and decency in the classroom; on the other, he wondered how much freedom he could grant his students without losing their respect and trust. In this precarious situation, Mr. McAuley was fortunate that his response dissolved Ben's challenge without further confrontation.

Another instance of signifying occurred during a class discussion of Toni Morrison's novel *Beloved*. In the context of the discussion, Mr. McAuley explained that some young men who were slaves and forced to live a life that was utterly dehumanized, had engaged in sexual acts with cows. While this explosive topic elicited only minor questions and surprise at the time, Ben brought it up again a week later. Mr. McAuley started to say, "Rules are made . . ." but was interrupted by Ben, who said: "to impress the Black man" and then used Mr. McAuley's surprised pause to ask him, "What were the exact animals Blacks had sex with?" Mr. McAuley wanted to know why he asked that question now. Ben answered: "I just wanted to know what Blacks are mixed with." Mr. McAuley, ignoring the feigned seriousness of this question, informed him that it was "biologically impossible for a human to have offspring with animals."

In both examples of signifying, Ben was playing on racist stereotypes. His comments forced Mr. McAuley, who was himself African American, to straighten out possible misunderstandings or otherwise run the risk that students could accuse him later of being racist against his own people. Such attempts by students to claim the course of the class—at least for a moment—were frequent in Mr. McAuley's English class. Students sometimes managed to withstand the teacher's claim for dominance and authority and set their own terms of engagement.

Through signifying, BusTech students managed to break up the school monotony, and maybe more important, demonstrate to their teachers and other authority figures that they could manipulate them and earn laughs from their peers. But these practices of signifying could make it difficult to teach, and they reinforced teachers' views of BusTech students as having discipline problems; as a result, many of them refused to teach in BusTech.

"Acting White"

Although Mr. McAuley's English class was sometimes loud and his students made regular attempts at sabotage through signifying, he had managed to earn the trust of many. Once he asked them to write their thoughts on Whites and whiteness in their daily journal entries. Some wrote of their frustrations after learning about the history of White oppression. Jamal recalled that he got mad at White people when he first learned about slavery in seventh or eighth grade: "It was the time of life when I really understood about slavery and for about a year and a half I called white people names. I remember once I made one get to his knees and say sorry for no reason. I socked a white girl in her mouth for telling me to shut up. I used to be in the office about every other day. Once I got suspended for telling her I was going to sock her in her face."

Others resented being labeled as "acting white" by their peers or their family. Henry commented on an article about talking White: "If they're black and they have a high intelligence level, they are considered a sell-out or just because a person dresses with their pants 23 slim and wears tight shirts they're considered white. I don't understand why."

One of the most passionate responses to the insult of "talking white" came from Tasha. She wrote:

My mom and boyfriend and family members all say I either talk, act, or dress white. Sometimes I didn't let it bother me, but what the people you love say and think about you does have an effect on you. [. . .] I don't think that your dialect should be limited because of where you are from or who you're with. If a person can be so interested in learning Spanish, French, or Japanese, why can't that person be well educated in their own language? How can you learn to say proper phrases or sentences in your foreign language classes if you have no intellectual skills in English? My boyfriend has said that I "act white and talk white," but now he has begun to accept it. [. . .] My cousin and aunt say that I am a white girl and I act white because of how I dress, but I feel I dress casual and comfortable. My cousin also said I needed to get more clothes because I dress white. But according to whom? Because I ain't dressed like her? It's my choice. If any person wears Hilfiger and another wears Guess, should they conflict over which pair of pants are "better"? A lot of my associates say I am a white girl, but it's me. I do not need to "act ghetto" to kick it.

In her passionate response to the charge of "acting white" by her peers and family, Tasha demands the rights of privacy and self-expression. She does not mention doing well in school as an explicit example of "acting white." Rather, "acting white" seems to be reflected in her choice of language and clothes and thus covers a broad range of personal expression that her peers and family consider alienating. This is an example of generalized and emotionally charged discourse surrounding "acting white" among BusTech students.

On a number of occasions I witnessed this discourse in action. During one of Mr. McAuley's English classes, in a discussion about how to react when someone called you "nigger," students explained the difference between the pronunciation "nigga," which they considered an insider term, and "nigger," which they saw as a racist slur. Sylvie, an African American student associated with Ben and his buddies, said: "Some Black people really act like niggers. They just have kids to draw welfare." Other students got mad at her, and Ben commented: "You are White yourself."

The reading of subtle nuances in speech variations as attempts to "act white" was common in Mr. McAuley's classroom. Once, he asked Max, a student who had recently transferred from another county, about his peculiar accent. Max picked up the suspicion and answered: "Oh, you mean my White accent?"

These snippets show how the accusation of "acting white" is not linked exclusively to performing well in school, but is based on a broader critique of the right to be who you want to be on one hand, and the charge of seeking individual advancement at the cost of disavowing blackness on the other. This either/or discourse, and the intense emotional reactions it generated, were intensified in the "family-like" BusTech environment, where peer groups were more dependent on each other, more formidable, and more inescapable, and where contacts with students outside were more limited than they were in other school academies.

Blaming somebody for "being," "acting," or "talking white" was a powerful insult for many in BusTech. Aligning one's actions with those of the dominant White culture was seen as a form of treason, as rejecting one's obligations to "Black fictive kinship" in favor of individual advantages. "Acting white" in these examples was a form of social control against those who violated the imaginary boundary of this in-group. Students' testimony about past or present anti-White sentiments in response to the realization of White racism were another aspect of the strength of "Black fictive kinship."

Avoidance and Conformity: High-Status Low Achievers and Low-Status High Achievers

Some students actually liked their BusTech classes and the program's "family-like" atmosphere and felt that the teachers were caring. Others did not worry much about school generally and saw BusTech as an opportunity to have fun with a close-knit group of friends in a program that provided more freedom than other programs and teachers who were more tolerant. But there were other students who were frustrated about being "treated like fools" by their teachers. They felt trapped, they found the program limited in its scope, and they felt marginalized within the close-knit "family-like" atmosphere. Fordham's analysis of Black underachievers and overachievers provides an explanation for how BusTech students themselves might have contributed to the reputation of failure. While underachieving students emphasize their connections to "Black fictive kinship" and the spirit of egalitarianism, overachieving students see themselves in opposition through their conformity: by showing that as Black students they can perform as well as or better than White students, they challenged the stereotype of Black inferiority:

> Among contemporary African Americans, resistance is constructed as power and appears to take two primary forms: conformity and avoidance. As conformity, it is interpreted as unqualified acceptance of the ideological claims of the larger society; within the African American community, it is often perceived as disguised

warfare in which the Black Self "passes" as (an)Other in order to reclaim an appropriated humanity.[55]

The position of the high achiever in relation to her fellow classmates, however, is precarious. As Signithia Fordham writes:

> For high-achieving African-American adolescents at Capital High *warfare* is the appropriate term for academic achievement because they are resisting two competing yet similarly debilitating forces: the dominant society's minimal academic expectations for Black students and their classmates' internal policing for group solidarity.[56]

Such under- and overachievement strategies played out in Mr. McAuley's classroom of fifteen to twenty students. The most popular group was Ben's clique, which consisted of five boys and two girls, all of them African American. They often sat close to each other and exchanged comments and gestures that signaled their intimacy. Sometimes they went together to malls or sports events. On the fringe of this group was Jorge, who was part Mexican and part African American; a Samoan girl, Ebony; and for some time Mickey, who was Cambodian. These students were tolerated but not considered "in." On the outside was a Mexican girl, Maria, who had few allies, and Melanie, who was also African American.

This friendship group regarded Melanie as an overachiever. In contrast, she presented herself as working hard. Melanie hovered at the margins of the class, ostracized by her peers for "acting white." Melanie's family was poor, and her father, who had abused her mother, had recently died. Melanie was desperate to be successful. Ben, who was the center of his clique, represented the category of the underachiever. As one of the main instigators of signifying in his class, Ben had secured a reputation as an entertainer, which, together with his impeccable wardrobe, granted him a relatively high status among his peers. Interestingly, Ben's family was more stable economically than those of many of his friends, and his writing abilities stood out among his classmates. His conspicuous performance as a low achiever could be interpreted as an expression of his desire to downplay his social differences to his peers and instead emphasize how "down" he was with them.

When I first interviewed Melanie, in eleventh grade, she was very ambitious. She wanted to become a figure skater, and she had taught herself how to play cello and had joined the school orchestra. She also wanted to become a writer and was one of the few students who took Mr. McAuley's writing assignments seriously. She often criticized her classmates for being what she thought was extremely disrespectful. When I asked her several years later about her experiences in BusTech, she explained that she had tried to be popular in ninth grade, before she began caring about her GPA. Her guidance counselor then recommended that she enroll in BusTech, which she was told helped students who had high test scores on standardized tests but also discipline problems and low grades. The BusTech Academy, with its promise of field trips to local businesses and cultural events, sounded promising to her. In tenth grade, though, Melanie explained, she had learned that "Miss Popular" was not her true self, and she became a more serious student again. Her grades improved, but she also became more marginalized by her peers. She explained that her peers laughed at her for her thick African braids and called her "loudmouth" for her outspokenness. The guys in her class ridiculed her, calling her "ugly," "fat," and "stupid." Even those who had been friendly with her outside of class allied themselves with her antagonists in the classroom. Melanie's cries for help were often ignored by her teachers, even though some of them had a chance to witness how her classmates had ostracized her. Some told her it was her own fault for not fitting in. She interpreted this as a sign that teachers did not want to side with an outsider and thus lose their popularity in a situation where allies were important but hard to come by.

Melanie was also disappointed with BusTech academically. Despite assurances from her guidance counselor that BusTech was for talented students, where she would be exposed to the same materials as the students in the advanced and gifted classes, she felt BusTech had denied her these opportunities, and some teachers had even ridiculed her for her ambitions. After she told her counselor that she wanted to become a writer, she overheard the director of BusTech laughing, which she interpreted as laughing about her. Three years after she graduated, she said, "They told us we were smart, but they treated us as if we were stupid."

After Mrs. Lewis had ignored Melanie's complaints about her classmates, Melanie ditched several of her classes to avoid the constant harassment of her peers. She ended up receiving a grade of Unsatisfactory, despite the fact that she got A's on all of her tests. In twelfth grade, Melanie befriended Craig, who was also shunned by his peers in BusTech for "being a nerd." Melanie later managed to leave the program, after which her grades improved dramatically.

The degree to which her classmates made Melanie an outcast indicates how close-knit BusTech was. Her classmates used gendered stereotypes in their own acts of resistance and policing, by pointing out how she differed from "popular" girls and thus deviated from male expectations.

Fordham's concept of underachievers and overachievers provides an explanation for the social pressure and social status surrounding Melanie and Ben. Coming from a solid middle-class family, where both his mother and father owned businesses, Ben's ostentatious behavior could be read as camouflaging his differences from his peers. He sacrificed his academic performance in school for the social rewards of being accepted. In contrast, Melanie, by attempting to prove wrong the notion of "blackness as inferior" and to move out of poverty, took the risk of being ridiculed by her peers, but experienced rejection even from some teachers and counselors.

While these descriptions of the culture of BusTech and its students provide only glimpses of the ongoing interaction between students and the institution, they do show that despite the additional resources and at least partially positive label of being "smart but discouraged," some BusTech students developed an ethos of opposition; this was evident in games of signifying, in their readiness to engage in conflict, and in their use of the insult "acting white" as a tool for social control. These were vocal attempts to maintain a tight-knit community of blackness against an imposing White power structure.

The label "smart but discouraged" was outweighed by the much stronger label "at risk," which framed a majority of their daily experiences. The family-like atmosphere in BusTech, in conjunction with the laissez-faire and sometimes negative attitude of several of their teachers, the racializing label "at risk," and the strong conflation of giftedness with whiteness, reinforced a peer culture that made it difficult for some BusTech students to identify positively with school.

For Melanie and those who did identify with the school and believed that education could be a means for social advancement, positive identification came at the very high cost of being stigmatized by her peers. This became even more evident in her senior year, when she was able to enroll in regular classes and was no longer ostracized.

As mentioned above, critics of the theory of "acting white" have charged that it blames African American students and their allegedly "deficient" culture for the achievement gap, at the expense of recognizing the institutional constraints, and even oppression, to which students respond collectively. Subsequent studies have pointed out that rather than constituting a self-contained characteristic of Black culture per se, oppositional identities are linked to environments where Black students are underrepresented in demanding courses or where peer cultures are racially homogeneous in a particular educational tier. The study of RHS and BusTech concurs with those findings. Recognizing this context helps us understand students in BusTech.

The concept of racial formation and its link between structure and representation has helped here to explain the interplay between institutional structures and student as well as teacher cultures. The students manifested different common sense narratives of race and ability. A discourse of sanctions against "acting white" included a broad range of behaviors and expressions, from dress style to speech to educational achievement. But a number of students also challenged and resented this discourse. The signifying games Ben mastered so well were one form of opposition. Another way of dealing with the charges of "acting white" was to "conform" to educational demands, a path chosen by Melanie.

Blackness as Inferiority

The racial project of BusTech worked differently from the racial project of GROW. While a series of students stated that the gifted magnet was only or primarily for White students, none explicitly stated that BusTech was only for Black students. Neither did anybody say that they believed Black students were intellectually inferior, although Black students and others referred frequently to the widespread stereotype of Blacks as being less intelligent than Asians and Whites.

The disturbing fact about BusTech was not only that it provided a somewhat limited education to a largely Black student body. It also represented itself as a program for smart students that offered challenging courses and training for future employment, when in fact it trapped them in a program widely considered a "moron academy" and a holding tank for troubled students whom some teachers saw as "not capable of success," thus contributing to a vicious cycle of the stereotype of Black inferiority.

Like GROW, BusTech provided "the link between structure and representation." It linked the organization of people—that is, "at-risk" students who were mainly African American—to a special educational program with particular resources. At the same time, by contributing to a teacher culture that often disapproved of the program, and by creating an environment where oppositional peer culture thrived, BusTech also generated an image of itself as a holding tank and of its students as academic failures.

As a racial project, the program for "learning-discouraged" or "at-risk" students "routinized" and "standardized" [57] its students as "inept" and "unlikely to succeed," despite its claim to be a college preparatory program. The interpretation of racial dynamics implicit in BusTech, then, was that African American students, the majority of students in the program, were educational failures. In BusTech as in GROW, how students positioned themselves, internalized, explained, or interpreted their own racial positions varied and was sometimes contradictory. Rather than presenting an image of racial formation as a process that leads to a homogeneous or unitary common sense notion of race, the conceptual framework of racial formation helps to highlight the contradictions and discontinuities in the making of racial meanings, as well as the role of agency that students and teachers exhibit in the interface between structure and representation.

Racial Privilege and Racial Stigma

The two programs exemplify two kinds of racial projects. In the case of GROW, the reinvention of racial privilege through race-neutral meritocratic discourse occurred through institutional mechanisms and discursive practices. In contrast, in BusTech, the reinvention of racial disadvantage occurred only partially through institutional mechanisms and discursive practices. BusTech students' responses to their subjugated status within the dominant society and within the school also played a part in reproducing this inequality.

Comparing the two different programs—GROW as entrenching the notion of Whites as gifted, and BusTech as entrenching the notion of Blacks as inept and inferior—shows important differences in the dynamics of forming the meaning and structure of the racial category blackness in contrast to whiteness. Given that students frequently acknowledged the stereotype of White intellectual superiority and Black intellectual inferiority, it was apparent that White students knew that teachers and others tended to think of them as smart, and that Black students suspected that teachers and others tended to think of them as inept.

Discursive practices that equated whiteness with giftedness were used to lure White students into this inner-city school. In contrast, no comparable efforts had to be undertaken to lure Black students into BusTech. Most students were advised by counselors to apply for it. In fact, the label "at risk" often remained concealed from BusTech students and parents. BusTech was less accountable to the parent audience than to other educational administrators, who decided whether to continue funding the program, and to the state educational establishment, which represented schools to the public.

For GROW, in contrast, the label "gifted" enhanced students' and parents' standing in the school. As others have shown, parents of gifted children exert substantial political power to retain their privilege and are therefore a force that the school has to reckon with.[58] Parents of "at risk" children, in contrast, are more likely to feel that this label limits their rights to demand educational equality in the first place. The processes of racial formation thus vary accordingly. In both cases the school organized the categories and assigned people to them.

I used Omi and Winant's concept of "trajectory" earlier to explain the anti-busing movement and the growing awareness of whiteness. It describes the dynamic relationship between social movements and the state, where a social movement emerges in response to racial issues, confronts the state, and then, to various degrees, becomes incorporated into, absorbed by, or insulated from the state's institutions and policies. This relationship between state and movement shifts between "unstable equilibrium" and "disruption." Racial projects such as the magnet program can be seen as having embedded in their organization the history of this pattern of conflict and accommodation.[59]

The social movement at the root of the magnet program, at RHS and elsewhere, was the civil rights movement and its demand for desegregation; the state was represented by the practice and legality of segregation. *Brown* forced the state to begin instituting desegregation. But the roots of this project also lie in the historical construction of giftedness as a predominantly White and upper-middle-class phenomenon,[60] and of intelligence as linked to whiteness. Through the inherent racial bias evident in the implementation of "gifted" programs and the ongoing entitlements conferred through this label, it appears that the school as a state institution addresses demands for desegregation through a practice of "insulation," where "the state confines demands to terrains that, if not entirely symbolic, are at least not crucial to the operation of the racial order."[61] Thus the gifted magnet at RHS illustrates the characteristics of an unstable equilibrium between social movement and the state, where different constituents and their interests are aligned with different aspects of this desegregation instrument.

Accommodating demands for desegregation was a progressive move by the schools. However, using gifted programs to lure White students into a predominantly non-White school and retaining practices and policies that continued to exclude non-Whites did little to disrupt the preexisting racial order. In fact, both practices may have emphasized the "badge of inferiority" that was the mark of segregation. It is not surprising that the gifted magnet became a tool for preserving White privilege rather than for attaining racial equality. This raises the question of whether the compromise of enticing White and wealthier parents with the carrot of giftedness[62] was acceptable in the first place. Furthermore, given the links between this racial project and other projects of White privilege, it can be asked whether giftedness can ever be institutionalized without lending itself to racial exclusion and social control.

The position of BusTech was different. Unlike the gifted magnet, as a California Partnership Academy, BusTech was not the direct product of any social movement comparable to GROW. Instead it reflected state and industry desires to improve the educational and career chances of students at risk and to provide a better-trained body of workers.[63] Parent audiences did not need to be lured, but institutions within the educational structure needed to be motivated to set up such educational programs. Thus the state itself produced the programs, evaluated their effectiveness, and made decisions about their future funding.

The state's accountability structure was also very different. In the case of GROW, its goal was to demonstrate schoolwide integration, whereas for BusTech it was to show improved student performance. By offering a carrot to the privileged White constituency and state stewardship for underprivileged non-White youth, these programs reflected the inherent power positions of both populations and set the stage for the likely outcome of such interventions. The racial and program identities (whether explicit or implicit) orchestrated through the school structure were critical influences on the racial identities and hierarchies that students developed themselves. But although the pairing of educational labels with racial labels was expressed in a number of ways, students and teachers were not passive recipients of those messages. Neither students nor teachers accepted these presumptions in a monolithic or homogeneous fashion. The students' viewpoints were diverse and complex and often reflected contradictory constructions of race. The students negotiated, rejected, and sometimes internalized "common sense" notions of race. But this was only one domain in which they were forced to come to grips with racializing structures and meanings. Another was in their school-yard interactions, where adult supervision was more limited, and where they could temporarily escape the pressure of the classroom regimen. As the next chapter shows, the school-yard interactions illustrate how they actively negotiated a racial order quite different from the White/gifted and Black/at-risk dichotomy.

4 | RACE POLITICS IN THE SCHOOL YARD

Alliances, Dominance, Subordination

ACCOUNT OF A RIOT

On March 15, 1995, after almost daily reports about racial conflicts in many New-town schools, a "race riot" also erupted at Roosevelt High School. Watching the scene unfold from a distance, I saw a crowd moving toward a fight at the other end of the school campus. I learned later that some African American girls had thrown water balloons at a group of Latinos, who, as usual, had gathered under a certain tree that everybody referred to as "the tree where the Mexicans hang out." More a prank at first, the skirmish soon started to look like a provocation.

A fight broke out and quickly escalated. More Latinos joined in support of the Latinos at the tree, and more African Americans came to support the African Americans who initiated the conflict. Cambodian students, who themselves had a long-standing feud against Latinos in this part of town, joined the melee, fighting on the side of the African Americans against their arch rivals, the Latinos. The fighting, which caused several broken fingers and a number of expulsions from school, ended only after some Samoans allegedly intervened on behalf of the Latinos and after more than thirty police officers in riot gear appeared in the school yard. Or so the story went as it emerged in the subsequent mediation meetings.

Racial confrontations continued over the following days, apparently fueled by gang rivalries in the neighborhood. African Americans and Asian Americans continued to attack Latinos in what some described as "open hunting season on Mexicans"; school administrators tried frantically to prevent further escalation and to restore the school's image of racial harmony. They quickly recruited students they thought to be influential among their peers as "peacekeepers" to visit classrooms and ask their fellow students to leave their gang fights outside the school and practice racial tolerance. Banners in the school colors with the slogan "Everyone Together for RHS" were placed in hallways, overpasses, and windows. Speak-out sessions were scheduled for students to vent their feelings, and parent meetings were set up to mend Latino–African American relations. During the following days, racially separate meetings were held with those involved in the event. White students, who constituted almost a quarter of the total student population, were entirely uninvolved and in many cases unaware of the conflict.

The fight was a rude awakening for RHS's administrators, who until then had preached the gospel of RHS as an integrated and harmonious haven in a crime-ridden inner-city environment, which through sound educational practices had been spared the racial conflicts so rampant at other schools in the area. RHS's staff had not seen racial tensions of this intensity since the turbulent 1960s and 1970s, when fights between Black and White students were frequent. Similar, well-publicized conflicts in neighboring schools had blemished the reputation of these schools and resulted in the demotion of their principals. Administrators were particularly sensitive to RHS's public image because two sets of outside visitors were at the school that week: a group of German exchange students and an accreditation team.

While this incident was the most serious, further confrontations occurred between Latinos and African Americans in the following days. African Americans repeatedly singled out Latinos as targets for provocation. Cambodians, involved in a decade-old conflict with Latino gangs in their neighborhood, took the opportunity to get even with Latinos and forged a conspicuous alliance with African Americans, who appeared to enjoy uncontested dominance. White students, half of them isolated in the magnet program, were clueless about the racial tensions that had become so tangible during the previous days. Like the first confrontation, several of the fights during the following days began between girls and then were carried on by boys. Female students, particularly Latinas, initially took on a leading role in the mediation meetings, but after the first few sessions were no longer part of the reconciliation effort. During these days of "racial unrest"—as the principal called it—racial divisions, alliances, and hierarchies among students came into sharp relief.

In the previous chapter, I described educational labels and the organizational structures that went along with them as racial projects. As such, they contributed to a representation that linked Whites with the label "gifted" and Blacks with the label "at risk," although different people interpreted these links in different ways. The school as an institution of the state played a significant role in creating and representing these identities. But racial projects can also be recognized in other, less obvious arenas, for example in the way they craft new racial identities, or in the way they express or change common sense notions of race.[1]

In this chapter I explore how students retold and explained an event, which later was often referred to as a "race riot," in light of their own insights into what race meant and how it functioned at RHS. More often than not, their interpretations split along racial lines, and the collective actions linked to their interpretations reflect the dynamic process in which race emerges as a representative and substantive phenomenon. And while students expressed racial attitudes based on their personal experiences, their interracial interactions were nevertheless shaped by the school, the city, and the larger racial discourse at work. The analysis of the race riot—and the underlying conflicts it signified—were linked to these larger domains and influenced the formation of common sense that emerged from students' explanations. But students also retained a significant degree of autonomy in the making of these identities and in the way they inhabited them.

Using this "riot" as a crystallization of racial alliances and antagonisms, this chapter describes how students, collectively, worked out racial identifications and configurations. Observations, conversations, and interviews with a wide range of students across the racial and academic spectrum provide insights into how they conceptualized and created their own systems of racial order and how these orders operated at Roosevelt High School: what racial boundaries they erected and how these related to their own locations within the educational race hierarchy; what frame of reference they used to describe their racial identity and how they positioned themselves in relation to others: whom they recognized as worthy opponents or allies, and whom they ignored.

RACE, SCHOOL VIOLENCE, AND THE ROLE OF GANGS

Various racial classification systems operated at Roosevelt High School. The formal classification system adopted by the school district used the categories African American, Native American, Hispanic, Asian, Filipino, and Pacific Islander. This contrasted with the one employed in the school yard, where Filipinos and Asians were lumped together as Asians, and where Cambodians often were seen as representative of all Asians. Various Latino ethnic groups were often called Mexicans, while Pacific Islanders were referred to as Samoans. But which racial lines underlay the so-called "race riot," and to what extent were other forms of identity involved in the racial conflict?

Race was not the only form of politicized identity addressed in the meetings; gang activity and racially motivated violence were often spoken of in the same breath by students and by administrators. Sometimes they used them interchangeably, leaving it unclear what the connection between gangs and race was, or where gang conflict ended and racial conflict began. According to newspaper reports, both gang and school violence had become widespread in the city and in the region during the previous years. Although the district had managed to lower crime rates significantly for younger students, crime statistics for all Newtown students rose again by the end of the 1990s, and gangs, often associated with school violence and with instigating large-scale racial conflicts, continued to flourish in the city.[2]

Newtown gangs had acquired notoriety, particularly in the attendance area of Roosevelt High School, where Latino, Asian, and African American gangs were engaged in a multilateral conflict. But despite the abundance of gangs in the neighborhood and graffiti on school walls, it was not always clear whether wall scribblings indicated the presence of violent gangs or just taggers. Unlike gangs, taggers generally make a name for themselves not through violence, but by competing to tag the most walls in the riskiest places, such as freeway dividers and barriers, where cars pass by closely and at very high speed, or on places that are dangerous and difficult to reach. Taggers are usually not affiliated with gangs, but to the uninitiated eye there is little difference between the marks of a tagger and those of a gang.

As my tour with the school painter had made clear, tags were abundant at Roosevelt High School. Gang initials and names of gang members were painted on walls throughout the school. Following the conventions of semiotic warfare, other gangs often crossed out the tags or "throw ups" of their enemies to signal an imminent attack.[3] Many such tags were racially identifiable to the RHS community. Southeast Asian gangs were particularly easy to identify from their graffiti because they often used their ethnic origin as part of their gang name. The walls also bore the initials of the Dawgs, a prominent African American gang, but evidence of Mexican gangs and of White supremacist groups was rare.

The administration went to great lengths to minimize the gang presence on campus. Several police cars were parked in front of the school every morning and afternoon; a police officer was assigned to patrol the school grounds during breaks; students had to show their identification cards (to prevent nonstudents from staging an attack on the school grounds); paraphernalia associated with local gangs was outlawed, including belt buckles with initials, hats, oversized pants, and certain sports jackets; and finally, a painter had been hired to clean up graffiti every day.[4]

However, it was not always gangs who were responsible for defacing walls, and groups who called themselves gangs were not always involved in illegal or violent activities. One day, while I was taking a picture of a small scribble on a classroom door, a group of Cambodian students asked me whether I knew what it stood for and then went on to explain that it represented their gang. When I told them that I was doing research for a book, they got excited and offered to print it for me, because printing was a business that they wanted to develop. I had not expected gangs to be engaged in this sort of entrepreneurship.

Another demonstration of gang semiotics among RHS adolescents occurred when I asked a group of White males—all members of a high school fraternity—whether I could take a picture of them in the school yard. They were happy to pose, but not without throwing a hand sign for their fraternity, a practice outlawed by the school because it was associated with gangs.

Before I describe how different actors rationalized the so-called race riot, often without drawing clear distinctions between gang and racial affiliation, the position of Samoans requires an explanation. Samoans had acquired the reputation of peacekeepers in the riot. They had played a crucial role in the fight by coming to the aid of Latinos, who were the most vulnerable of the three opponents. Roosevelt High had only a handful of Samoan students, which is why I did not systematically focus on them as I did on the four larger racial groups. But despite their small numbers, Samoans had a noticeable presence on campus. Many had large physical builds, which made them prime candidates for the football team, and they stood out from their classmates because they looked more physically developed. A Samoan in ninth grade could easily appear to be a grown man. Samoan males at RHS regularly wore their traditional clothes, a skirtlike wrap, unbothered by what their classmates might think of them. Many of the male Samoan students wore their hair long, even though the fashion standard dictated short hair for guys. Samoans were proud of their heritage and not afraid to stand up for themselves. They were not star students, but neither were they particularly prominent in the lower-tier programs. In fact, Samoans held their ground in more than one way. One teacher described them as having nobody to fear because of their large bodies, and as so self-confident in their masculinity that they could remain calm and even shed tears without losing their manhood.

This reputation explains why the Samoans were not afraid to intervene on behalf of Latinos. Even if they were numerically a minority, they were so respected that nobody dared to challenge them. The high status of Samoans, and the power it afforded them, was underscored in a scene I observed after one of the mediation sessions about the fight on campus. After they had finished their deliberations and were about to return to class, one of the Cambodians involved in the fight walked up to Joe, a Samoan, and proudly showed him the new tattoo on his arm. It was an Aztec face. Obviously, the Cambodian student wanted to get the Samoan's approval of what appeared to be a gesture of reconciliation toward Latinos.

LATINOS: BEING THE TARGET OF PROPOSITION 187

It was not insignificant that the confrontation that ignited the "racial unrest" took place at the usual Latino hangout, "the tree." Its location outside the central area of the school yard signaled the Latinos' marginal position. Considered by many as the place where the Mexicans hung out, "the Mexicans" were really only a group of fifteen to twenty students who had managed to gain name recognition among their peers through their opposition to Proposition 187. They had staged meetings and organized protests to alert their fellow students about the imminent threat of school expulsion for students who belonged to the undocumented. With the help of a young and dynamic Chilean teacher, who himself criticized the racial politics of Proposition 187, this group organized Club Mexicano and Cultura Latina and with other activists in the area fostered a Latino presence and consciousness on campus.

Rather than being concentrated in one academy or educational tier, Latinos were enrolled in a large number of different programs. Even those who met regularly at the tree were from upper- and lower-tier programs. Their wide representation in the educational tiers was matched by the wide range of subcultures with which they identified. There were those who fit the media image of urban Latino youth dressed in baggy jeans and seams cut open at the cuffs; some called themselves "greasers," slicking back their hair with gel and wearing wide-cuffed Levi's; some called themselves "Rastas" and grew dreadlocks; and others called themselves "grungers," wearing drab and baggy clothes, notwithstanding that several of these styles, particularly "grungers" and "Rastas," were more often associated with Whites than with Latinos by RHS students.

The conspicuous heterogeneity and solidarity of Latinos was related to their marginalization in the classroom. Not only were they usually the smallest group among students in any track; they were also often the target of African American and sometimes Cambodian students' taunts. Months before the confrontation over the water balloons, Cambodians and African Americans had routinely used the arguments of Proposition 187 to make jokes at the expense of Latinos.

One such incident took place in a multiculturalism class taught by Mrs. Williams. Mrs. Williams was an African American teacher who had spearheaded a districtwide training camp for racial tolerance and had over the past twenty years worked tirelessly for a culturally diverse curriculum. The class she taught in the school's Academy for Social Work, typical in its racial composition of students in this tier, consisted of predominantly African American and Asian American students, with a few Latinos and Whites. In connection with the ongoing conflicts in the city, Mrs. Williams's lesson plan for the day was to discuss with her students the cultural differences between ethnic communities in Newtown. Half-serious, half-joking, Otis, an African American student, commented: "A lot of Mexican people come here, have babies, get MediCal. Yeah! We talked about that in Health." The class responded with a laugh. "They take over," he added. Jamal, another African American student, added: "The Mexicans come over here and the Haitians get put in the concentration camps! They shouldn't allow Mexicans to come in." Latino students, sitting spread out in different areas in the class, remained silent. Otis and Jamal might have tried to stir up their African American teacher and her multicultural agenda into a lesson about racial tolerance. But as these Latino students later complained, they experienced these jokes as hostile and directed personally at them. In fact, they described it as a form of bullying typical of the way African American students treated them at the school.

Such events were central to Latino students' descriptions of their situation in the school. Enrique, a regular at the tree, was a first-generation Mexican American who often looked after his younger siblings. He explained:

> A lot of people, from other races, yeah, they were going around, you know, "187, yeah, 187, we're gonna pass it." Like, I be walking, and there is, like, one Black guy coming behind me and saying, "We're gonna pass it, we're gonna pass it" and all that stuff "and get rid of you guys!" And I, just, like, turn around and, I don't do anything cause there is like twenty of them around, and I am sitting all alone, and also, I don't believe in violence. [. . .] I didn't like how it went around, in the classroom, in the hallways, everywhere, and people everywhere saying, "Oh 187, we're gonna pass it." Like, after it passed, it continued on. But then, since you didn't hear it in the news, there was not a lot. Since it died down, you didn't hear it so much any more. And you don't hear it now at all.

Enrique was a kicker on the varsity football team, one of two Mexicans among mostly African American teammates. Enrique described an incident in which his teammates had harassed and ridiculed him for losing the game because of a supposedly timid performance. He also said that his teammates ganged up on him at strategic moments during practices and games and deliberately tried to hurt him. Although he was frustrated by and resented this treatment, he refused to inform his coach. Instead, he preferred to wait for the right opportunity to get even on the field.

Latino students' vulnerable position at Roosevelt High, however, was not only a result of the racially exclusive rhetoric of Proposition 187 used by their African American and sometimes by their Asian American peers, or of their underrepresentation on the school campus. Latinos were also vulnerable because they were highly concentrated in the immediate neighborhood of the school and because Latino gangs had a reputation as fierce warriors who were not to be messed with. During the reconciliation meetings, Cambodians and African Americans had blamed Latinos a number of times for the riot because they were affiliated with gangs. But Pablo, another regular at the tree who enjoyed an influential position among his friends and whom the principal handpicked as one of the "peacekeepers" after the riots, vehemently rejected this charge. He explained:

> Latino gangs don't come here. See, the only reason why there is riots in other schools is that a lot of Mexican gangsters, they just like to start crap. [At other schools] there is, like, this gang called Locos, and no one likes them, and that's why there is no riots here! 'Cause we don't have gangsters here, really. And, so [. . .] if you know there is no Locos, or, if you know that there is no one from your gang at one school, and you know there is a rival gang, like Dawgs or something, you're not gonna go to that school. Because, especially if you don't get along, you're just gonna get jumped every day, and you gonna get sent home from the school anyway, for fighting or something. You know what I mean? So, there is something like one Locos coming here, but he keeps, like, low key, a low profile.

In Pablo's understanding, the idea that Latinos had brought their predicament on themselves because they were gangsters did not make any sense. In a school with such an overwhelming number of enemy gangs, revealing one's gang identity would be very risky. Like many of his Mexican friends, Pablo also went on to debunk the myth of racial warfare between Latinos and Cambodians. He rejected the idea that the conflict between Cambodians and Latinos was based on racial hatred. Instead, he blamed Cambodians' conflict with Latinos on their opportunistic alliance with African American gangs, who themselves were involved in a long-standing feud with Latino gangs. In his view, Cambodians joined African Americans not because they hated Latinos so profoundly, but because African Americans enjoyed the reputation of being the dominant racial group on campus:

> Asians, they just want to be with the majority. It's like, if there are more Blacks than Mexicans, then the Asians would go on the side of the Black people. Just because they know that they wouldn't lose out. They wanna be with the stronger force. Like, if there were more Mexicans than Blacks, they would be on the Mexican side. No matter what problems they had had before. It's just whoever has the most power. Let's say there are two gangs, let's say one gang is more powerful, maybe not in the school, but maybe they have more outside power. But the neutral force, the neutral people, they go with the stronger people.

Pablo did not consider Cambodians to be a force in their own right. In his eyes, they were mere opportunists who tried to raise their status by aligning themselves with a stronger force. Pablo's analysis of the racial politics of Cambodians reflected the views of several of his friends from the tree. Cambodians and Asians, supposedly their arch rivals, were rarely topics of conversations when Latinos talked about race. Instead, the only racial antagonists that Pablo, Enrique, and many of their friends identified were African American students, whom they described as domineering. Pablo explained:

> Everybody is more than the little Latinos, the Hispanics around here. You don't see, like, Asians going around, you know, like, bossing people around, like a lot of Black people do, so that's what makes them more of a, I guess, a bigger force [. . .] like a lot of the bigger ones, that have a lot of influence, they are talking head to everyone. So it is just . . . there might be a lot more Asians than Black people, but it's just that the Black people have a lot more that, . . . that way of going around, of carrying themselves that, that the Asians don't, like, really stand up to.

When Latinos at Roosevelt High talked about race, they portrayed themselves primarily as the target of a racial discourse of exclusion, notwithstanding the fact that formally, through Club Mexicano and Cultura Latina, they were one of the most politically organized groups on campus. But rather than expressing pride in their Latino roots and in their mobilization against Proposition 187, they presented themselves as the victims of African Americans' and Cambodians' racial aggression. They did not invoke an explicit discourse of race to situate themselves in relation to Whites, Asians, or African Americans. Instead, in their account, racial confrontations at RHS derived from political race-baiting in the media—primarily the political rhetoric of Proposition 187, problems of numbers and representation, and gang politics. Thus they described themselves as being perceived in racial terms by others, rather than perceiving themselves in that way.

Latino students' strategy of understating race as a cause of conflict with their peers was consistent with their position as underdogs in the school yard hierarchy. Emphasizing differences and producing exclusionary discourses themselves could weaken their fragile position even more. White students were their only potential allies. This alliance was expressed sometimes in similar styles, and in the number of people who moved back and forth between their Latino friends at the tree and their White friends elsewhere in the school yard.

Latinos' heterogeneous group of activists was useful in mobilizing against the threat of larger political discrimination around Proposition 187, but did little to fend off peer aggression. In fact, it might have even added to their being ostracized and marginalized by their African American and Cambodian peers. The irony was that Latino students at RHS associated much more with Whites, who, in the world outside the school, were those who put Proposition 187 on the ballot. They hardly mentioned their relations with Cambodians, or with Asians in general, and denied the existence of the supposed warfare between Cambodians and Mexicans in the immediate neighborhood. Similarly, their relationship with White students was not a subject of their discussions.

AFRICAN AMERICANS: A MATTER OF STYLE

According to the comments of students during the week of reconciliation meetings, African American students were clearly seen as the instigators of the fights, although most, including Latinos, seemed to agree that Latinos contributed to escalating the violence. Another fight broke out later in the locker room, where African American girls started a fight with a Latina. In the meetings that followed, however, Cambodian students were singled out as the culprits, not Latinos and African Americans.

In the classrooms of the middle and lower tracks, African American students were often a majority, and jokes were often made at the expense of Latinos.[5] In the school yard, African Americans' favored location was in front of the administrative building, where they occupied a position as gatekeepers to vital spaces in the school yard: the principals' offices, the teachers' offices, the attendance office, and the counselors' offices. Everybody who went to these places from the school yard had to pass through this territory. Occasionally, as I experienced myself, a passerby had to endure stare-downs and hostile remarks. Several students explained that the concentration of African American students at this nodal point on the school grounds had been the subject of intense conflicts between them and others in the past. Just as "the tree" was recognized on the racial map of RHS as Latino territory, the area in front of the administrative building was generally recognized as the hangout for African Americans. And just as Latinos' location on the periphery of the central school yard underscored their marginal position in the school hierarchy, the central location of the African American students underscored their dominant position.

Their peers, particularly Mexican Americans and other Latinos, often described African American students as the most dominant and largest group on campus, despite the fact that they were smaller in number than Asians. Charles Gallagher has found that, nationwide, Whites overestimate the number of African Americans and underestimate their own numbers, suggesting that Whites regard themselves to be under siege.[6] Mexican American and Latino students at RHS who overestimated the number of African Americans at the school justified their misperception by saying that African Americans were intimidating and domineering. During one of the weekend camps RHS had instituted to improve interracial relations, White and Latino students described their African American schoolmates as bullies who cut the lines in the cafeteria, blocked the stage during noontime rallies, and staged unexpected provocations. As Enrique put it, African Americans were considered to be overbearing by their peers not because they were "more in numbers, but [because] they [were] bossing everybody around."

Other facets of this perception of dominance were a conspicuous style and an intense policing of racial boundaries. African Americans' conspicuous style involved wearing brand-name clothes such as Eddie Bauer, Guess, and Tommy Hilfiger, gold necklaces and bracelets, expensive brand-name shoes and sneakers, and pagers. Even teachers recognized that African American students had a distinct style and that they were much more fashion-conscious than Asians, Latinos, or Whites. Many—boys even more than girls—were proud of their style: some African American girls complained that "all the guys can think about is clothes and what they are going to wear the next day."

If style played a role in creating and maintaining collective and racialized boundaries, style had a very different gender valence in the four different groups.[7] Among Latinos and Whites, who tended to cluster in mixed-gender groups, style was more unisex, and it was often the women who were identified as trendsetters. In contrast, African Americans and Asian cliques tended to be more gender-segregated, and there was a clear distinction between male and female styles. African American males treated style as a primarily male endeavor, whereas females were less concerned with clothes in the first place and less constrained by peer pressure to be "decked out." For African American males particularly, style was a defining element of a larger racial identity.

Daniel, an African American student who had recently moved to the area and was still somewhat of an outsider in his class, described the important role of style among his new peers in Newtown:

> Some guys, if they don't have their Eddie Bauers on, or their Timberland shoes, they won't come to school. I am not really into clothing lines, so when I came to school, in some Levi's, I was, like, the laughing stock. Levi's!

A friend, Max, joined the conversation. Max wore a keychain with a picture of his baby, and a thick gold necklace. He told us that his baby's mother had bought it for him, and that it had cost about $600. Daniel commented:

> People will literally die for this chain. They snatch it off your neck, and this is so materialistic, this is an item that maybe shouldn't even be worn, because it is so expensive and . . . it looks so nice. Yeah, people are literally cutting your neck, they taking your shoes.

While style was a crucial marker for racial dominance and an indicator of inclusion or exclusion among Black students themselves, it was also a major domain for describing racial differences and for gauging racial relations. Rob, a ninth grader, for example, used style to describe Blacks, Latinos, Asians, and Whites:

Latinos . . . they wanna wear big, big, big clothes. Like their pants, they cover their whole shoes, until right to the [tip], and then they cut 'em up right at the sides. And Asians are kind of like a twist with the gnarly White boys and the Mexicans. You mix 'em together, you got your baggy pants, you got your khaki shirt, [. . .] it's that swap meet stuff [. . .] and then, you got your Brothers. They wanna dress, you know, they wanna dress to impress the Black women, 'cause if we don't look nice to them, they don't look nice to us, and we sure as hell don't wanna have no ugly women, you know.

The importance of style as a marker of dominance was particularly evident in an interview with Albert, a small-framed, Hispanic-looking student from Nicaragua who despised Mexicans and their culture. He himself associated primarily with African Americans and belonged to a Black posse called Black Brothers. His nickname was Nawty Dog, which he had tattooed on his wrist. Albert was explicit and reflective about the importance of Black style as a marker of dominance and status. To him, wearing expensive jewelry and clothes was a sign of power and showed that one had the means to protect and defend oneself against those who might want to take it away:

A gold chain is, like, for decoration. Who gets the biggest chain, who gets the best shoes, like brand-name shoes, like Nike and Fila. Who got the brand name clothes? [. . .] Kind of, like, to identify with each other, like, a style. To be a man [means] to be able to handle any problems that may occur. If someone messes with you, you gotta be able to handle that, 'cause [. . .] you know [. . .] if someone wants to snatch your chain . . . If I had a chain, I feel, it's necessary to back it up, to make sure that it's . . . , that nobody can take it. Because, if not, what is the point of having a chain, if somebody is gonna take it away? [. . .] It's kind of like a strength, how big you are . . . [Because if you were weak and didn't have a lot of backup], you wouldn't wear a gold chain. Yeah, you wouldn't wear nice shoes, because you would get your shoes taken away, or nice clothes, 'cause your clothes will get taken away too.

Jewelry, according to this logic, was a sign of power, both because it was expensive and because it showed one's political clout; it portrayed a sense of the wearer as confident, invincible, and most important, powerful and ready to activate a large network of allies. If style was a central topic of many interviews and conversations with African American students when we talked about race and power, gangs, so frequently mentioned by Latinos and Cambodians, rarely came up. It was only in a conversation with a Cambodian, who told me about his gang and its affiliation with the Dawgs, known in the area as a large and influential African American gang, that I heard about African American gangs and their significance at RHS. Only then did I start to see initials of the Dawgs and their various subsets on walls and desks. And suddenly I became aware of the overwhelming appearance of black—the color associated with Dawgs—and the gang initials on clothes, backpacks, sports jackets, and other personal items. Sylvie, an African American senior about to graduate, provided an answer to my question about the Dawgs:

> Basically, everybody around here is Dawgs, cause you won't find any Mob really in Newtown. Period! [Asians], I mean, they formulate their own little posse or whatever, and Dawgs is just, like, the thing to be in Newtown. I mean, I don't think you'll survive if you're a Mob unless you are a Samoan. You know what I am sayin'? I's[8] like ... [...] As I told you, in this side of town, you're kind of automatically considered a Dawg, no matter what kind of gang you're from. On this side of town, i's like automatically you wear black. You know what I am sayin'? And especially, if you're a new gang, or a new posse coming out!

The Mob and the Dawgs are two legendary gangs, generally thought to be African American, who have had a long-standing and widely publicized feud in the larger metropolitan area. Explaining the Dawgs' territorial prominence over the Mob, Sylvie referred to African Americans in a dominant, unmarked discourse. No matter what one's race might be, you would have to succumb to and ally yourself with one of two African American gangs if you wanted to survive in the neighborhood. Blackness was the critical color through which others had to identify themselves, whether in their style or their gang alliance. New posses, gangs, or crews would have to declare themselves as Dawgs—rather than Mob—independent of their racial and ethnic classification.

This was the only time that the topic of gangs came up in any of the conversations and interviews I had with African American students. In contrast, Latinos had denied the existence of Latino gangs on campus, and Cambodians had said gangs played a major role in determining the racial climate at RHS. Sylvie explained that Black students distanced themselves consciously from gangs. Even if they were in gangs, they would try not to reveal it because of the stigma associated with gangs that severely limited one's possibilities in the larger social arena. Instead, she said, they were more likely to call themselves posses or school gangs. An African American football coach, a graduate of RHS and of Newtown's African American gangs, confirmed her view. He added that distancing oneself from gangs was also an act of consciously maintaining a boundary between oneself and Latinos and Asians, whom African Americans tended to consider lower in status. In a similar vein, African Americans' use of style as a marker of dominance and an instrument for assessing racial differences was meant to demonstrate their dominance over Latinos and Cambodians.

African Americans' distancing from Latinos and Asians contrasted sharply with their positioning in relation to Whites. While they often treated the former as a nuisance, not worth serious consideration as enemies or allies, it was the latter they identified as worthy challengers.

As discussed earlier, among the students in Mr. McAuley's English class, topics such as "talking white," "acting white," and "being an Oreo cookie"—that is, Black on the outside and White on the inside—frequently came up in conversation. Academic success, using specific vocabulary, and speaking in Standard English with one's peers could all be interpreted as "trying to act white." Such policing against behavioral characteristics of whiteness did not apply to appearance: girls with long and straight or wavy hair and a light complexion were regarded as more beautiful than girls with cornrows and darker complexions.

African Americans, more than anyone else, thus rigidly enforced racial boundaries, particularly between themselves and Whites. Because the cost of "selling out" to Whites was so high,[9] sanctions were severe, and internal policing and conformity were necessary by-products.

CAMBODIANS: "WE'RE ALL DAWGS HERE"

As the largest group of Asian Americans at RHS, Cambodians were considered by many to represent Asians generally. This view obscured the distinction between the academically competitive Chinese, Japanese, Koreans, and Indians, who tended to be U.S.-born (the second- or third-generation children of immigrants) and the "1.5 generation" of Vietnamese, Cambodian, Laotian, and Hmong children who came to the United States as refugees during and after the Vietnam War.

While the former were more concentrated in the magnet programs and uninvolved in the racial conflict on campus, it was the latter who were important players in the "race riot." Although not involved in the initial confrontation with water balloons, Cambodians soon joined in and fought on the side of African Americans. A few days later, several Cambodian students brought some balloons, filled them up, and walked around the quad showing them off. Security staff soon spotted and reprimanded them for bringing objects to the school that had been declared contraband.

Several cliques of Cambodians, some of them self-declared members of gangs, ordinarily met in front of the library. Others met between the cafeteria and the quad, a less exposed area. Still others sat on the benches in the middle of the quad, with their buddies or their girlfriends. These locations positioned the Cambodians strategically between African Americans around the administration building and Latinos at the tree.

During the week-long series of mediation meetings, administrators watched Cambodians closely. It is quite likely that they considered the visibility, if not growth, of Cambodian gangs to be a serious problem for school security. Cambodians had been singled out as instigators of the riot and had also emerged as the most defiant of all the parties involved. The original conflict between Latinos and African Americans had become secondary to the agenda set by the school's administrators, which revolved around containing a potential Cambodian backlash against Mexicans. In the final meeting, Cambodians still seemed the most resistant to calls for tolerance and cooperation. In response to questions about what kinds of activities students thought might improve race relations on campus, some Cambodians suggested, in writing, "to beat up more Mexicans." Needless to say, after an entire week of reconciliation meetings, counselors and administrators found this remark dismaying.

The long-standing conflicts between Cambodians and Latinos was reflected in a conversation I had with a Cambodian student, Bo, following a mediation session. Bo explained how he had been caught in a fight with a Mexican gang and ended up with a bullet in his back, even though he himself had never been in a gang. He said Cambodians did not trust Mexicans at Roosevelt High because Mexicans would not admit their association with gangs. As Bo put it, Mexicans wore nice clothes in school, but as soon as they were outside the school they put on their gang clothes and fought for their race. Bo assured me emphatically that Cambodians would gladly vote for Proposition 187. Cambodians, he said, hated Mexicans because for every Asian there were about forty Latinos in the city.

Many Cambodians described their relationship with Mexicans—their generic term for Latinos—as fraught with fear and hate. Mexicans, to them, were synonymous with Mexican gangs. Living in neighborhoods that were often controlled by Mexican gangs, Cambodians experienced a constant threat of "getting jumped" or even killed by Mexicans. Stories about fights and barely escaping attacks by Mexican gangs were a staple of their conversations. Many Cambodians joined gangs during junior high school, either as a means of protection or as an inevitable consequence of living in these neighborhoods. Joey, a Cambodian from the Social Work Academy, described the relationship between Latinos and Asians as exclusively determined by gang conflicts:

> It's all about race now. You can even be a nerd. Now there are so many gangs out there, so much race hate, it's like, if you're Asian, it's like, they're making you a gangster.

In the eyes of many, the conflict between Cambodians and Mexicans had turned into generalized racial warfare that affected entire communities. Even adult Latinos and Cambodians were often scared to walk on certain streets, worried that someone might attack them because of their race. This tension existed side-by-side with a cultural affinity between Cambodians and Latinos, expressed in the many romantic relationships between Cambodian girls and Latino boys. And interestingly, interracial couples, rather than creating further interracial strife, found that their partners provided effective protection during the riots.

Eight out of twelve Cambodian and other Southeast Asian students I interviewed at length indicated that they had been in or currently were in a gang or a tagging crew. Gangs were as conspicuously present in their conversations about race as they were absent in African Americans' discussions about race. In Cambodians' understanding of the gang war as a race war, they were also eager to portray themselves as allies of African American students. Mickey, a Cambodian veteran of neighborhood warfare, supported Joey's notion of a race war and explained:

> So mostly, Black and Asian together, you know, it's like, united, like all mens, I mean all mens from, I mean like all ethnic mens, you know, just, [. . .] Blacks and Asians together, [. . .] we don't, mostly Black and Asian don't like Mexicans right now. You know, Mexican[s] used to be in a lot of trouble with us.

In the racial politics of Roosevelt High School, Cambodians allied themselves closely with African Americans. Even more, Cambodians identified themselves as the "Blacks of the Asians," as one student put it. This was expressed also in self-conscious and joking allusions, as the interview with Babe G and Li'l Monster, both members of the gang Asian Deuces, reveals:

ADS: You're Cambodian?

ALL: Yeah.

BG: You could tell? [laughs]

LM: You could tell by our skin.

ADS: Cambodian are darker than . . . Vietnamese?

BG: Na.

LM: Some Cambodians are light.

ADS: Yeah? So why do you say you can tell by the skin?

BG: It's just like, just, I don't know how to say [laughs, embarrassed].

But Babe G and his friends associated themselves with blackness not only because of their skin color, but also because of the stigma associated with it. In discussing the events following the riots, I asked Babe G and his friends why they thought that Cambodians were almost exclusively blamed for the riots at the school. Their spontaneous, though increasingly self-conscious and stifled answer was because Mexicans, their major enemies in the fight, had the same skin color as Whites, who also controlled the school.

ADS: One thing that I was noticing during that meeting in the cafeteria [the postriot mediation], it seemed to me, everybody was saying to the Cambodians, you guys, you need to get it together.

LM: White people's skin color is close to Mexican [who were the opponents in the fight].

ADS: What was that?

LM: Just kiddin'.

ADS: White people call you Mexican?

LM: No, I was just kiddin' around. I don't know what the FUCK [emphatic] I am talking about.

Contained in Li'l Monster's stifled remark—which I understood only after listening to the recorded tape—was the implication that because their skin was dark, like that of African Americans, they were seen as troublemakers, as were African Americans in general. Their identification with blackness and their political alliances with Blacks might be rooted in the more widespread color discrimination among Asians, who often distinguished each other ethnically by referring to their skin color. This was also evident in a statement made by Lance, a member of the Cambodian gang, the Newtown Kings, when he said: "We're all Dawgs here, it's, like, our nationality." Racial differences between African Americans and Cambodians, from the Cambodian perspective, were insignificant. Racial warfare among "ethnic mens," as Mickey said, produced a unified front against Mexicans, whom they considered to be White.

The acceptance of Black dominance in this one-sided coalition between Blacks and Cambodians was also manifested in Cambodians' adoption of Black cultural elements. Thus Cambodian students usually spoke to me in a form of African American vernacular, which they called "street language." In contrast, African American students switched to Standard English when talking to me, but used Black vernacular to talk to each other or their teachers. The primacy of Black cultural expressions in Cambodians' self-representation was also evident in their appreciation of Black style, as Mickey explained: "In high school I am into style, girls, and money." They also adopted the term "Mack Daddy," a term that describes a man who knows how to attract women's attention with his talk, although Black students and others had abandoned it after junior high school.[10] These inconsistencies between Black students' culture and Cambodians' emulation of it indicated that the alleged Cambodian-Black coalition was not based on actual social interaction, but was rather a one-sided form of alliance.

WHITES: "RACE DOESN'T REALLY MATTER TO ME"

Where did White students fit into this picture? Which space did they occupy in the school? Where were they when the "riot" broke out? As the emerging literature of whiteness shows, being White is a fundamentally different experience than being Black, Latino, or Asian American in the United States. Ernesto Laclau writes:

> Derrida has shown how an identity's constitution is always based on excluding something and establishing a violent hierarchy between the two resultant poles— man/woman, etc. What is peculiar to the second term is thus reduced to the function of an accident as opposed to the essentiality of the first. It is the same with the black-white relationship, in which white, of course, is equivalent to "human being."[11]

Mary Waters writes that White "racial" identity is more often structured in reference to European "ethnic" ancestry than in reference to other non-White groups.[12] One characteristic of whiteness consists in the expectation that racial privilege is a birthright of whiteness and as such not tangible.[13] Whiteness becomes tangible only when this privilege is threatened or absent, or when Whites assume a minority status within a non-White majority. But as is true of other racial identities, the meaning of whiteness depends on context and locality; some Whites experience significantly greater race privileges than others.

No White student was involved in what the school administration called "racial unrest." When the fight broke out at "the tree," White students remained at the other end of the campus. No White students participated in the subsequent mediation meetings either. Hours before the conflict took place, I had interviewed two White girls from the gifted magnet GROW about the racial climate at RHS. They denied that any tensions or conflicts existed and emphatically described RHS—unlike other schools in the area—as a place where everybody got along.

Their unawareness of the pervasive racial tensions, which were about to erupt into a fight, reflected their limited social interaction with non-White students. Because so many White students were concentrated in the accelerated track, in different classrooms from non-White students, the possibilities for interaction between White and non-White students were spatially restricted. This was especially true in the predominantly White gifted magnet, where White identity was nurtured around the discursive practices of being "gifted" and "in need of protection." Extracurricular activities, such as student government, drama clubs, speech and debate, and Model United Nations, where participation consisted primarily of students from the two top tiers, followed the racial distribution in the different tracks and thus amplified the spatial segregation of the classrooms. However, a small number of White students were enrolled in the school's other academic programs, where they usually were a small minority.

A few years earlier, RHS had been in the news because one of its students was a member of a White supremacist group that had planned to start a race war in the region. This flashed through my mind when I saw a swastika scratched on the desk in front of me.[14] I was attending a history class in the racially mixed, middle-tier City Academy. As curious as I was alarmed by this discovery, I scanned the classroom, the students' clothing, and their accessories for more indications of White supremacists. I was shocked to see one White student wearing a T-shirt with a VW logo on the front and the Nazi slogan *Kraft durch Freude* (strength through joy). This slogan was associated with Nazi recreational camps, just as *Arbeit macht frei* (labor liberates) was associated with concentration camps. After class I asked Jim about his T-shirt and what it represented. He said he wore the shirt because he was a VW fan. He had gotten the shirt from a VW exhibit. After I translated the slogan for him and explained its connotations and history, he was embarrassed and insisted that he had had no idea what it meant and denied any association with neo-Nazis or White supremacists. When I brought up this subject with students later, they said there were some neo-Nazis at the school, but that they kept a low profile because so few at RHS shared their views. As one Latino student put it: "They don't dare to show themselves, because they would just get their butt whipped."

In the school yard, White students tended to gather around the rally stage, located near the administration building, the area identified as the African American hangout, and opposite the library, which was identified as the Asian hangout. White students' territory branched out into the center of the school yard and toward the gated entrance. What was considered the White student hangout was at the opposite end of the school yard from "the tree," the Latino hangout and the site where racial tensions had erupted. This generally recognized White hangout was the home of some well-defined cliques, one of them being the notorious Trojans, a fraternity whose members were enrolled in the second highest educational tier, the Agriculture, Business, and Industry (ABI) Academy, and the "Surrealists," mostly from the gifted magnet, who defined themselves as the school outcasts. During the Friday noon rallies, when student groups regularly performed on the small stage in the school yard, White students largely vacated this territory. Some decided to establish a club that would meet during that time; they called themselves the Surrealists, in reference to a discussion of surrealism in one of their courses. Club members were allowed to stay inside a classroom during the break. One member of their clique, Rick, explained that they felt they were overrun by African American students, who claimed both the stage and the space for the audience.

Rastas were another group of Whites located around the rally stage. Their location between the White territory around the rally stage and the African American territory near the administration building signaled in several ways an intermediate or hybrid position between White and Black students in the school yard. With their various degrees of matted hair and their ritualized speeches about "living righteously," spiked with references to Rastafarian religion, they exhibited an appropriation of a specific Black cultural identity. Some regulars of this group were Latinos who also hung out at the tree, and some were from Latino-Anglo families. Just as they worked against their racial categorization as White through their style and their location, Rastas vehemently avoided using racial labels when talking about their non-White peers. For example, Allison, a senior from a middle-tier academy, passionately argued that there were no different races of people; rather, there was only one race, the human race.

Rastas, most of whom were enrolled in the middle range of the academic programs, were a minority in their classes. In addition, most of them lived "in the hood" and were therefore also a racial minority in their neighborhoods. Allison, who lived in the suburbs, was an exception. She described her own neighborhood as uninteresting and sterile and praised the liveliness, friendliness, and communal spirit of people in the "hood," where she spent a lot of time visiting her boyfriend. Zach, also a senior and a friend of Allison's, was a surfer and a skater, whose dreadlocks, he said, had proven to be an asset in his neighborhood. As one of few Whites there, he said, he might be considered an outsider and raise suspicion among his neighbors and the informal economy that flourished in his neighborhood. But because of his dreadlocks, he said, his neighbors assumed that he was smoking marijuana and maybe even sold it. His dreadlocks, he explained, thus seemed to help him blend into his neighborhood.

The Rastas conveyed a strong sense of group cohesion through their explicit references to religion, their often neglected physical appearance, and their common practice of smoking marijuana, which set them apart from others. But they were oblivious to their classmates' criticisms that they were unclean. They masked their racial identity, often White and sometimes Latino, through their identity as Rastas, a subcultural style associated with blackness. While Rastas did not have access to or acceptance in the world of African American students at RHS—who often called Rastas "filthy"—their style signaled an appreciation of a specific Black subculture, which softened their relations with African Americans.

Sports, like the noontime rallies, were also spaces of racial isolation. Softball and water sports were played primarily by Whites and Asians, and soccer was played primarily by Latinos and Whites. Baseball was a bit more integrated, and basketball and football—considered to be the most "masculine" and prestigious of all the school sports—were played mostly by African Americans.

Jake, a White senior in the second-tier academy, was an exception in this regard. He explained that he had not let himself become intimidated by the almost exclusively African American basketball team and was the only White student on the team. Asked how he felt about this experience, Jake answered:

J: Race doesn't really matter to me, I feel comfortable with it. [. . .] It wouldn't matter if it did make a difference to me. I love playing basketball, and making race a problem wouldn't help me at all.

ADS: It's kind of courageous to be the only White guy in an all-Black sports team. I heard White guys say they would love to play basketball, but they just feel it's not for them.

J: The first day I got here, it was the day after I graduated from junior high school, I came here during the summer, and, I didn't know anybody, and, it was for sports only, and, there weren't any White people here, and, then, and I came out, and everything looked so big to me, and, I just did it 'cause I love playing basketball, and I signed up, and, I's . . . I was one of the better guys, and, they respected me, and it wasn't about race at all.

Jake, like many other of my White interviewees, first responded with a color-blind statement about the racial climate on campus. But unlike most of his White peers, Jake's involvement with basketball required interacting with his African American teammates and had made him aware of the tensions between African Americans and Mexicans. Asked about the school's riot, he explained:

J: Well, it seemed White people weren't involved in it at all, you know, it's like, a Mexican and Black thing, and I, kind of stayed out of it.

ADS: Would you have expected something like that? [. . .]

J: Well, yeah, it seemed like, I wouldn't say just recently. But, it seems like there's always some animosity between Mexicans and Blacks. [. . .] It's just, like on the basketball team. No Mexican plays basketball, and, like, there is some Mexicans who hang around there, and try to play basketball with us, and, they'll be like Blacks against Mexicans. They trying to make it personal, they be saying [changing his voice] "Mexicans against Blacks," and sometimes they won't even let me play, cause they wanna make it just a racial game I guess.

At the beginning of our interview, Jake presented himself as immune to thinking in terms of racial differences. During the course of our conversation, Jake became more explicit about his experiences of race and racial differences. He confirmed others' opinions of African American students as domineering, and described how some imitated what they thought were Black speech patterns, particularly in using the inflammatory term "nigga." They used this term to portray themselves as hip. Jake explained the term "wigger"—a contraction of "white nigger"—in this context:

Well, there's some people which I call wiggers, White guys trying to be like Black guys. That's an expression, uh, I don't know why, maybe because Blacks get a lot of respect, 'cause they're the athletes and stuff, 'cause this is one of the best schools for sports around, and if you're like one of the best athletes in the school, you're one of the best athletes around, and most athletes are Black. [. . .] I don't know, sometime even when I play basketball, I have like . . . a Black friend of mine, the way they deal with . . . I don't know, the way they play basketball is the way I play basketball too. And it seems, like, I act Black when I play basketball too. [. . .] If I dunk on somebody, I be like, "Oh, look in your face," like Black people do. I be like, taunt them, you know, or I scream "Oh, that's in your face," or whatever, or just scream "aha," or whatever. [. . .] I don't know, sometime, even when I, like, play basketball, [. . .] the way they play basketball is the way I play basketball too, and it seems, I act Black when I play basketball too, and it seems like, if I dunk on somebody, [. . .] I be like, . . . like Black.

Jake here turns from a description of wigger to an explanation of how he himself identified as Black, that he was Black in the way he played basketball, stopping short of calling himself a wigger. But once our conversation turned to girls and sex, Jake's identification with being Black changed. He described his African American teammates as continuously boasting about their sexual conquests, which he found was quite the opposite of his White friends' behavior:

Well, in my experience, um, Black people have a lot more sex, than I know White people do. I hear, I hear, it's like commonplace for Black students. Maybe my . . . , my perspective is unique, cause I am on the basketball team, and I hang out . . . I don't hang out with them, but, the time I spent with them in practices, and in the weight room, or whatever, we talk, and I hear a lot, like, "Yeah, yeah, I just got back from my next door neighbor, my groin hurts" and I swear, like, this guy, like, this guy on my basketball team, he has sex before practice, and after practice, and, um, during ga . . . not during games, but, I mean, all the time, well, that's all he thinks about, and I don't know, I think he got his girlfriend pregnant too, and he still has sex with a lot of girls and stuff.

Jake's pursuit of what others considered to be racially exclusive spaces set him apart from many of his White peers and made him more aware of the racial dynamic in his environment. Jake's racial identification shifted with the composition of his social environment. On the basketball court, he described himself as acting Black, almost like a "wigger," but when it came to sex, he was White.

For Jake, as for the other White students I have described, African American students were the critical "racial other," more visible than Latinos or Asians. Jake's contact with his teammates was limited, and beyond the basketball court, Jake remained an outsider to his African American peers, whose sexual norms he described as disturbingly different from those of his White friends. Latinos and Asians were peripheral to his experience. Despite the fact that the buddy who gave him a ride to school every day was a second-generation Mexican American, Latinos were outside his field of vision, visible only as rivals to Blacks. Asian students were also invisible to him, as was his own White racial identity.

Paul did not have the same courage as Jake. A good-looking junior in the ABI Academy, with an athletic build and short brown hair, Paul was on the varsity swim team. I first met Paul during an interview with Ben, when the two of them greeted each other with a hand slap. I remember that at the time I was struck by this rare display of intimacy in Black-White interaction at RHS. After warming up to our conversation, Paul explained to me that his primary interest in athletics had been basketball, not swimming. But when he came to RHS, he found that basketball was accessible only to Blacks. Paul later became the president of the Trojans.

Members of the Trojans made the most racially explicit statements of all the White students with whom I spoke. In a conversation about the racial climate at RHS, Caleb and Thomas were quick to point out that although Whites were a minority on this school campus, they represented the top tier of the educational hierarchy: "If there was to be, like Caucasian, or whatever, it would be in the ABI or gifted program. There aren't too many White people in the regular classes." Similarly, they were quick to remind me that whatever racial tensions there existed on campus, White students were not involved in it. They described the apartment buildings adjacent to RHS as "Roosevelt Housing Project" and warned me not to park my car in the school's parking lot because Asian guys would break into it and steal my stereo. Theirs were certainly the least color-blind comments regarding race.

Finally, there were the self-described outcasts, the Surrealists from the gifted magnet, GROW. In their openness toward others, their liberal views, and their self-reflection, they were in many ways the opposite of the Trojans. Though mostly White, the Surrealists also included Norman, who was of mixed African American and White heritage; Jorge, a third-generation Mexican; and occasionally two African American girls, Jessie and Shanarah. Otherwise, the Surrealists had little contact with Latinos, Southeast Asians, or African Americans. They defined themselves primarily as different from the regular GROW crowd, and especially the Trojans. Any distinction between themselves as White and African Americans, Latinos, and Asians as non-White was largely muted in an environment where the discourse of giftedness had become interchangeable with whiteness. However, on the flip side of whiteness as giftedness, in the realm of the dominance relations in the school yard and peer cultures, they were aware of their relatively low status. Being referred to by their GROW teachers and staff as "in need of protection" from their peers was clearly also a statement about their relative naiveté and powerlessness in relation to the non-gifted, non-White student body.

Unlike their peers, White students did not have a strong or explicit racial solidarity to appeal to in their everyday life in the school. As a Mexican American student put it pointedly, "It's no fun to beat up a White guy, because most likely none of his friends will back him up." Whiteness did not need to be asserted in the predominantly White environment of the top-tier programs. However, the farther down one went in the educational hierarchy, the more White students became a minority. This did not necessarily mean that White students had more social interaction with others, but their self-awareness about being Whites increased. White students here reacted in several ways: with an increasing sense of alienation and a demand for a White space, as the Trojans did; by subtly or unconsciously displaying symbols of White supremacy, as Jim did on his VW logo T-shirt; or by appropriating a subcultural identity that emulated Black elements and thus softened their appearance of difference, as the Rastas did.

What all these different groups of White students shared, however, was a primary perception of African Americans as racial others. African Americans were their racial point of reference, not Latinos and not Asians. When they talked about their experiences with and perspectives of racial others, they only described African Americans and eclipsed the Latino or Asian identity of some of their closer associates. Even Asians, particularly East Asians who were more prominent in the upper-tier programs, were not in their field of vision, as they might have become whitened through the "gifted" label.

THE RACIAL CONFIGURATION OF THE SCHOOL-YARD HIERARCHY

The relational nature of how students identified themselves and others was unmistakable. Whom each of them perceived as a racial "other" depended on their own location, and such perceptions were often not symmetrical.

In the post-riot meetings, for example, Cambodians and Southeast Asians generally described Latinos as their biggest racial antagonists, but Latinos were challenged mostly by African Americans. African Americans paid little attention to their interactions with Latinos or Asians and instead situated themselves in relation to Whites. White students, similarly, were almost oblivious to the presence of their Latino or Asian peers, but based their sense of racial identification on their relationship with African American students, whom they found aggressive but also admired.

How this racial configuration was interpreted as a political act gradually became transparent through the stories they told. According to them, Cambodians exploited the momentum of the riot to escalate their own animosities toward Latinos. Their conspicuous and strategic alliance with African Americans during the riot tapped into the cultural capital and dominant position that African American students at Roosevelt High School controlled. African Americans, on the other hand, not only did *not* reciprocate this one-sided alliance, but sent clear signals distancing themselves from both Cambodians and Latinos. They considered neither group to be a worthy challenger or ally.

Latinos showed the strongest mobilization of a race-based political identity, although this identity was limited to official school culture and thus was of little use in the arena of peer culture and the school yard. There, Latinos adopted a more race-neutral identity.

White students, finally, as long as they were engulfed in the discourse of whiteness as giftedness, were the most unmarked racial category: they were the least conscious of their own racial status and that of their non-White peers. However, outside the protected space of the gifted program and in the quad, where they were more likely to see and interact with others, they became increasingly aware of their whiteness and relative lack of power in the school yard. The Surrealists demonstrated this, for example, by surrendering "their" spot to an African American crowd during the lunch rallies. The lower White students were located in the educational hierarchy, the more acute was their awareness of being a minority, and the more in need they were of finding either compensatory or accommodative strategies.

THE SCHOOL-YARD GEOGRAPHY OF RACE

Studies of race and school have often focused on the institutional and curricular aspects in which schools produce and reproduce race or on individual accounts of racial identity.[15] However, RHS students' analyses of racial conflicts shed light on a quite different aspect of race-making in schools: adolescents' collective maneuvering in the school yard and neighborhood. Adolescents cannot escape the racial order that emerges in the institutional setting and the curriculum, but they also form their own explanations of the racial order based on their collective experiences with identifiable racial others, and on the local "folklore" to which they actively contribute.

In their systematic study of racial and interethnic conflicts at school, Rosemary Henze and her colleagues found that conflict is manifested not only in physical clashes, but also in taunts, ethnic jokes, and racial tension. In schools where resources are shared more equally and tracking is not systemic, they found students to be relatively cooperative across racial lines, more likely to engage in interracial friendships. But conflicts that did occur tended to be explosive. In contrast, schools with greater gaps in resource distribution were most likely to suffer racial conflict.[16]

Roosevelt High administrators encouraged meaningful interracial interaction in some instances, such as at the Human Relations Camp, but hindered it in others. Following Henze and her colleagues' analysis, this would suggest that the most volatile conflicts would take place between the gifted magnet and the rest, or between White students and non-White students. As it turned out, though, there were no physical conflicts and few noticeable tensions between these two most segregated populations, although they were also not neutral toward each other. Actual clashes involved only Latinos, African Americans, and Southeast Asians, with Samoans acting as peacekeepers. These were all members of populations that were disproportionately poor, lived in crowded areas, and received a small share of the school's educational resources.

In contrast, the picture that emerges from students' narratives is one of racial identity as relational, instrumental, and scale-specific. First, that adolescents constructed racial identity through relations with each other was evident in the way each group defined itself in relation to one or maybe two "others," but never in relation to everyone. But these dyads were often not symmetrical. For example, Latinos' "other" was African Americans, but for African Americans, Latinos hardly registered.

Second, that racial identity sometimes was also used as a political strategy was evident in the racial alliances, dominations, and exclusions that were formed for political expediency. The Cambodian students, for example, bolstered their position against Latinos by forging an alliance with African Americans and portraying themselves as the "Blacks of the Asians"; and Latinos engaged in a generalized alliance with Whites. Groups allied themselves racially with others according to their own collective interest and the context in which they found themselves.

And finally, that racial identity was scale-specific was illustrated by the ways in which Proposition 187 was used. At the state level, Prop 187 was seen as a backlash against Mexicans and Mexican Americans on the part of White California voters. At the school, though, Latinos and Whites were cautious allies, and Cambodians and African Americans used the proposition's racially divisive discourse in their alliance against Latinos. Similarly, during the 1992 Los Angeles riots, Blacks and Asians were often portrayed in the media as arch rivals. But in the school yard a few years later, there was a strong, if unilateral, alliance between the two. Seen from a different perspective, new immigrant groups, here Latinos and Cambodians, adapted to and molded themselves according to the well-established racial positions of Blacks and Whites.

But although racial configurations are scale- and context-specific, the complex reframing of Prop 187 at Roosevelt High School also showed how racial conflicts in one context are linked in unexpected ways to racial conflicts elsewhere. Proposition 187 loomed large in the low-level racial tensions at the school. It was a discursive resource for bolstering racial boundaries. But every so often racially explicit talk turned physical. Surprisingly, though, Prop 187 did not lead to increased conflict between Latinos and Whites, as it had done elsewhere. Instead, it fueled the conflict between Latinos and African Americans on one hand, and between Latinos and Cambodians on the other.[17] This was one unpredictable ramification of a political rhetoric that scapegoated a vulnerable disadvantaged group.

Race politics among students, then, was not unrelated to or uninfluenced by state and national racial politics. However, how adolescents acted on their conflicts at the micro level depended on their own position and on the social and political resources available to them.

The racial tensions that erupted during the fight at the tree can also be regarded as a racial project. The racial mobilization and the physical confrontation that it entailed can be seen as the structural aspects, while students' narratives about the riot can be seen as the project's representational aspect.

Students are not usually regarded as political agents, and their power struggles with each other are not as significant as power relations in the wider arena. After all, they are operating from within an institution and do not have access to formal power. But either as individuals or collectively, they negotiate power relations and they conduct politics in their sphere of influence. The racial meanings that emerged in their narratives of the race riot reflected their collective maneuverings. In fact, their analyses of the event illustrate how they forged their own "common sense" notions of race. But the common sense notions students volunteered went beyond "preconceived notions of a racialized social structure" as a basis for interpreting race.[18] They deviated from the more common "common sense" by tailoring their notions of race to their own living environments and experiences. Although they incorporated some elements of the larger racial discourse, such as Proposition 187, alliances between Blacks and Asians against Whites and Latinos also contrasted sharply with the existing pattern of racial tension between Whites and Latinos. Adolescents at RHS selectively appropriated, redirected, and transformed racial meanings. Their agency in creating those meanings was evident in their active construction of a racial common sense, as well as in the identities they exhibited and inhabited and in the social relations they created with others.

However, the common sense they developed through their analysis of the riot differs from the one discussed in the previous chapter. There, students' and teachers' notions of whiteness/gifted and blackness/at risk were more closely linked to the state, since both "gifted" and "at risk" are binding educational labels.

Interpreting the riot as a racial project complicates the links between the micro and the macro level. The relationships among adolescents in the school yard can only to some degree be considered a product of the state. Certainly the institution dictates (by virtue of its license from the state) that adolescents go to school, it influences whom they meet there, and it directly or indirectly influences which educational program they enroll in. But the social space they generate through their interactions with each other is of importance to the state only when problems occur, such as a riot. Otherwise, students' social space in the school yard generates discourses that are only indirectly linked to the state, and an environment where common sense notions of race operating at the level of the state (such as Prop 187) are selectively appropriated and rearticulated.

The collective racial positions students were hammering out were means of asserting their location within the racial hierarchy in which they operated. The state merely provided a backdrop and resource for the selective racial positioning of

Cambodians and African Americans on one hand and Latinos and Whites on the other. More tangible than the racial hegemony in the larger domain was the racial hegemony operating in the school yard, where African Americans dominated their peers. This brings into focus the process of racialization among subordinated groups, and with it their agency in racial mobilization in the semiautonomous sphere of adolescent school interactions.

5 PERFORMING MANHOOD THROUGH THE RACE MATRIX

The significance of gender in the race riot and its aftermath was ambiguous. African American girls had been portrayed as instigating the event, and more fights between African American girls and Latinas erupted during the days following "the riot." Physical conflicts occurred either between girls or between boys, although the balloon fight was coed. Girls were present during the initial mediation meetings following the event, but eventually it became an all-male affair. Girls rarely mentioned gangs in interviews or spontaneous conversations, and neither females nor males ever volunteered information about girls being affiliated with a gang. Finally, ideas about who started the "riot" were contradictory: some said gangs did; others blamed girls.[1]

Roosevelt High's administration took racial conflict among boys far more seriously than similar conflicts among girls. Popular images and research support such priorities.[2] Whether in the Columbine High School shooting and the many copy-cat events that followed it, or in the violence more often associated with urban schools, the perpetrators tend to be predominantly male.[3] This is true for violent crimes generally, the vast majority of which are committed by men.[4] But the fact that so many students had interpreted the race riot at Roosevelt High as an exclusively male affair suggested that ideas of masculinity were mobilized to produce racial identities and that ideas about race were mobilized to produce masculinities. Building on the racial configurations I have examined in the urban, educational, and school-yard domain, this chapter shows how peer cultures within the setting of a school produce distinct racialized masculinities through their interaction with each other.

SCHOOLS AND MASCULINITY

As Connell has shown, schools play an active part in the making of masculinity. They teach students what it means to be masculine directly and indirectly through "textbooks, career counseling, [and] teacher expectations"; by condoning violence in sports; by silently endorsing homophobic practices; or through sorting practices that encourage high-tracked youth to adopt a hegemonic masculinity and push low-tracked youth into marginalized masculinities. But schools are also settings in which peer cultures generate different masculinities through their dynamic interplay. In schools, peer cultures provide the authority to endorse masculinities, particularly those that are opposed to the dominant gender norms represented in the school curriculum. As both agents and settings, schools produce a "marketplace of masculinities."[5] How racial identities are shaping and shaped by this relational formation of masculinities in peer cultures is the focus of this chapter.

Masculinity can be understood as being formed and performed around three social axes: men's relationships with women, men's relationships with other men; and men's relationships within a collective. By conquering, defending, and controlling women as sexual objects, men often use women as the prime social referent to validate their masculinity.[6] This is endlessly showcased in popular culture, where the male hero wins the most beautiful women, and it is lived in schools, where a male's status is judged by the beauty of his female friends. But equally important is the "idea of woman" as a means of policing against other men and masculinities. Michael Kimmel writes: "In large part, it's other men who are important to American men; American men define their masculinity, not as much in relation to women, but in relation to each other. Masculinity is largely a homosocial enactment."[7]

For example, calling another male a "wimp" or a "pussy" and other forms of feminization are effective weapons for challenging his masculinity and subjugating him symbolically. An everyday example of this is the insult "Fuck you," where sexual domination is a metaphor for the domination of another male. Similarly, the ubiquitous use of "faggot" in schools illustrates the extent to which feminization of other men has become a tool of social control.[8] In their relationships with each other, men use masculinity to exclude or include, or to exploit or intimidate: in other words, to create a "gender politics within masculinity."[9]

This points to the third axis, the performance of masculinity in relation to a collective or an audience.[10] As a performance, masculinity is not identical to the thing it performs, but an approximation of an ideal. Gender performances follow a script and thus are limited in what can and cannot be performed, but such scripts also leave room for variation and agency. How successful one's masculine performance is is ultimately determined by the audience for whom the performance is intended. In his ethnography of Crete villagers and how they construct a specific ethos of masculinity, Michael Herzfeld illustrates how masculine identity is performed in relation to a collective. Which collective or imagined community Crete villagers consider critical, however, shifts with the context. Whether as a male kin group, a village, or a nation,

> the successful performance [. . .] depends upon an ability to identify the self with larger categories of identity. [. . .] Whereas the cognate English word "egoism" suggests a pure focus on the self, the Greek term can only be understood as a *social* category. The fierce mustache and insouciant cigarette of the truly successful *eghoistis* are recognizable precisely because they fit a pattern. [. . .] One has *eghois-mos* on behalf of a collectivity, be it kin group, patriline, village, region, island or country.[11]

Eghoismos thus characterizes the male self, a self that is recognizable because it defines itself through the conventions established by his collective.

These three axes of masculinity, the male-female, the male-male, and the male-collective, are not necessarily separate. Instead, they are often overlapping and complementary, as is readily visible in the feminization of the nation as the mother and in mothers as producers of the nation, as well as in the use of feminizing put-downs as attacks on other men's masculinity.

MASCULINITY AND RACE

American popular culture and folklore are filled with racialized images of masculinity. Popular representations of White masculinity represent an image of White men as naturally powerful, successful, and superior. In contrast, Black men are often imagined as violent and hypersexual, an image circulating at least since D. W. Griffith's 1915 film *Birth of a Nation* and in seemingly endless reincarnations in such icons as Mike Tyson and Snoop Dogg. Mexican men are imagined as macho types who father numerous children and demand exaggerated masculine respect. But maybe the most derogatory stereotype of racialized masculinity is that of Asians as a "castrated race."[12] From the effeminate Fu Manchu character of the early twentieth century to the image of the nerdy Asian student who excels in academics but fails in athletics, Asian men's bodies have been portrayed as soft and hairless[13] and their masculinity as "lacking sinful manhood."[14] As Song Liling says in *M. Butterfly*, "I am an Oriental. And being an Oriental, I could never be completely a man."[15]

While such stereotypical images of racialized masculinity are ubiquitous in our culture, they are distortions that are challenged in numerous ways. The Million Man March in 1995, for example, organized around the idea of atonement for African American men, countered the stereotype of the African American man as uncaring, irresponsible, and exploitive. The 1990 film *Paris Is Burning* showed gay and cross-dressing Black men, often thought of not only as hypermasculine but also homophobic; Latino men are also described as caring fathers,[16] and Asian men have become prominent heroes of martial arts movies.[17] Whether through the eyes of others or through one's own, racialized masculinities are composites; to be understood they need to be situated within their relational contexts.

Two central aspects of masculinity, as of race, are power and domination.[18] Like race, masculinity is a category of embodiment that, in order to be performed, requires an audience.[19] Moreover, the new attention to the study of whiteness brings into focus how whiteness and masculinity are linked to each other and to the relational construction of racial "others." For example, White men's backlash against affirmative action and what they perceive as reverse discrimination underscores how naturalized both superordinate identities are. Furthermore, it exposes the deep-seated assumptions of White male privilege[20] and the aggressions that can be unleashed if these taken-for-granted privileges are challenged.

If different groups of men produce competing masculinities, racial discourses intensify the fomentation of multiple masculinities. By fixing and sometimes challenging status hierarchies, racial discourses give rise to niches of masculinity that enable the performance of masculine dominance. The boxing match between Jim Jeffries, the White boxing champion, and Jack Johnson, an African American newcomer, that took place in Reno in 1910 provides a telling example.[21] The event was publicized internationally, and Whites all over the world anticipated the victory of Jim Jeffries, dubbed "the Hope of the White Race," which they believed would confirm White men's supremacy not only in civilization, but also as a symbol of masculinity. African Americans, though, saw the fight as a chance to finally show the "White man" his weakness. When the fight ended with Jack Johnson knocking out Jim Jeffries, White fans' disappointment turned into rage and riots ignited in some U.S. cities. The individual defeat of Jeffries had become a racial defeat of Whites generally. Because Johnson defeated the hegemonic White order represented by Jeffries in an arena that appeared to be securely dominated by Whites, Whites resegregated this arena of masculine performance in order to prevent future defeats.

In this chapter, I argue that a similar process is at work among youth at Roosevelt High School, where each peer group identifies and secures critical arenas in which to perform masculinity; these masculinities in turn shape and are shaped by existing racial hierarchies.

RACIAL FORMATION, MASCULINE PERFORMANCE, AND RACE BOUNDARIES

Omi and Winant say that race and gender are both "regions" of hegemony, and thus of the racial state. Such regions are not isolated but "overlap, intersect, and fuse with each other in countless ways. [. . .] In many respects, race is gendered and gender is racialized."[22] While this statement echoes the positions on race and masculinity mentioned above, it provides few clues as to how racial formation theory can shed light on the making of racialized masculinities through peer cultures. In fact, although one could argue that racialized masculinities, like racial formation itself, are formed through dynamic processes of creation and recreation and are linked to the state through its gendering practices, they are even more removed from the direct influence of the state than the narratives about the race riot in the previous chapter.

In addition, it is hard to know exactly what we can regard as racial projects in the way peer groups develop niches of masculinity to differentiate themselves from others. If masculinities are viewed as racial projects, how do such projects create a link between structure and representation? Or do they belong completely in the realm of representation? Is their structural component the embeddedness of a particular racial group within a specific location, such as a particular program within a school's different educational tiers and the flow of resources and expectations associated with this particular location? Or is the structural component of this racial project the gender practices they engage in and the political mobilization that it accomplishes by cultivating—and rallying around—certain collective ideals of manhood? Similarly, because the peer culture expressions of masculinity were more defined and subculturally specific than the students' racial assessments of the race riot, would not any attempt to understand masculinities as production sites for "common sense" notions of race lead to sweeping and misleading generalizations?

Considering that students' ways of generating masculinities at the school entailed boundary maintenance as well as negotiations over territory, I suggest using theories of ethnicity[23] and identity[24] to complement racial formation theory. Both offer theoretical frameworks about collective identities with or without the immediate presence of the state[25] and provide concepts through which to interpret not only the interactions and conversations between individuals, but also the larger discourses operating at the level of group and collective identities.

Creating niches for masculine performances goes hand in hand with boundary formation, and studies of ethnic boundary maintenance have often examined competitive ritualized masculinities as arenas for creating and maintaining ethnic boundaries. Describing Yemeni men's competitive performance of improvised poetry in front of an audience of other Yemeni men, Barth argues that such a poetry contest provides an "arena of convergence." Improvising poetry "locks the actor into an agonistic tournament that makes participants converge significantly in action and style, creating a shared consciousness within a group, and discontinuity between them and outsiders."[26]

Improvising poetry becomes for these men a practice "where members of a group converge in behavior and style because of a widely embraced code or value in terms of which they struggle to excel."[27] Such an "arena of convergence" accomplishes several tasks in regard to masculinity. First, men demonstrate to other men that they are what Herzfeld has called being "good at being a man" rather than "being a good man."[28] Second, by creating a shared consciousness or collective identity with other men, they also show that they are good at being Yemeni men, thus creating boundaries with non-Yemenis who do not share their cultural institutions.

Such practices of creating a collective masculinity are not limited to gender-segregated societies such as Yemeni and Crete villages. Playing the dozens, a verbal tradition of ritualized insults in African American culture, allows a similar performance of masculinity. In fact, practices of collective masculinity occur on every level of society: in organized sports, in the development of subcultures such as the Rastas and the greasers, and in institutions such as prisons and schools. Willis found that working-class boys in England developed a distinct working-class masculinity in opposition to school.[29] African American males often do the same thing in American schools. Disproportionately assigned to lower tracks and frequently subject to disciplinary actions, they often are forced into oppositional masculinity lest they be considered effeminate by their peers. This shows that the content—or "arenas of convergence"—of these subordinate masculinities is not arbitrary, but in a complex relationship with the subject position of the collective group and its relationship with others. Particular arenas of convergence, then, might offer solutions to conflicts that marginalized groups of men experience.[30]

Like other forms of identity, masculinities are formed through contact and competition rather than isolation. Stuart Hall and others argue that identity is always structured through what it excludes, through the creation of an outside.[31] Similarly, Barth argues that differentiation and boundary maintenance occur not in isolation, but in conditions of intense contact.[32] This describes the situation of American schools everywhere and of Roosevelt High School in particular, where several thousand students crowd together daily in a small area surrounded by a twelve-foot fence.

In the following pages, I show how friendship groups devise codes of masculinity within a racial hierarchy and how these codes, in turn, contribute to a dynamic racial order. I rely on the analytical tools Barth developed for studying processes of ethnic formation. First I use the concept of "symbols of identity [that promote] an imagined community [. . .] by making a few diacritica highly salient and symbolic."[33] Then, I look at what Herzfeld has described as "lines of contest" or the spaces that a specific group has carved out for itself to demonstrate to its members that they are "good at being a man."[34] Finally, I locate these lines of contest in three domains: first in relation to women; second in relation to other men; and third in relation to a collective.

This analysis provides answers to a series of questions about how small groups of men—and sometimes women—construct codes of manhood within and through the race matrix. Focusing on the "symbols of identity" provides clues about the "zones and modes of contact"[35] that certain groups highlight in their self-identity, and thus how peer groups position themselves in relation to others. These "lines of contest" or "configurations of social practice" (as Connell calls them)[36] are what a peer group devises for competitive performances. They show how each group positions itself in relation to meaningful others. They also show how a peer group stakes out arenas in which its members can enact dominance. Which niches are available to a group at RHS, however, depends on the racial order in which adolescents operate in the educational and the school-yard hierarchy. Within this landscape of racial order, each group has to situate itself along the two entrenched axes of alliances: the Cambodian-Black alliance and the weaker Latino-White alliance. It is in these landscapes of power, in which competing racial orders intersect with interracial alliances, that peer-cultures negotiate and devise their own distinct codes of masculinity.

METHODOLOGICAL CONCERNS

An examination of four different peer groups at Roosevelt High School—each one representative of the racial distribution of students in different educational programs—shows how students express their sense of selfhood and masculinity through the idioms they use and the competitive arenas in which they perform it. Through their specific ways of talking about masculinity and performing it, each group positions itself within the racial orders of urban space, educational structure, and school-yard hierarchy. How a peer group decides which groups are worthy opponents, which ones are desirable allies, and which ones to ignore reveals the frame of reference of a group and how it positions itself, while simultaneously establishing arenas in which to perform dominance. Accordingly, the repertoire of each group's masculinity is influenced by the existing racial order, and at the same time produces, sustains, or challenges this racial order and its characteristic patterns of dominance and subordination.

My analysis relies primarily on the way adolescents talked about masculinity, directly and indirectly. As discussed earlier, discourse generally can be regarded as a set of linked ideas and concepts that provide conceptual frameworks.[37] While discourse involves language and the making of reality and social relations through language, discourse is also made tangible in the shape of institutions that inform and structure everyday practices and in the distribution of resources (as in the making of whiteness as giftedness and blackness as deficiency). Discourse analysis provides a context for an analysis of "modes and zones of contact between dominant and dominated groups, between persons of different and multiple identities, speakers of different languages, that focuses on how such speakers constitute each other relationally and in difference, how they enact difference in language."[38]

These "modes and zones of contact" between groups differentially empowered and the relational constitution of identity through difference is what I seek to uncover by examining the stories through which young people at RHS perform masculinity.

Although several studies have shown how masculinities are forged through a dialectical process in institutional and peer cultures, few have ventured into a complex multiracial site such as Roosevelt High School. There, racial stereotypes are formed, clash, and are remade through complex local power relations and in the interrelated domains of urban culture, the educational institution, and school-yard hierarchies, as described in the previous chapters. Approaching the question of masculinity-making from the perspectives of the four peer groups will broaden our understanding of the processes that forge racialized masculinities.

It has to be remembered, of course, that while schools are an important place for the making of race and masculinity, they are not a microcosm of race and gender relations at large. Politics, families, media, popular culture, history, and multiple other contexts influence how masculinities are constructed and how they are linked. However, as other ethnographers have shown, gender and race are always locally made.[39] The local and concrete experiences observable in a small site such as a school allow us to examine the process of masculinity-making as a relational and strategic practice.

To highlight the uneven racial distribution of students in the different academic tiers at RHS, I chose to examine friendship groups from educational programs in which one racial group was predominant. Accordingly, I selected a White group from the gifted program, an African American group from BusTech, a Cambodian group including students from middle and lower tracks, and a Latino group comprising members across educational tiers. The different groups did not usually share an intimate social space. Indeed, the group of African Americans from BusTech had hardly any exposure to Whites, and Whites in the gifted program had very little exposure to African Americans. The only time they interacted with students of another race was during lunch in the school yard, which itself was also highly segregated spatially. Although the peer groups I selected tended to be monoracial, all except the Cambodians included at least one member of another racial group.

These peer groups are not meant to represent entire racial groups in the United States, or even racial groups at RHS. There were numerous other groups, some racially homogeneous, others more integrated. Among the former were the Trojans, a predominantly White fraternity described earlier, and among the latter were the multiracial Rastas. Some peer groups were associated with student clubs, such as Club Mexicano and the Asian Club, while others were bound by athletics. Some were associated with gangs, and there were "wannabes," who wanted to be associated with gangs. Some of these groups were clearly identifiable by others through the territory they claimed during lunch or a distinct style of clothing or appearance; others had less defined or recognizable boundaries.

I chose to study the peer groups described below for the following reasons: they were visible to outsiders as discrete groups of friends; they were representative of the educational stratification by race; and they had some points of contact with each other. To regard them as manifestations of generic Black, White, Latino, or Asian masculinities, or worse, as general racialized identities, would be a mistake. My goal here is not to provide a typology of racialized masculinities. Instead, the focus of this exploration is on the making of masculinity through relations with others, through the "modes and zones of contact" between collective masculinities, and what these tell us about the link between race and masculinity. More important than showing the content of a particular peer group's masculinity, the intent of this chapter is to show the connection between race and masculinity and how adolescents position themselves in relation to others through the particular masculinities they develop. In this process, they find some competing groups to be more significant and ignore others.[40]

AN AFRICAN AMERICAN GROUP PORTRAIT: "PIMP, HUSTLER, PLAYER"

Ben's group of friends consisted of about six people, all of whom had been encouraged by their counselors to apply for the BusTech Program. I first met this group of students when I visited Mr. McAuley's English class, and came to know them better through the extensive interviews I conducted with several of them. The most noticeable student in this class was Ben, the tall, well-groomed, and handsome young man, introduced earlier, who enjoyed a reputation among his peers as the best dresser and for his quick comebacks. Although nearly all of the men in BusTech dressed neatly and fashionably, Ben stood out: he came to school almost every day wearing what looked like a new matching outfit. In addition, classmates and friends described Ben as the "class clown," who made people laugh and who was good at derailing, stalling, or otherwise interfering with the classroom agenda.

A close friend of Ben's was Ryan, whom others called, fittingly, "Ben's tagalong." He usually sat next to Ben. Ryan rarely emerged from Ben's shadow, mostly imitating—but careful not to challenge—Ben. Ryan and Ben were cousins and had been living together with Ben's family after Ryan's mother moved out of the school district. Much shorter than Ben, Ryan was a no less careful dresser. He compensated for his obvious submissiveness by habitually referring to Mr. McAuley as Mr. McCrawly, hoping to gain some attention from his peers. Steve was another cousin and close friend of Ben's. He played on the varsity football team and enjoyed a solid status among his peers.

Closely associated with Ben's clique were also two women, Sylvie and Luanda. Both were light-skinned and had long, wavy hair, two characteristics essential for being considered good-looking in Ben's clique, as Melanie explained to me. During class, Sylvie and Luanda usually sat close to Ben, Ryan, and Steve. At some point, Steve and Luanda were dating, exchanging backrubs and kisses. But during most of the time I knew them, they were just members of a larger friendship group around Ben. These friends spent time together in school and also enjoyed going together to an upscale mall twenty miles south, in a predominantly White coastal community.

On the periphery of Ben's clique was Jorge. His father was African American and his mother was Mexican. Unlike Ben, Ryan, or Steve, who often engaged in verbal challenges with each other and with their teacher, Jorge was usually quiet, but knew how to hold his ground in various taunts and games, such as playing the dozens. John was another very careful dresser and, like Ben, often impressed his classmates with what looked like brand new clothes. Toward the end of my stay at RHS, John cut his ties with Ben because he found him too arrogant.

As I have shown earlier, "styling" was considered by many a distinct characteristic of African Americans and marked racial boundaries.[41] This was also true for Ben and his clique. Their styling revolved around physical appearance, gold accessories, and specific brand names: Eddie Bauer, Guess, Polo, and Tommy Hilfiger.[42] Styling also involved wearing brand-name sneakers and shoes, such as Timberland. Mr. McAuley routinely commented on their new outfits and at times included their favorite brand names in the skillful sketches he drew on the blackboard.

The clique's meticulous attention to style and dress contrasted with the dress of many of their peers in other racial groups. In this inner-city school, where almost 50 percent of the students came from families who received AFDC,[43] teachers and other students often remarked on the display of expensive brand-name clothes and accessories of many African American teens. They expressed a mixture of admiration and surprise about it, because it did not fit their image of African Americans as being poor.[44]

Styling was an element of the discourse of race for African American youth at RHS generally, as discussed in the previous chapter, and so it was for Ben's friends. But despite the centrality of style as a way to establish racial difference and personal signature, Ben and his friends did not foreground style as a characteristic of their clique or subculture per se. Instead, in their narratives and self portrayal, their references to style signaled an identification with a broader identity of African American culture generally. As such, style was itself a sign of difference, a difference that afforded them superiority over those who did not share or understand this style. Style was a way to make a difference that needed no further explanation. Ben and his friends knew that they belonged to the racially dominant group in the school yard. Therefore, there was no need to position themselves in relation to others. Clothes and style were signs of power that spoke for themselves.

They did not mark style as a specific collective identity beyond race, but they did use style as an arena to compete with their male peers, possibly more than they competed for women. Like the two African American girls from the student commission mentioned earlier, Luanda complained that instead of thinking about what to do after school, her friends focused on clothes and on being well groomed. Luanda noted that the boys manicured their nails more than she or the other girls did.

Confirming Luanda's assessment, Jason described in a journal entry how much he enjoyed being well dressed. He liked to model in front of his brother and discuss with him what to wear the next day so they would not go to school in identical outfits. Being well dressed, Jason wrote, made people treat him differently. Ryan responded similarly to Mr. McAuley's question about what was most important to him. He explained that he loved to get new clothes, jewelry, and cologne and would miss those things sorely if they were taken away from him.

There was no doubt among Ben and his friends that styling was a masculine endeavor. Asked how men were different from women, Ben explained:

B: Men are strong, more powerful, but also more, I feel women are more sensitive than men, I feel that, we value possessions and material things more than women do, I know that.

ADS: [. . .] When you say men are more interested in material things, what do you think about?

B: Like cars, and, well just the guys that . . . , my friends we're all into clothes and money, just . . .

ADS: What type of clothes for example?

B: Eddie Bauer.

ADS: And what kind of shoes?

B: Timberland, Eddie Bauer, Nike, Polo. We mainly have Eddie Bauer and Polo and Guess. I don't have any Guess shoes but I wear a lot of Guess clothes.

Styling, or the sporting of specific brand-name clothes, shoes, and accessories, worked not only as symbols of identity for the larger community of African Americans at Roosevelt High School. It also functioned as an arena for competition among the small group of friends surrounding Ben. It was the venue in which one could show one's sophistication and gain status among peers, as Ben's reputation as best dresser illustrates.

Style was a performance that indicated competence in other lines of contest as well. Expensive brand-name clothes and jewelry might also signal a man's access to women's resources and thus his "pimping" abilities. The agonistic tournament over styling among men, therefore, also played a significant part in the performance of the pimp and the player.

Pimp and player were two representations of masculinity that sometimes had the same meaning.[45] For Ben and his friends, "pimp" and "pimping," however, meant something different than "player" and "playing on somebody." For them, a pimp's skill was in extracting as many material possessions as possible from a relationship with someone of the opposite sex. In contrast, the player's goal was sexual access to as many women as possible. In this scenario, guys often referred to women as "hoes." Although no one ever used it in the context of prostitution, the connotations associated with pimp and whore provided a very specific script for male-female and male-male relations and in the group's discourse on masculinity.

During a substitute assignment in Mr. McAuley's class, I learned the hard way how significant the idioms and performance of the pimp and player were in Ben's clique:

Throughout the class period, several people had asked me if they could read the poems they had written for an assignment that was due that day. Flattered by this somewhat unexpected interest in scholastic matters, I suggested that we leave the reading of the poems for the last part of the almost two-hour class period. When the last half-hour arrived, I asked a few girls to read their poems, which were about God, their feelings, and their friendships. This changed when I got to the boys. The first poem started out, "Ah distinctly I remember, watching hoes in late

November." As it turned out, almost all of the guys' poems centered on the three personas pimp, player, and hustler, with "hoes" as essential background characters and sexually explicit plots. Torn between my curiosity as ethnographer on the one hand and my fragile substitute authority and job to maintain decorum on the other, I restrained myself from intervening, pretending that I did not know what they were talking about. Finally, however, Henry's poem, a toast about Jorge's mother, brought what had become more and more like a rap session to a halt. Jorge was part African American, part Mexican. His mother worked at the school as a staff assistant and over the months had become a dear friend to me. Henry's stanza went something like this: "Jorge's coming home, sees his mama's all messed up, sitting in his bed, she fucked a nigga and looks half dead." Jorge laughed, a bit embarrassed it seemed. Henry's comment, after I reprimanded him, was just, "ah, we friends."

In this setting, the rhymes about pimps and players, which took the form of playing the dozens, constituted an agonistic tournament with other males as the critical audience. Who composed the most daring stanzas, or toasts?[46] Who could create the baddest pimp or player? Obviously, both pimp and player suggested a male-female relationship. But it was not hard to see that the performances the young men gave that day were directed primarily at other males, to some extent even at Mr. McAuley, the teacher who had assigned the stanzas as homework. Ben made that clear when he ended one of his journal entries about his pimping abilities with the following words: "I became the playa and pimp you guys know and love."

For Ben and his friends, both "pimping" and "playing on somebody" were used to describe status relations between men. Of the two, it appeared that the pimp was referred to more often. The language of love and romance did not enter this discourse. A person who showed romantic feelings and emotional attachment was considered gullible, weak, easy to control and manipulate, and therefore an easy target to be pimped. The name of the game was to always remain aloof and thus unexploitable. Women in this performance were primarily vehicles for conveying status to men, who were competing with other men.[47] But in order to attract women in the first place, the pimp or player needed to be skilled at presenting himself as a man who made women fall for him. Rather than treating these two aspects jointly, I will first look at the pimp and the player as idioms of masculinity in male-male domains, and then examine them within a male-female relationship.

On the day of our interview, Ben wore a new black leather jacket, an Eddie Bauer shirt, Eddie Bauer pants, Timberland shoes, and a gold necklace. Admiring

Ben's clothes, I wondered aloud how much he had paid for his outfit and how he was able to finance his style. Ben explained:

B: My friends, females give me money, and my parents.

ADS: Females give you money? Like . . .

B: [. . .] Girls that like me [. . .]

ADS: That's new. I thought always it was the other way around.

B: Oh no. Oh no! I feel it takes money to get money. To make money you have to spend money. I'll buy them [girls] little gifts, like about forty to fifty dollars, to let 'em know that I care, at the beginning of the relationship. But as we get deeper, like about . . . a month [they will spend a lot more on me]. [. . .] They think that they are serious to me, but they are not.

ADS: I understand now why the girls say they want an honest guy.

B: Well, I make it seem as if I am honest, but . . .

ADS: But you're really a "dog"?

B: I wouldn't say I'm a dog [laughing]. Just, I see my opportunity, and act upon it, money is power to me, and [. . .] a lot of the females at Roosevelt High, they judge you by the physical, by the physical person. They may say, "Oh, I wanna have a guy that cares," and that's honest, but that's not what it is. They judge you by the physical, [. . .] meaning the build, the clothes you wear, the way you wear the clothes, if you keep your hair . . . You know, it's just [. . .] what I did, in the beginning of the school year, I bought clothes that make me look well, and . . . [The females] also look at your walk, and, and I let the way I think come through the way I walk, and through my gestures and all that, [. . .] that's what puts me above everyone else, I feel. Because, I know, I've talked to a lot of people, and, they're stupid with the things that . . . you know. I think, I take it a lot deeper, because money and clothes are serious to me, so I take it a lot deeper than most teenagers, because I feel it's like something I have to have, and, yeah [. . .] I just feel it's like something that I have to have. [. . .] Like every few months, I have to get at least, like, four new outfits, like . . . four new outfits and about two pairs of shoes.

ADS: Outfit, you mean like . . .

B: Hat, shirt, jacket, everything I have on, watch, everything, [. . .] 'cause females are always there just to give me money, and I am there to spend it.

Much of what Ben described addressed the way he manipulated women into providing him with resources, but his audience were his male friends, to whom he showed off his success through the clothes he wore. Such outfits, particularly if they included a leather jacket, could easily cost several hundred dollars, an amount to which he readily admitted, and the reason why some girls, as he stated, needed to get jobs to stay with him.

The girls Ben "recruited" were usually from other schools. He found new girls through his network of friends at other schools. Seeking girls from other schools prevented his reputation as a pimp from spreading too quickly, a reputation that could have made it difficult for him to continue finding new girls:

> [I meet girls] at schools, because, I like to go to different schools all the time after school. So, [I go there with my friends] and they have friends that go there, that are female, you know, female friends, and then, [. . .] , I'll meet her, I'll get her phone number, she'll get mine, whatever, and, we'll talk, and I'll pretend to be something that I am not.

He explained his strategy as a series of carefully calculated steps he had devised to reach his goal, all the while emphasizing that he was manipulating girls with the goal of "recruiting" them in order to extract material things from them. He portrayed himself as a con man who worked to gain the confidence of girls as a way to lay the groundwork for successful pimping.

In the public sphere of the school, Ben reserved his time for his male friends. Only in the private sphere of the home did he spend time with girls:

> Weekends I spend with girls, and during the school time I spend my time with boys. [. . .] It's like, during the weekend, I'm getting money from the girls, and during the weekdays I gamble, [. . .] just a dollar a hand, sometimes two dollars a hand. Black Jack. [. . .] That's about it. Like yesterday, I won thirty dollars. Today I lost two dollars. It's not a big deal. Money, money to me comes as quick as it leaves, so, if I spend a lot of money on a certain situation, it doesn't matter to me because I can get it back real quick.

It was important for Ben to appear affluent in front of his friends. Having cash was critical for his life style and signaled to his friends that he was a successful pimp. Judging from his extensive wardrobe and gambling habits, his need for money appeared substantial. The question was, how was a young woman supposed to come up with such large amounts of money on a regular basis? Ben explained:

> B: They got jobs. The current girl that I'm with, she got a job so that she can stay with me.

ADS: That she can stay with you?

B: Yes. Because . . . she didn't have enough money to give me, just, all the time that I needed money. So, she had to get a job.

What was important about a girl were the resources she provided. Ben did not have any racial preference for his girlfriends or care particularly about their looks. What he did want were girls who were inexperienced in relationships and preferably from other schools. Inexperienced girls were more likely to be "gullible" and therefore exploitable:

B: Well, it doesn't matter about looks, [. . .] she may be ugly, I would talk to her to get her money, to get everything she has to offer, all her resources, and then I leave her alone. [. . .] I don't [. . .] like to meet the girls at the skating rink, because they go, they go like every week and then they . . . I mean, it's, I don't like to meet girls who go out all the time, I don't like that [. . .] I like . . . , I like girls [who are] very vulnerable, I like that, I like females who [blush] 'cause I can take advantage of them a lot easier, a lot. If you can think for yourself, if you have a mind of your own, it's kind of hard.

Throughout this interview, I was tempted to ask if he considered himself to be a pimp, but finally decided not to, afraid to insult him. Ben himself never used that expression. Several months later Latasha, an African American girl from a different academy, shed more light on this subject. Latasha, already recognized as a promising rap artist, explained that "pimping her niggas" was what she wrote and rapped about, but not something that she was actually doing herself. Latasha, joined by her boyfriend Jamal, explained:

L: [Pimping is not] necessarily [making people] do things, but gettin' you things. It's like, you got a boyfriend, or some boys, and you just like, you be like "give me some money." And they just, like, give it to you. They don't ask no questions about it. [. . .] If you pimpin' 'em, you just, like, get whatever you want, you know. You be askin' 'em, like, "can I have five dollars," and you can be like, mean to him and everything, and he like "sure." The idea is, get money from them . . . , and like, anything you want, really. [Because they want you.] You act like you like them, but you don't.

ADS: But why would the girls go for that?

J: Because, like she said, they like the boy, they love him a lot, so they tryin' to keep him happy. So he could stay with them, so they just keep on buying him stuff.

L: Like some girls, if it's like the boys, like, he likes them a lot, like he's sprung or whatever, and they be like, "buy me this, buy me this," and if he's gonna keep doing it for them, they gonna keep doing it, 'cause, they think, you know, they can go away with it. And actually, they pimpin'. 'Cause he jockin' her . . . [Boys do it to girls and girls do it to boys.] Like, I be expectin' that they pay for everything. Right? [. . .] But [I] don't do hardly nothin'.

Echoing this definition of pimping, Ben wrote this in a journal entry in answer to the question "Why I am unique?": "It is unbelievable what I can make people do for me." He went on to describe how he had written to his girlfriend, Hannah—who was in Japan at the time—that he had had an affair with a girl who then had become pregnant. In response, he wrote, Hannah sent him money. He left it open whether he had asked her for money for an abortion. But his journal entry ended with the lines: "McAuley, can you believe that?" In contrast to Latasha, who only rapped about pimping, Ben deliberately portrayed himself as a pimp, without actually calling himself one. His provocative revelations about how he exploited women did not prevent him from being extremely polite, respectful, and even charming.

His account of how to "pimp" girls resonated with lyrics in hip-hop culture (Snoop Dogg, Dr. Dre, and others). However, Ben did not particularly care for rap. He preferred the music of Pearl Jam, the Red Hot Chili Peppers, and Nirvana, as well as other "alternative" music more often associated with White teenagers. Ben came from a middle-class family that lived in a relatively affluent, racially mixed neighborhood. His father owned a printing shop and his mother a paralegal business. He was the second of five children and lived with both of his parents, a rarity among teenagers I interviewed, regardless of race. Ben was also a Jehovah's Witness and regularly attended church. His family background was far removed from the "street culture" that he seemed to model in his pimp performance.

Pimping as performed by Ben was a manifestation of masculine ethos in which Ben and his friends gave primacy to establishing masculinity within a male-male domain, and literally, at the expense of women. The greater the degree of exploitation of girls, the higher the status of the male. Ben seemed extreme in the way he prided himself in pimping people, even to his peers. Girls like Latasha and Sylvie knew all about pimping, but distanced themselves from actually adopting the pimp pose. According to Luanda, a member of Ben's friendship group, while pimping might be a strategy practiced by men and women, only men used it as a way to develop a reputation. Girls were more likely to keep a low profile when acting as pimps, or, like Latasha, they did it as an act, rapping about it on stage. "Pimping guys" and "making them do unbelievable things" was not something that girls could translate into status currency with other girls or with guys. Too much talk about it could cause them to be called gold diggers or worse, whores, and ruin their reputation. In contrast, the more outrageous a boy's demands were, the greater his reputation as a pimp, and the more unlikely it was that a girl would fall for his demands and his game.

Another idiom of masculinity circulating in Ben's clique was that of the player. Unlike the pimp, who showed off the material possessions he extracted from girls, the player showed off by flaunting the number of women with whom he was involved. Ben's friend Ryan explained this in a journal entry about what made him happiest:

> To get to know a nice-looking girl and then to have casual sex. I enjoy spending time with her afterwards if she is very attractive. That allows me a chance to have sex with her again and again. Showing her off to my friends is very important because they are more important to me than the girl anyways. If she is not so attractive I will spend as little time with her as possible, and try never to be seen in public with her.

An indication that being a player was no longer in vogue was expressed by Steve in a self-critical account. Steve was Ben's cousin and close friend. He played football on the varsity team. However, that was not the reason his friends called him a player. As he explained, he had given up trying to be a player after an embarrassing incident where he found himself the subject of ridicule by his friends and relatives:

> When I was in eighth grade I thought I was a Mack.[48] I had four different girlfriends at the same time. They all went to different schools. But when I went to a RHS football game it all came to an end. Somehow they were all sitting in the same area. So the first half I walked around so I would not get caught. When halftime was here I just kicked it with the boys. When the third quarter came I sat in a bad place because, somehow, they all found me. At first it went pretty good. They were all just talking to me until one of the girls' big-mouth friend said "who are these other girls you were talking to?" I started to smile and say that's my friend. They knew I was lying so they asked her and she said that's my man. So they started to clown on me. I was so embarrassed because people were looking at me getting clowned. My mom and my sister were laughing like they were watching live comedy show.

Rather than enhancing his status, being a player made Steve a focus of ridicule after one of his girlfriends realized his game.

How did the boys in Ben's group prove their masculinity to women? What were the qualities they thought women would find masculine and therefore attractive? The pimps and the players proved their masculinity to other males by exploiting women; but both of them also needed, at least initially, the approval of women since women had to be attracted to them in the first place. This required guys to be familiar with women's romantic expectations.

Ben was very explicit about what he thought women needed or liked in men. He found that women looked at the physical appearance, even if they said they were only interested in character and honesty. And he knew it took start-up capital to be competitive: clothes, a well-groomed appearance, and initially, presents to give the impression that he was seriously interested.

Another critical element in making women believe that he was a sincere, respectable man and in keeping a relationship with a woman going was spending "quality time" with them. Ben explained:

> I don't usually go for formal dates [formal dates generally require the male to spend a lot of money]. When I meet a girl, I like to go to her house, meet her parents, and play this role that I'm that nice guy, like this and that, and basically . . . [. . .] See, females love quality time, that's what they call it, quality time, going to their house, kicking it there, going to the park, going with their sister to the park, or playing with their little sister, little brother. Quality time, females love that. Feelings come on strong when you spend quality time, when you talk to them all the time on the phone, and that's what my night consists of, just talking on the phone.

Ben's account of himself as an unscrupulous, misogynist pimp seemed somewhat contrived. He admitted that he bought some clothes with his parents' money—something I in fact had overheard in favor of the more provocative statement that girls financed his style—and that he also was thinking about looking for work so that he could buy himself a car. But Sylvie, one of the two female friends in Ben's clique, confirmed that Ben's portrayal of himself as a pimp was not uncommon among guys she knew. And, she said, she knew plenty of girls who would fall for the guy Ben claimed to be, even to the point of stealing from their parents to support him. She knew the tricks of guys who pretended to spend "quality time" and said romantic things if they felt it opportune:

ADS: Are girls going for such a guy because he knows how to talk and stuff like that, or is it because . . .

S: Oh yes, that's sure.

ADS: Or is it that they think that they need to have a man around?

S: Nowadays, it could be both. But nowadays, guys are coming smooth, they know what to say, and they learn, like, just how to, what . . . , what women like, like, you know what I am sayin'? Like, the cuddling, and all that. They'll find that out [. . .] and this quality time. They'll do anything. There are some guys, I have friends, that know how to cry on cue. [. . .] They know how to cry on cue. They'll sit there, and the guy will cry "Oh I love you, I wanna be with you. I'll give you the world." I's a game, i's a game. It's all a game, the whole thing, the whole, the whole teenager thing.

Sylvie also was aware of the shifts in strategies that guys used to prove their masculinity to each other. When I asked her about the difference between a pimp and a player, Sylvie explained:

s: Players are played out. I's, like, i's a fad. You know what I mean? I's goin'. Everything is like a phase with the adolescents.

ADS: So you say that it is a matter of time, they are getting too old for that player thing?

s: Oh yeah, most definitely that. But some people, it takes longer than others. But yeah, right now, i's just gone. I's just fading away. You find a few people who tryin' to call themselves like, . . . But you, you rarely . . . I don't think anybody nowadays call themselves a player. They're more, they're more on the side of calling themselves a pimp. Which is something, kind of, different. [. . .] You know what I am saying? A player is just somebody who like, "Oh, I'm gonna play on this girl, or I'm gonna play on that girl." And a pimp is somebody who gets females, or, vice versa, a female who gets males they get things from them. Like, "oh, I got this from this female and this female." [. . .] Like, "she bought me this, she bought me that." [. . .] A player is just somebody who has a lot of girlfriends. And that's about it. And probably, havin' sex with all o' them. That's what a player is. [But a pimp], that's more now. Like, Snoop has that new, um, a new tape or whatever, and there is an intro on it, and it says something like, "a hoe is done until she all hoed out, a player can be played out, but pimp is for life." See what I am sayin'? So a pimp is forever.

Sylvie gave the pimp a much higher value than the player. Pimping, as she described it, was primarily a male endeavor. At the same time, though, by making it clear that she knew about men's tricks, she presented herself more on the side of the pimp than on the side of the ones being used, gullible girls.

Although Ben and some of his friends made much of portraying themselves as guys who exploited women, they were not without romantic feelings and respect for them. But, as Latasha explained it when introducing me to the concepts of pimping, "Love is like a whole different level."

Ben himself made a clear distinction between Hannah, the girl he loved deeply, and the rest of the girls "down here," for whom he had little respect and regard other than for their ability to finance his style. They might call themselves his girlfriends, but he did not. In his understanding, his relationship with Hannah, who was at a safe distance in Japan, was untainted by the emotionally distant encounters he had with those Sylvie called "gullible girls." In addition to Hannah, his loyalty was exclusively to his friends, as he expressed to Mr. McAuley in a journal entry: "I became the playa and pimp that you guys know and love."

After a long interview, in which Ben provided me with an exhaustive introduction to the art of pimping, he went on to explain:

B: Really, I am caring, and I am very honest, I mean, it just depends on who you are. Like, my girlfriend Hannah, in Japan, she means the world to me. If she would come back now, I would drop everything I have for her. [. . .] But, if you are just one of the girls here, I'm going to lie to you, I'm going to tell you that there is no Hannah, I am gonna tell you that there is no . . . anybody else out there. I will make you feel like it's only you in this world. [. . .] So, like, everyone out here is just until she gets back, I wouldn't take any girl down here seriously.

ADS: Hannah doesn't know about your . . . ?

B: She knows.

ADS: She knows and she doesn't mind?

B: She knows I don' like 'em. She's . . . I'm not having sex with any . . . Well, if I do, then it's not . . . I mean, our relationship is just different, it's totally different, it's like, . . . very understanding with Hannah. [. . .]

ADS: Since when are you together with her?

B: Two years and a couple of months.

ADS: That's pretty good, you are 17 or something like that?

B: Yeah, I'll be 17 tomorrow. [. . .] If someone was to disrespect her in any way, I either beat 'em up or [they'll] die, just, point blank, there'll be no discussion, no . . . , none of that, it's just they'll either get beat up or they will die. [. . .]

ADS: Do you think she could have a Japanese lover, could you imagine her to have a Japanese lover?

B: Of course not.

Despite emphasizing his emotional involvement with Hannah, he made sure that I understood that Hannah was not pimping *him*. In a journal entry he wrote that Hannah, his true love, had been waiting for him on her birthday, but that he had decided at the last moment to go out with his buddies instead. And he did not give her a birthday present the next day either. Thus, while he described himself as being sincere about Hannah, he went to great lengths to make sure he was not seen as the one being exploited or manipulated.[49]

For Ben's friends, other men were more important than their relationships with women. Styling and pimping were the central arenas in which they established their masculinity. Little effort went into developing clique symbols per se. Rather, idioms and performances of masculinity were self-referential and accessible to African American students outside Ben's group, but often inaccessible to others.

The boundaries set through style were race boundaries. No particular discourse of masculinity emerged from this particular style because it represented what many of their peers would describe as urban Black style generally. The main frame of reference relevant to Ben's group of friends was the larger community of urban African Americans and the experience of living in a White-dominated world.

The importance of style as a form of a resistance is not a new phenomenon in African American culture. Style has a long history as a cultural resource for creating an arena of self-expression and identity separate from the dominant White culture:

> Styling as a form of resistance and nonverbal social comment was [historically] a way to evade punishment. It created a space of social communication inaccessible to White sanctions.[50]

Style is primarily a person's statement about him- or herself in relation to others:

> Strategic style is the way a person deals with the definitions prevailing in the cultures most salient to him. It includes the way in which he defines situations in his own right, and the information about himself he expresses or "gives off."[51]

Self-expression through style has traditionally been interpreted as resistance or rebellion. This was most evident in the popularity of the zoot suit worn by African Americans, Filipinos, and Mexican Americans during World War II. To support the country's war effort, the government issued an order prohibiting the waste of cloth. Because the typical zoot suit had a knee-length coat and billowing pants, wearing it could be interpreted as an unpatriotic statement and a violation. In the Los Angeles Zoot Suit Riot, the zoot had become the scorned subject of patriotic sailors who stripped the zoots from African Americans and Mexican Americans who wore them.[52] I suggest that style and pimping function in a similar way across racial boundaries because they maintain a space for the Black self that contrasts with White values. They allow the production of an arena of dominance in which they remain unchallenged.

By choosing certain brand-name clothes, Ben and his friends continued an established pattern of one facet of urban African American culture. Their response to the stigma of being seen as the manifestation of inner-city failure and poverty was to appropriate the White prerogative: an expensive and sophisticated style. Through this emphasis on style, they also set themselves apart from Latinos and Cambodians, who favored a gangster style consisting of White T-shirt and Dockers, as well as from the White grunge style. After all, "style is not simply a reaction to cues given by others in a particular interaction, but is a person's way of acting, creating, and redefining his self in relation to others."[53]

Just as style was not Ben's and his clique's invention, the pimp and the player were also part of an African American urban folklore that was popular during the 1960s and 1970s and again in the 1990s.[54] Both pimp and player are firmly located at the nexus of White dominance and Black resistance. Whites have historically viewed African American style as "conspicuous" and "outlandish" and not infrequently regarded a well-dressed African American as a pimp or "shiftless Negro" who lived off his wife's hard-earned money.[55]

Ben's clique reenacted the pimp, and to a lesser extent the player, by deliberately positioning him in relation to a White discourse of privilege and dominance. Through their style and their focus on the pimp, they also set themselves apart from Latinos and Asians, whom they regarded more as a nuisance than a serious challenge. However, the frame of reference reflected in their performances was their location within the larger system of White domination against which the pimp performance and style provided an arena for rewriting power relations and self-image.[56]

A CAMBODIAN GROUP PORTRAIT: "MACK DADDIES AND GANGSTERS"

Mickey and his friends were definitely not "schoolboys," a derogatory term they reserved for those who did not know anything about street life. In conversations, Mickey and his friends revealed sooner rather than later their associations with Cambodian gangs. Mickey was a member of the Asian Posse, and Babe G, Mickey's friend and idol, had acquired a certain reputation among the Asian Deuces, as had Li'l Monster. Another friend of Mickey's, Joey, had been in the same gang as Mickey in junior high but had since turned his attentions to graduating and pursuing a career in graffiti art. And finally, Veasna, who had never been particularly close to Mickey but knew him well, was a former member of the Cambodian Kings, a notorious Cambodian gang that had lost its position of power only after many of its members were sent to jail.

I met Mickey during a visit to Mr. McAuley's class, where Mickey was the only Asian in a class of mostly African Americans. In this class, Mickey played the role of an agreeable, nonconfrontational underdog, very unlike the influential role he played among his friends. This came out clearly in a class assignment where students were to retell a newspaper report as a first-person narrative. The plot of the story was that a battered wife and depressed mother of two had thrown her small children over a bridge before jumping off it herself. While almost every male in the class assumed the role of the abusing husband, cursing and blaming his wife, Mickey took on the role of the toddler who died in the floodwaters. His narration of the story from the perspective of the small child and convincing description of "his" cute baby features earned the praise of his teacher.

Mickey's contact with others in the BusTech class was limited. Although he tried several times to make inroads into Ben's clique, he remained an outsider. Mickey eventually had to leave BusTech because of his frequent absences and low grades. A few months after he was forced out of BusTech, I saw Mickey in front of the school, driving a brand new Honda Civic. When I tried to contact him at his home toward the end of my fieldwork, his brother informed me that he was in jail. I remembered later that he had told me he would have to go to jail because of the "work that he put in" for his gang, the Asian Posse.

Mickey's allegedly closest friend and—as he described him—"road dog" was Babe G.[57] He symbolized for Mickey not only what it meant to be a good friend and a real man, but also what it meant to be a Mack Daddy. Unlike Mickey and most of his friends who were juniors, Babe G was a freshman. He had recently transferred to RHS after being suspended from another school. While Mickey was ambiguous about his loyalty to the gang, Babe G was explicit about it, and while Mickey was happy to have found a good-looking girlfriend and to call himself "married," Babe G was a real Mack Daddy who could talk any girl into going out and even having sex with him.

Another buddy of Mickey's was Joey. He was the only one in this group who also had connections to White students, primarily through his interest in art and design. This linked him to some members of the White peer group I describe later. With some of them, Joey shared art classes and clubs and had the support of an enthusiastic and engaged art teacher.

Only loosely associated with Mickey's friends was Veasna. He had left the Cambodian Kings several years earlier, after one of his friends got shot. This traumatic event, he explained, had made him realize how high the stakes were in being an active gang member. Veasna knew the gang life well, maybe better than Mickey, but no longer regarded it as the measuring stick for his masculinity. In contrast, fearing reprisal from his former buddies for getting out of the gang, Veasna kept a low profile and avoided areas where the gang members hung out. Having outgrown the gang, he described himself now as moving on to what he considered more mature challenges of Cambodian masculinity. He planned to join a Buddhist temple to become a monk for some time and later go on to college.

Mickey and his friends created their identity through skin color, tattoos, and language, all of them symbols of embodiment. For them, these symbols represented a sense of community at the level of race. They justified their association with Cambodian gangs such as the Asian Deuces, Newtown Kings, and Cambodian Kings as part of their manly duty to stand up for their honor as Cambodians. Moreover, the gangs represented not only Cambodians, but also their larger racial identity and loyalty to the Asian race. In this context—and notwithstanding the sometimes severe conflicts between Asian gangs—for Mickey and his friends, all Asian gangs served as militant outposts for the defense of their race.

Mickey and his friends, like other Cambodians mentioned, borrowed heavily from African American culture in their assemblage of symbols of identity. Cambodians identified with African Americans on the basis of skin color, their own experience with racial stigmatization, the language they used, and what they considered Black style.

Cambodians at RHS considered themselves and were often seen by their Asian American peers as the darkest-skinned Asians. One day, while chatting about this with a Chinese American counselor, he gave me an instant demonstration. He asked a Vietnamese American student who happened to knock on his door how she would recognize Cambodians without knowing their names, and she answered, "You can tell easily by their skin color. If they are really dark-skinned, they are most likely Cambodians."

Several of Mickey's Cambodian friends also demonstrated their color-consciousness by stressing their multiethnic heritage, which often included Vietnamese, Chinese, and/or Thai ancestors. They viewed these ancestors as lighter skinned, as well as superior culturally and intellectually. In contrast, they described their Cambodian relatives as backward, lacking in education and style. For example, Mickey explained that he much preferred his mother's refined Thai culture over his father's rural Cambodian culture. His friends referred to Mickey often as the "the light-skinned one," and referred to others by their skin color or mixed racial parentage. Expressions of color-consciousness were common among Asian American students generally. But such expressions acquired a different quality in the self-presentation of Mickey and his friends, for whom skin color was a way to demonstrate affinity or identification with African Americans.

Like skin color, tattoos served as embodied symbols that set up boundaries between Cambodians and others, between those who were similar and those who were different. The power of the tattoo consisted in signaling a lifelong association with a group and an identity that could not be washed away. The pain associated with getting a tattoo strengthened this bond. The more conspicuous the tattoo and its location on the body, the more loyal and "down with the set" that person was thought to be. In an interview, Babe G and his friend Li'l Monster explained:

BG: If you are in a gang, you stay in it for life.

LM: I mean since you have tattoo all over sayin' AD [Asian Deuces], what's the reason of quittin'?

ADS: What is the reason to quit?

LM: Yeah, what is the reason to quit? I mean, you have tattoo sayin' AD and all that.

Often, tattoos were artfully decorated gang names, initials, or one's gang moniker.[58] But the tattoos of Mickey and his friends also indicated wider systems of allegiance. Mickey's friends proudly showed me tattoos on their hands that consisted of five dots between the thumb and index finger, the five dots representing the five letters of the word "Asian." Gang identity, again, for Mickey and his friends, represented racial identity, and vice versa, racial identity was made real by the signs and practices of gang affiliation. In another context, racial identity was described as encompassing "all ethnic mens" against Latinos, as Mickey said when he described the Black-Asian alliance as an alliance of "ethnic men" against Mexicans.

Cambodians' use of Black vernacular was another striking feature of their identification with African Americans. Unlike them, however, Mickey and his friends did not switch codes as easily and as frequently as African American students. African American students who used this vernacular usually did so in conversation with their friends and sometimes with their teachers, where it became a statement about their cultural identity. In interviews with me, however, African American students generally switched to Standard English.

Many African Americans at RHS used the term "nigga" among their buddies and distinguished it from the derogatory—and racial outsiders'—pronunciation of "nigger." In my conversations with Mickey and Joey, however, "nigga" had become a constant reference, not used as a racist remark but as a term signaling they were insiders to the culture of their Black peers.

Like, say, I, kick it with them, right, and I put in work? It don't matter whether I'm from it or not, right? And they gonna say this and that, "Oh, I'm down with you now," this and that, and then I'll be known. And everywhere I go they like, "Oh man, that nigga down," you know?

Veasna himself, for example, was aware of the exclusive nature of using African

American vernacular when he explained that his White classmates often "don't even know what we're talking about."

Roger Hewitt argues that many inner-city neighborhoods develop multiracial vernaculars that cannot be interpreted as "crossing" into another culture. Rather, he argues, they should be considered languages shared by residents of the inner city that result from their coresidence in the same environment.[59] The context of Roosevelt High School and Cambodians' strong reliance on an African American ally, however, suggests that adopting the Black vernacular was another way for Mickey's clique to identify with their conception of Black culture. Maybe they had not learned it consciously, but they nevertheless used it strategically to emphasize their dissimilarity from those who were not familiar with the code, particularly "schoolboys," some Latinos, and Whites.

Mickey and his friends did not appropriate a particular style of dress, but rather seemed to blend in with the rest of the student body, which—given the alleged dominance of the Dawgs—wore lots of black to avoid being identified as members of the rival gang, the Mob. The black jackets of the Los Angeles Raiders were especially popular. Despite their deliberate and self-conscious identification with African Americans, Mickey and his friends did not copy their impeccable wardrobes or their ostentatious display of expensive jewelry. Some wore a gold necklace with a Buddha pendant for protection. But conspicuous gold necklaces, gold earrings, and brand-name clothes were not part of their appearance, as they were for Ben and his friends and for many other African American students. Mickey usually wore baggy jeans and a T-shirt, while Joey sometimes came to school with jeans cut open at the bottom, in a fashion more characteristic of Latinos at the school. Veasna, in contrast, often dressed neatly in new, perfectly matching clothes. Nevertheless, when I asked how they would describe their style, they explicitly called it "Black style," which they described as the most popular style. Mickey's clique deliberately presented themselves as identifying with African American culture in language, style, and skin color. They regarded Latinos and Whites as outsiders and lumped them together racially as Whites.

Among Mickey and his friends, language, tattoos, and skin color were symbols of a racial frame of reference in which blackness was the mold for their own experience as Cambodians. Their allegiance was more to the collective of the gang, and by implication the race, than to individual friendships or competition. Being associated with a gang was a means for developing an identity and provided a framework for establishing masculinity. Of twelve Southeast Asian students I interviewed, eight identified themselves as being or having been associated with a gang or a tagging crew. In contrast, African American students never mentioned an association with gangs despite an abundance of Dawgs graffiti all over the school. Latinos, likewise, questioned the sense of revealing one's gang affiliation to an outsider like me. And the White students also did not bring up any gang affiliations.

Whether Cambodians emphasized their ties to gangs because of the widespread image of Asians as "unmasculine schoolboys," or because of their families' experience of war, genocide, and terror, violence and crime were constants in their lives. Many saw joining a gang as an inevitable course of action. It was a means of self-protection and a matter of defending one's "race." How Mickey and Joey wove together masculinity, gangs, and racial identity became evident in Mickey's and Joey's response to my question about how they defined manhood. What they described was a notion of masculinity that was specific and was situated in a spatial context they referred to as "the ghetto," where gang warfare was endemic and where gang membership was an almost inescapable necessity for survival:

ADS: Tell me, what does it mean to you to be a real man?

M: Real man is like, like, you gotta be strong, strong from the inside, from, from your heart, you know. [. . .] You gotta learn how to survive. [. . .] Yeah, we live in [. . .] the ghetto, right, the bad areas, and we run away from guns to knives. [. . .] We live in a bad situation right now, and mostly all of us, us mens, trying [. . .] to survive, you know, tryin' to get good life [. . .] you know, have a good girlfriend, have a steady family. [. . .] It's all about race now. [. . .] So mostly, Black and Asian together, you know, it's like, united, like all mens, [. . .] I mean like all ethnic mens, you know, just, [. . .] Blacks and Asians together, [. . .] we don't like Mexicans right now.

J: Looks like we don't, we argue . . . [inaudible]. Now there are so many gangs out there, and we, so many race hate. If you're Asian, they assume that you're a gangster, you know, it's like, they're makin' you a gangster.

Babe G, a seasoned gang member, and his friend Li'l Monster made an even clearer link between one's honor as a man and as a Cambodian. This honor required defending one's race against racial insults by others, particularly Mexicans:

BG: I have a lot of reasons to be in a gang. I hate Mexicans. I hate the Locos [a Mexican gang]. They say, they say, every day I see them they say "Fuck Cambodians!" Stuff like that, we can't take that no more. So I fight it back.

LM: [. . .] I mean, if somebody is dissing my race, I have to stand up for my race. So I'm not gonna stand there and let somebody diss my race, you know, "Fuck Cambodians this and that," you know. I mean, there is no right for them to say that.

Their performance of manhood was tied up with the honor of the gang, which itself was intimately tied to the larger social identities of ethnicity and race.

"Putting in Work"

In the gang, the way to establish and gauge one's manhood was measured by "how much work one put in," that is, how many risky and sometimes criminal acts someone committed to contribute to the gang's reputation of fierceness. Through one's "work" one was able to command respect within the gang, enhance the reputation of the gang, and defend one's race. As Mickey and his friends described it in extended interviews, the "work" could entail "stealing cars and rob[bing]," "snatching stuff," and first and foremost, "going around shooting and beating people," ideally Mexicans. Those who just enjoyed an affiliation with the gang without putting in work were considered "boys." Going to jail for one's work was an honorable duty that conferred the status of becoming an OG, Old Gangster. Mickey and Joey explained this concept of "putting in work":

M: I got in a gang for AP, Asian Posse, I'm still from it right now, now, like, I'm going to court for it and everything, you know? 'Cause, ah, I've been putting in a lot of work for them, for the gang, you know. That's why I, like, have to disappear now.

J: Putting in work means doing things for the gang, like . . .

M: Like, steal cars, and go rob.

J: And beat somebody, yeah, it's like, it's like, you put in work they give you more respect than if you're not putting in work.

M: You have more [pros(?)]

J: Yeah, because like, if you don't put in work, you is nothing but a buster, you know it's like, you're in a gang for nutt'n', just for the name, if you like . . .

ADS: When you're a wannabe?

J: Yeah it's a wannabe, say, like see you put in work, that mean like, "Damn, you know, he's down for it, you know." [. . .] Yeah, like more man, it's like more being a man if you put in work. Like if you don't put in work, they call you a boy.

If putting in work meant being a man, not putting in work was like getting a free ride; it was enjoying the reputation of a gang without risking one's skin, without paying one's dues, and thus was evidence of one's lack of manhood. This construction of manhood was crucially embedded in gang membership and the wider network of associates. By "putting in work," a gang member showed a loyalty and willingness to sacrifice for the gang. Through this work, he gained a reputation for himself among friends and associates of the gang, as well as among hostile outsiders. Babe G and Li'l Monster explained:

ADS: In order to be considered well among your friends, in order to be popular and well respected, what do you need to have?

LM: You gotta put in a lot of . . . , if you wanna be well respected . . .

BG: You gotta put in a lot of work, and you gotta get around, you know, to be known.

LM: Si.

BG: A gangster, yeah. But it doesn't matter if you a gangster or not, you know. I mean, you kick it with them, you put in work, you be known. Like, say, I kick it with them, right, and I put in work? It don't matter whether I'm from it or not. Right. And they gonna say this and that. "Oh, I'm down with you now," this and that, and then I'll be known. And everywhere I go they like, "Oh man, that nigga down," you know? They tell people that, you know, "He fucked up that dude" that and that. So they say this and that about you.

But putting in work and gaining a reputation were not the only criteria for proving one's manhood. As Mickey and Joey explained, it was also a matter of having self-control, of not getting carried away with bragging about one's trophies. Mickey recounted the story of a friend who killed a Mexican gang member, but instead of keeping it to himself he wanted to cash in by telling everyone about it:

M: It's like, you know, like some people they shoot, they shoot or kill people, like, last year, I got a friend, he killed this one dude, right, he killed him! With a gun he shot and killed him, and he started braggin' to everybody about this and that and now the police want him real badly. He's now, like, the American Most Wanted one. [. . .] Yes, if you're a gangster and kill somebody you need to keep your mouth shut, you don't wanna know everybody.

J: And that was like, you know, 's like, some people, they wanna brag.

M: They brag . . . , they wanna be some'n'. They wanna get credit, you know what I'm sayin'?

J: They want like, "Oh yeah, I shot someone," and they go to everybody, and, then the word gets passed around, [inaudible]

M: That's like a boy right there.

J: That's like a bragger, a kid.

ADS: A bragger is a boy?

M:/J: Yeah.

M: But, it's like, be a man you gotta keep it to yourself.

Changing Role Models and Objectives: From Gang to Family

Veasna and Joey recognized the importance of putting in work to prove one's loyalty to the gang. But in contrast to Mickey, and particularly to Li'l Monster and Babe G, Veasna and Joey distanced themselves from their involvement with gangs and from this code of masculinity.

Having been active gang members themselves, their focus had shifted from the gang to parents and their relationship with women as more significant for establishing manhood. Joey was now concerned with graduating (his parents' wish) and keeping a steady girlfriend. Likewise, Veasna was trying to leave the gang behind and had started to focus on finishing school and preparing for college. Spending time with their girlfriends had become more appealing than spending time with other guys. Both of them had outgrown the gang as a measure of masculinity. They now considered it a symbol of immaturity and boyhood:

> V: [Gangs] it's not, it's not dealt with, [. . .] like manhood, it's just like, they just hate each other for some reason, it could be over territorial, or . . . danger[?] something, but I don't think it's about manhood, you know, they don't show how tough they are, you know, just because they want to. It's because, like, they, you know how, like little kids, like, they fight with each other because, you know, they do something wrong [to] each other and then they gettin' them problems like that. I think this is what happened too, like, between races of Mexican and Asian people.
>
> ADS: So, what do you mean by little kids that fight?
>
> V: Yeah, see little kids fightin' 'cause they say someth'n' wrong and they misinterpret it, right? And I think this is what is like, is going on with the Mexicans and the Asians, 'cause, I think we can all get along, you know. Everybody can get along, but it's just something that happenin', 'cause, before, like the gangsters, like, the Mexican gangsters and the Asian gangsters, they got along and everything, but, then, they like, started name-calling each other and guess, they started havin' a rivalry, the gangs, fighting.

Veasna had transferred his loyalty to his mother, whom he wanted to help, and to his younger siblings, for whom he wanted to become a role model. His shift toward the family reflected an appreciation and awareness of Cambodian culture and traditions, which included respecting one's elders. His goal to become a monk after graduation would show his gratitude to his mother. And joining the temple, he explained, would boost the reputation of his family. In Cambodia, he added, he would have most likely joined the army after becoming a monk, which would have enhanced his family's reputation even more.[60] Thus, for Joey and Veasna, the relevant collective for establishing one's masculinity had shifted from the gang to the family. Their identification with Cambodian identity remained, but in different forms.

In Mickey's clique of friends there was little concern about establishing one's manhood in a dyadic, male-male interaction. Mickey appreciated and even adored Babe G, whom he considered to be his idol, and Joey greatly supported his friend Mickey. But there was little evidence that Mickey or any of his friends engaged in competitive games with their friends to prove their masculinity. That was taken care of entirely by the gang. In Ben's clique, in contrast, masculinity was performed, mostly, through male-male relations, within an enclosed space of African American culture.[61]

There was no doubt that their relationships with women were a crucial domain for scoring points for manliness. But whose approval they actually sought was ambiguous. Did manliness derive from women who signaled their attraction, or did it derive from their male friends? Ben's clique clearly sought each other's approval, but it was less clear which strategy Mickey's friends preferred. Being a "Mack Daddy" or a "player"—or having a "wife," as Mickey and Babe G put it—was an important element in proving one's masculinity. But their use of "Mack Daddy" and "player" differed from the concept of the player used by Ben and his friends, for whom being a player meant having sexual access to lots of females, rather than the ability to have a long-standing relationship with one.

M: This year, like, mostly I'm popular, 'cause, like, because I was being a Mack Daddy.

J: You know it's like getting' the girl, you know it's like . . .

M: Getting' the girls like that [snapping his fingers].

M: Yeah, 's like, like, you know i's like damn, you're with your girlfriend, and your friend says, "Ah man, if you think you're a Mack, go and see if you get her jumped" [have sex with her]. 'Cause if you get her jumped it's like being a player, you can play around, it's like boom boom boom. It's like me, I used to kick it with . . . 'cause like, the middle over there, that's where all the popular people [are], right, that's what called like the quad area, and it's like, that's where everybody, like, all the Mack Daddies are kickin' it.

ADS: What is it that made you so popular?

M: You know, I'd be macking all the girls . . .

J: . . . playing with the girls, you know.

M: Talking with them [establishing relationships] [. . .] a lot of people say I have a pretty girlfriend, but she ain't, she ain't all that, you know, but she's good enough, that's why I don't, I don't mack no more, I just keep the cool.

J: I's like he's more responsible, he knows he wanna keep this girlfriend, so he, he don't play, you know, he's like Mack Daddy, you know, but he's a cool one, you know, like he's not like a, like some, some of the Macks, you know, they will like, just . . .

M: They don't give a damn, as long as they got the girl and show it to everybody.

Describing his popularity as a Mack Daddy, Mickey was ambiguous about whether he was a real Mack Daddy in "gettin' all the girls" or whether he was a "cool" Mack Daddy who did not mack anymore because he now had a pretty girlfriend. Beneath this ambiguity, both Mickey and Joey seemed to derive satisfaction and prestige from their respective girlfriends that belied their ambiguous attempts to portray themselves as slick "players." It seemed as if they thought they should emphasize their ability to be "players," but really felt comfortable in their monogamous relations.

Just as Babe G was Mickey's declared "road dog," he was also Mickey's role model in being a "true Mack Daddy"—a guy who could get a different girl every day, whether it was a cheerleader or a White girlfriend from a nearby city. When I asked Babe G in front of his friends—both male and female—how significant he thought girls were to be considered cool, Babe G downplayed their importance, but not without earning some laughs from the girls, Monica and Giselle, next to him:

BG: I don't care about girls.

ADS: You don't care about girls?

M: [starts to laugh] Babe G!

BG: No, I just . . .

G: [laughs too] I heard that, Babe G!

BG: No, the girls is too, sometime, but we care more about . . .

LM: Yes for OG, uh huh OG.

BG: You know like, I tell you, you know girls, they come and go, you know, but like a friend, a homeboy, I's like, is [priceless], we can never replace them.

LM: So, the friends are more important.

BG: Unless you have a wife or something.

Babe G was downplaying his alleged success as a Mack Daddy, but he also made it clear that girls were secondary to the brotherhood of his gang. However, if one had a "wife" that was a different story. Li'l Monster explained to me what he meant by being married. Li'l Monster's own girlfriend had been living with him for a few months. He and his parents considered him "married," though they were not, of course, legally married. Li'l Monster explained that he had learned to appreciate her and had given up pursuing other girls. But he said that they had started arguing all the time and had grown tired of each other, so she would return to her parents in the summer.

The guys in Mickey's clique downplayed the significance of girlfriends within the context of the gang. It was more important how good one was at getting girlfriends with the snap of a finger. In contrast, homeboys were considered irreplaceable. At the same time, there was a parallel and often contradictory value of having a steady girlfriend, a pretty girlfriend, a girl to whom one was "married." For Joey and Veasna, who cut their ties with gangs entirely, this gained even larger significance.

This self-presentation as a Mack Daddy, on the surface similar to a player, however, was an incomplete emulation, a half-hearted adoption of a concept that was somewhat incompatible with having a long-term relationship. Mickey and his friends, in their discourse of masculinity, borrowed heavily from African American cultural concepts, but they often used these concepts differently.

In addition, Mickey and Joey were not familiar with the concept of pimping. For Ben and his friends, pimping was a deliberate strategy to con women out of money by pretending that they loved them. But Mickey and Joey could conceptualize pimping only as something *women* might do. When I told them what I had learned about pimping in Ben's clique, they started laughing, saying that they would never get a girl if they would ask her for gifts and money. Their perception was that even if African Americans, or guys in general, had nice cars, they still had limited success with women. In contrast, they themselves, even without cars, had pretty girlfriends:

J: These days, guys have like pretty cars, fine cars, and everything, but got ugly girlfriends.

M: I've been seein' ugly niggas with nice cars 'n' fine ladies.

J: I did too.

M: And see, girls like that, they just want you for your cars.

J: Yes.

M: And for your money.

J: Yeah fo' money, 'cause they know you got stacks, but like us, we ain't got no car. But you know, even though we can still get our Macks on, you know? Like other niggas, you see, have a fine girl, and we wonder, damn, I have, I have no money, I have no stacks, but, nigga, I've a pretty girlfriend.

Thus, in all their attempts to identify with blackness, there was a considerable gap in their cultural knowledge. Mickey and Joey did not seem to be aware that among their African American peers being a player was on its way out, and that the guys they were describing might actually have been pimping.

Mickey and his friends drew on Black culture and identity not only for their ethnic and racial identity, but also for their masculinity. This was evident in their frequent use of Black vernacular, their borrowing of the concept of "Mack Daddy," and their attempt to emulate Black style in dressing. Their adoption of Black cultural representations was particularly visible in their submissive relationship to the Dawgs, the prominent African American gang. Maybe most important, their identification with African American culture was evidence of a racial ideology that was similar to a Black perspective of race. They conceptualized their racial identity on a continuum of Black and White identities, where they aligned themselves with African Americans at one end against a block of racially conflated Latinos and Whites at the other end.

This influence of and orientation toward Black culture, however, was a one-sided relationship. For example, Cambodians' perceptions of what was popular lagged several cycles behind what was "in" among African American students at RHS. They misunderstood the concept of pimping in the Black culture, and in their focus on gangs, they emphasized an identity from which African Americans consciously distanced themselves. Through their code and discourse of masculinity Mickey and his friends allied themselves with "higher status" African American masculinity, but relegated themselves to a position as "lower ranking" dependents.

A LATINO GROUP PORTRAIT: "KICKIN' IT WITH A LOT OF PEOPLE"

The "tree group" met regularly under the shade of an oak tree, located between the snack shop, the library, and the graphic arts workshop. "Grizzly Square" was outside the main courtyard, the center of the school campus before decades of over-enrollment and prefabricated "bungalow" classrooms had turned the original symmetry of the school yard's layout into a haphazard assembly of spaces. It was in the central courtyard area, as Joey put it, where "all the popular people kick[ed] it" and where Mickey's friends, the White peer group, and Ben's friends hung out.

By contrast, the marginalized group at the tree symbolized Latinos' marginal status within the school; and, as everyone knew since the riot, their location was a visible sign of their structural vulnerability.

The "tree group" consisted of about twelve guys and girls, most of them juniors and seniors, some involved in romantic relationships with each other. They called themselves Mexicans, except Marco and his sister Eva, whose parents immigrated from Chile. None of them used the term Chicano to describe themselves. Many Latinos and non-Latinos alike identified this group as "the Latinos" or "Mexicans" generally and its location as the place where Latinos generally kicked it. But although others regarded them as the prototype and most conspicuous group of "Mexicans," they were in several ways not very representative of the school's Latino or Mexican population.

Many in the tree group were born in the United States or arrived as young children and thus had been schooled in English mainstream programs. This set them apart from the more recent Latino immigrants who attended bilingual classes. In addition, the tree group tended to come from middle-class, sometimes even upper-middle-class families, while many other Latinos at the school came from working-class families. More reflective of Latinos at the school generally, though, the members of this group were enrolled primarily in the middle tier of educational programs; one of them was in the gifted magnet.

Eva had mentioned their attempts to include more recent Mexican immigrants from the bilingual classes, but it had not worked, Eva regretted. She explained: "We try hard, but we don't seem to have much in common." In fact, many had more in common with White students, with whom they shared classes, interests, neighborhoods, and sometimes styles. Marco, for example, was surprised when I asked him whether the keychain he carried every day had anything to do with the zootsuiters, a subculture of the 1940s that many associate with a Latino style. But Marco informed me that the keychain was rockabilly style. Eva said that she and her brother had only recently begun identifying themselves as Latinos. Similarly, Pablo, a regular in the group, had spent much of his childhood and youth with White kids, and, as he recalled, often had deliberately tried to hide his Latino culture.

The tree group had existed for more than a year. With some more loyal than others, its membership fluctuated. What had brought the group together and what kept them together was their common opposition to Proposition 187, the 1994 ballot measure that sought to drastically limit services to undocumented immigrants in California. Although none of the students in the tree group were undocumented, all had become the targets of antagonism by some African American and Cambodian students: in the classrooms, in the hallways, and on their way to school.

The tree group was very heterogeneous in its style and class. Marco, whose parents were from Chile, established an identity around music and clothes. He was in the process of changing from "rebel" to "greaser," a style associated with Harley Davidson boots, cuffed Levi's jeans, and music from the 1950s. Marco's interest in art also made him an associate of "two-tone skinheads,"[62] and their arts posse. Marco's personality was adaptable, moving swiftly with the style and composition of the groups with which he associated. He moved easily between groups and earlier had switched from associating with White students primarily to assuming the role of spokesperson for Latino politics in the school.

Through his mother's connections, Marco had access to a job for which he got paid ten dollars an hour. In contrast, many of his friends from the tree group were happy if they found a job at all, and when they did it usually paid minimum wage. And while Marco worked for a weekend so that he could buy himself a pair of Harley Davidson boots, his friend Enrique used his earnings to supplement his family's income. Similarly, while Marco planned to attend art and design school over the summer, Enrique prayed that his mother would not go to Mexico and force him to babysit, thus preventing him from going to summer school. Finally, while Marco was hoping to go to an Ivy League university, many of his friends from the tree group hoped they would be able to afford *any* college. Marco, it seemed, had joined the tree group in part to establish a more influential role for himself and to gain greater visibility.

Marco's sister, Eva, was also a central figure in the tree group. She had been one of the main participants in the riot. Although she was younger, her brother idolized her and her style. Eva's thrift shop wardrobe had become for some a trademark of the group. Both Eva and her brother had been associated with RHS's fraternities and sororities. But whereas Marco had left the Trojans—a predominantly White fraternity—shortly after he fulfilled the initiation requirement of collecting $200 in panhandling from other students, his sister, Eva, remained active with the Alpha Girls and sometimes abandoned the tree group to have lunch with them.

Pablo was a sophomore when I first interviewed him. I had noticed him earlier because of his striking hairstyle. He shaved the lower part of his head and tied the remainder of his thick black hair into a ponytail or a braid. Pablo was in the TechEng Academy, a program that emphasized modern technology. Immediately following the school riot, the principal had recruited Pablo because of his influential position among his peers for the post-riot reconciliation team, Let's All Get Along (LAGA). Pablo was born in the United States. He had an older brother, and both his parents were employed in low-level service jobs. Nevertheless, he described his family as "upper class" but not ashamed to always try to save a buck. Pablo explained that many of his friends in junior high had been African American. But since coming to RHS he had felt rejected by Black students and now kept his distance from them. However, through his pursuit of multiple activities such as music, BMX racing, and arts, he had a wide network of friends and considerable influence.

Enrique was a junior enrolled in a middle-range academy. He was tall and had a muscular build. He was a kicker on the varsity football team. Through football he had a lot of contact with Black and Samoan students. On his team, Enrique felt doubly stigmatized. As a kicker he got the least respect from his "teamies" and the coach, and as one of only two Latinos on the team he felt picked on by his Black and Samoan teammates, who mocked him with references to Proposition 187 and ridiculed his style of dress.

On the fringes of the group were Jorge and José. Jorge also hung out with the Surrealists, but shared the political interests of the tree group. Among the more flamboyant though irregular members was Mat, who went in short succession from gangster to Rasta to political activist and back to gangster again.

The tree group was co-ed. The women in the group were steady members and sometimes outspoken and influential. It was one of the girls in the tree group who was first assaulted in the riot. But despite their prominence in the riot, it was more often the guys who assumed the role of group spokespersons and leaders.

Every Thursday noon, Latinos abandoned the tree. The benches under the oak tree remained empty or were used by others. During this time, the group met as Club Mexicano, in the classroom of Mr. Figueroa, a young and enthusiastic teacher who sponsored the club. Mr. Figueroa was Peruvian and served as a political catalyst for the tree group in particular, as well as for many other Latinos who attended the club meetings.

The tree group's foremost symbol of identity was their race: being Mexican or Latino. For their non-Latino peers, they were representative of Latinos generally. Being seen at "their" tree was enough to be identified as a member of the group and to become the target of anti-Latino sentiments. The ongoing racial remarks of classmates with reference to Proposition 187 and the hostility directed toward them served as a unifying force.

Even though Proposition 187 did not affect any of them personally since none of them was undocumented, they firmly opposed the proposition and organized walkouts, rallies, and political protest sessions. Whereas the more recent Latino immigrants stressed their desire to blend in, the members of the tree group conspicuously emphasized what they were stigmatized for—that is, being "Mexican." When they were accused of wearing cheap, off-brand clothes and accessories, they made sure they didn't "look like [they were] wearing anything from the mall," as

Eva had put it, thus clearly distancing themselves from the fashion dictates of their classmates. They saw themselves as the vanguards of Latino consciousness and as fighters against racial oppression.

Like Mickey's clique of predominantly Cambodians, the Latinos from the tree framed their identity in essentialized terms: as members of the Mexican "race" or ethnic group. Their group was directly related to their Latino identity, an identity that came into sharp focus through the political rhetoric of Proposition 187. But unlike Mickey and his Cambodian friends, who justified their involvement in gangs by stating their need to defend themselves against the overtures of Latinos and Latino gangs, the tree group members let their group solidarity speak for them. By referring frequently to the riot and to animosities in the classrooms and corridors, they were able to establish a legitimate identity without having to engage in aggressive retaliation.

In contrast to the Cambodian clique, where all had links to gangs, this group of friends was assured of the administration's moral support in their tense relationship with African American and Cambodian students. Although the administration had suspended Latinos for throwing a trash can at African Americans, the administration also was under public pressure to provide safety for the shrinking number of Latinos after many had asked to transfer out of the school. Latinos thus were aware and assured of administrative support; the principal even joined the group for a photograph I took of them.

The tree group and their Club Mexicano were also supported by organizations outside the school, including the parent committee and the Coalition of Latin Americans (CLA), an influential Latino organization in the city. As Proposition 187 had earlier, the riot later provided powerful glue for the group.

As one of them put it, all of the people in the group had "tree pride." But unlike Mickey and Babe G, who had used their gangs to prove their virility and as a defense against Latinos, the boys in the tree group downplayed it as an arena in which to establish aggressive masculinity. Rather, their references to masculinity in relation to their group membership were framed around their role as interpreters of the riots and as spokespersons for their race. Marco's account of leaving the Trojans to become politically involved in Latino affairs illustrates this stance:

> Well, in ninth grade I pledged for the Trojans [the White fraternity], and I guess it was kind of my crowd for a few years, just [after a while], me and my girlfriend, we were starting to get into, like, CLA[63] [. . .] , Club Mexicano, Cultura Latina, [. . .] and we, I guess we're like, well, we organize things . . . Well, we go to meetings every other Sunday, and we come here and tell [the others] what happened. [. . .] When I go to clubs, and meetings, I speak out, especially, Proposition 187, I

mean I really got into that, I was one of the main people who helped to, like me, my friend Robert, we are the main people, like in Newtown, we were the ones that formed the rally. I mean I really got into it, and, what I heard a lot was that we should keep going to school, get an education, get a high, get a good degree, bring our names, bring our Hispanics a good name.

Marco not only presented himself as a political organizer, a spokesperson for Latinos, a liaison to CLA, and a Latino role model, but he also advertised his strong connections to parents and his special insights into the dynamics of the riot and its impact on Latino students and parents:

I know a lot of Latinos left, [. . .] 'cause I know, they were who started up the game [riot], 'cause, there is not much of a chance [to be in peace here], 'cause most of the school here is Black, so, a lot of Latinos left. I know, I talked to a lot of . . . , I know a lot of the parents. I am really close to a lot of the parents, and I know they told me that they didn't want their kids here anymore.

Pablo, whose insights into schoolyard politics I cited earlier, illustrates a similar performance as spokesperson for the group when he demonstrated his understanding of political psychology through a detailed analysis of the different factions and their motives for fighting. He presented himself as an expert on the riot, able to interpret the motives of the different parties involved. By providing insights into racial and gang thought processes, he presented himself as an asset to the group:

Asians just wanted to be with the majority. It's like, if there were more Blacks than Mexicans or Latinos, then the Asians would go on the side of the Black people, just because they know that they wouldn't lose out. They wanna be with the stronger force. Like, if there were more Mexicans than Blacks, they would be on the Mexican side. No matter what problems they had had before. It's just whoever has the most power. [. . .] There is a gang called Islanders, East Side Islanders, they are Asians. [. . .] The Islanders were gonna back us up, even though there is like seven that go here, but they're a really big gang. So, when the Islanders were to back us up, they calmed a lot of the stuff down, 'cause they said "they wanna start something, we can't do this." The Islanders knew we don't have a lot of representation, so they backed us up anyway, and they knew that no one would like mess with them, and no one would mess with us as long as they were like with us. [. . .] When they were, like, on our side it calmed down because a lot of gangs were like, "If we're messing with them, we have to deal with them on the outside" [and] on the outside [laughs] there is a lot of Islanders. But then, the other people who weren't really involved in gangs, they didn't really care, they just wanted a rumble I guess. They didn't care, they just kept it going.

Through this account and the intimate knowledge of racial and gang politics that it entailed, Pablo presented himself as a socially skilled observer, though not a participant in the scene he described, who debunked the myth of anti-Asian sentiments among Latinos. In his account, it was because of the Islanders, a Samoan gang that intervened on behalf of Latinos, that the riot came to an end. He also debunked the dominant story line that it was gangs that started the riot and kept it going. Instead, he blamed it on people who wanted a "rumble."

According to Pablo, the demonstration of political leadership and finesse was coupled with one's ability to withstand anti-Latino aggression. Pablo showed that he could keep his cool even in the face of adversity. He could withstand provocations by a hostile group and still seem morally superior. Pablo could stand up for himself even when cornered.

ADS: When [Proposition] 187 was going around, did you think that had an impression on people? What did you feel that was?

P: Even though it wouldn't involve me or any of my family because we are not illegal, but we've still like protested it. [. . .] Yeah, like a lot of people, from other races, yeah, they are going around, you know, "187, yeah, 187, we're gonna pass it." I be walking, and there is like one Black guy coming behind me and saying, "We're gonna pass it, we're gonna pass it" and all that stuff [. . .] "we're gonna get rid of you guys." And I just, like, turn around and, I don't do anything 'cause there is like twenty of them around, and I am sitting all alone, and also, I don't believe in violence.

Enrique, quoted earlier, explained further:

E: There was three freshmen kids, they were like "You fuckin' Mexican."

ADS: What were they?

E: Three Black guys. And I just looked back at them, stopped and turned around and looked back at them, and they didn't say anything. It's like just because I stopped they were intimidated, I intimidated them by reacting in a nonviolent way. You know? I was not gonna go "Come on, what's up?" I wasn't gonna threaten them or beat 'em up. I just looked at them, just looked at them in a funny way. You know they can say anything they want, they just can't do anything about it. I never got in a fight in my life.

Because Latinos had played a central role in the riot, the Latinos from the tree group distanced themselves from a merely racially motivated reaction and instead framed their involvement as self-defense. Pablo explained: "I am not just getting into a fight for racial reasons. People know that I am not racist. But if you get too close to me, if you break into my personal space, I will fight."

Through such strategies, Latinos from the tree distinguished themselves from Blacks and Cambodians, whom they accused of racial and racist reactions. Instead of retaliating on equal terms—an option unavailable to them because of their underrepresentation at the school, they invoked a position of moral superiority, presenting themselves as knowing better than to react on the basis of race.

Multiple alliances and larger social networks provided the tree group not only with a form of social capital, but also with the ability to escape confrontations with many groups who were potentially hostile toward Latinos. Instrumental in extending their social network was their ability to demonstrate expertise in different arenas: playing an instrument, engaging in different sports, or presenting oneself as an expert of a specific style. Instead of being known and making a name for themselves through the "work that they put in" for the gang, the guys in the tree group cultivated skills that allowed them to diversify their social relations and become known for their expertise. By assuming the role of interlocutor, interpreter, or spokesperson for Latinos generally, the guys in this group engaged a code of masculinity at the level of collective identity. In a seeming countercurrent to the homogenizing collective identity, they also engaged a highly individualized code of masculinity. That individualized code included being known for one's expertise among a wide, often cross-racial circle of friends. Crossing over to racial antagonists was particularly important and instrumental, because it proved one's neutrality and ability to "get along," to "kick it with a lot of people." Through such social connections, the guys in the tree group gained additional eyes and ears, additional sensors for recognizing potential conflict. Through multiple involvements with other organizations and groups, they were propelled into greater visibility and larger social networks. Pablo explained:

> I know a lot of gangsters, I like to kick it with a lot of different people, I don't stick with, like, I mean I hang around the tree, but I know a wide variety of people, like gangsters, like, a lot of people, a lot of people that do different things. So that like, that's what makes me . . . that's what makes me known. Like, when you go talk to skaters, they do know me, 'cause I skate. If you talk to the bikers that go here . . . like, if you talk to like basically any group, like the headbangers, you know what I mean? The rock musicians, I play music. I play guitar and drums, so it's like, a lot of people know me for different things. If you ask like, a Black guy, "Oh you know Pablo?" They go like "Oh, ya, ya, I know him from junior high, we used to play

basketball," and if you ask another person like a White person that stands over by the tree, "Oh you know Pablo," he goes "Oh, we jammed it at one time." And when you talk to an Asian, he would say, "Yeah, we go to church together, he is cool." You know what I mean? It's like, I kick it with a lot of people. 'Cause I don't like to just stick with one, with one group of people, 'cause then you get known for sticking with that group of people. You know what I mean? And then you get known like, "Oh, he kicks it with them." People think of me, oh you know, if you think of most people, you think of someone, "He is a skater, he is a greaser, or he is a . . ." With me, people think of me as the guy with the pony tail, who walks around." [laughs]. So, it's like, pretty crazy. Yeah, so I don't really have any problems. So, when the riots were happening, a lot of people, like, like one Black guy was coming, "Hey stupid Mexican, and i's like, . . . another Black guy is coming up behind him and saying "Hi, kick back." And I say, "it's all right." It's like, I got that with a lot of people.

The tree group was just one among several groups with whom Pablo hung out; he definitely did not want to be associated with that group only. For Enrique, who felt rejected and stigmatized by his Black and Samoan teammates, the tree provided a safe haven from his adversaries, where he could show his true identity, where he could prove to others that he was open and accepting of others, independent of their various group affiliations.

ADS: I heard a lot of people after these riots say that nobody likes Mexicans, everybody looks for beating up Mexicans, is that true?

E: That's true, [but] not to me! I didn't have any problems. Everybody is, "Let's get them." That's one thing, that's one advantage about me, I get along with everybody, I have a lot of, a lot of Black people from the football team, Samoan people, I have a lot of Cambodian friends, White friends. Nobody did anything to me, you know. I walked around like nothing ever happened. [. . .] Actually it is, like, all my friends, like, everywhere I go there is somebody there to say hi to. Everywhere I am, there is somebody to say hi to. And if I don't know 'em, like there is some people sometime they walk to the tree, I just shake everybody's hand, and I go up to somebody and say my name and ask "What's yours?" And I shake their hands. First time I've ever seen them in my life and I shake their hands. I make them gonna be my friend. I'm not, I'm not gonna disrespect somebody. You know, Ruby, at the Black History Show, she would, one of her poems or whatever, one of the things she did on stage was like, "Let's all be one, come on, let's all be brothers etc. etc., don't, um, like, get along in other words, in other words, let's all get along, and she's the main one that judges you by the way you look.

Marco also invested in diversification. He maintained strong connections to the predominantly White artist scenes that involved some of the Surrealists. And while he was on the one hand a sole representative of the subcultural style of "greasers," associated with rockabilly and music from the 1950s, he was also an active member of the Mormon Church.

A similar diversification regime is apparent in Jorge's self-presentation. A somewhat irregular member of the tree group, he was well informed about local and state politics and drew a large part of his identity from being aware of his roots and of his political obligations as a young Latino. In contrast to other Latinos in the gifted magnet, he openly identified himself as a Mexican American and supported Mexican Americans' rights. But besides being an occasional member of the tree group, Jorge made it clear that he also hung out with the rowers, most of whom were White, and that he was a regular in the White Surrealist group. Mat, another tree group member, epitomized this scheme of diversification sequentially. Over the previous two years he had shifted his style from dreadlocked Rasta to shaved-head gangster to member of the tree group.

Rather than emphasizing the autonomy of the tree group as an outpost of Latino identity and politics, its members, particularly the males, were affiliated with formal groups such as CLA and Club Mexicano, which helped to deflect attention on the tree group as an isolated outpost of Latino identity.

Some of the previous examples of withstanding racial aggression as an expression of collective Latino identity also can be viewed as performances of masculinity in a male-male arena. Although the conflicts were framed with reference to racial others, Enrique and Pablo proved their manhood to their adversaries as individuals. African American students taunted Pablo and challenged his status, but Pablo was alert enough to recognize the futility of giving in to their provocations. In his portrayal of himself as a nonviolent person, he managed to retain the moral upper hand and with this, a space in which to perform dominance.

Similarly, Enrique stood his ground in a nonviolent way when provoked by some African American classmates. Merely looking at them "in a funny way" was enough to get his adversaries off his back.

Psychological strength and nonviolent responses gave Pablo and Enrique a sense of moral superiority over members of hostile groups and thus a space in which to perform a dominant role and prove their masculinity to others: to guys in the hostile group, but also, in retelling the stories, to males in their own.

There was yet another facet of this code of masculinity as nonviolence. Implicit in their narratives was the idea that they were acting on their own behalf, not collectively as Latinos or even as members of the tree group. Their unspoken statement was that they positioned themselves against those they believed attacked them solely on the basis of their race: African Americans and Cambodians. Pablo and Enrique were not defending their racial identity; they were defending and demanding respect for their own "personal space," Enrique explained:

> To be a man is like, to have a kind of responsibility, to kind of look out for, . . . I know it seems like, like it may sound superior, but, in my heart, how I think, I always look out for other people. If you don't, if you always chicken out, like, if you see something wrong but you don't try to help it, it's just like, like, you're not living up to what you're capable. [. . .] Like, if I see something is wrong, I got to fix it. It's not like I sit and think, "Oh I have to or I am supposed to." It's just I want to. [. . .] Yeah, because they know that I am not prejudiced and *they* know when I am going to fight it is not because of the riots, or because he is Black or he hit my friend. But if you are touching me, you are invading my personal space I guess you would say. Yeah, it don't matter, you can be Mexican. If you touch me, you got what's coming to you. You're like, a lot of people know that. But then, a lot of people will just like wanna fight.

For Enrique the tree group was an escape from the racial hostility that he experienced on the football team, where he felt doubly stigmatized by his Samoan and Black teammates: first for being a Latino and second for being a kicker, a second-rate position in which he was little appreciated but often blamed for defeats. He felt particularly victimized by Sam, one of his Samoan teammates, notwithstanding Sam's reputation in the administration as a leader and spokesperson against racial violence. Enrique was also often ridiculed by Black students for the way he dressed, in off-brand jeans and T-shirts, which for him were primarily a matter of affordability. But instead of getting back at his adversaries in kind, he retaliated during a game, where, he said, "I got back at them really hard." For Enrique, playing football was a way to reestablish respect through the performance of a dominant posture. It was a sanctioned form of violence that did not contradict his creed of nonviolence. But it was also a strategy that protected him: it masked his retaliation behind the emotions of the game.

When I asked the young men from the tree about their personal definition of manhood, most of them described it as having a family and a sense of responsibility, of being a provider, of "having a son." Similar to the White peer group, the guys from the tree group never mentioned relationships with girls as male accomplishments. Even though some of the girls complained that guys were notorious for their disloyalty to their girlfriends, boys talked about girls not as commodities in a male-male status game, but as partners in relationships by whom they felt appreciated or insulted, accepted or rejected. Some complained that their fathers treated their mothers like slaves, and others envisioned marriage in traditional ways. But most were collegial with the women in the group and respectful of their girlfriends.

Pablo despised Black guys who called themselves "pimp" and presented themselves as G's, or gangsters:

> A lot of people here carry themselves like [gangsters]. Like no one messes with them, like they are OG.[64] Like, "I'm a G," but they're not really from anywhere.[65] They just think that they're like a pimp or something. So, you know what I mean? They go like, "Oh I am a G, I get all the ladies," all this kind of stuff.

Enrique showed his vulnerable side and his disappointment when he talked about his relationship with his former girlfriend, a friendship that broke up because of her mother's prejudice against Mexicans:

> E: I had a girlfriend, she just broke up with me, a month ago, and there is a sorority called Scarabs at school. She pledged for them, I didn't really like that, and, I started seeing changes, you know. She would ignore me a lot of times, but, every time I saw her, she's like Ecuadorian, you know. She, um, she doesn't act, she act more like a White girl, you know, she wasn't acting the way she was. That is one thing I would have never liked, I would never act like, you know, I have a lot of White friends, I have a lot of Black friends, I have a lot of Asian friends, but I would never forget where I come from. [...] Me and her broke up because of her mom. [...] [Her mom] didn't like me. [laughs] Mainly because her last boyfriend was a White guy, and I guess I wasn't enough. You know, she told her that she can do better, or that I was a bad influence. [...] That's what her mother said. And you know, I ask myself, I laugh sometimes too, how can I be a bad influence, you know? I go to school every day, I never ditch, I maintain a 3.0 average, or at least I try to, I am on the varsity football and soccer teams, I'm in the jazz band, I try to do my best to stay alive, and still her mother says I am a bad influence on her daughter. I just . . .

> ADS: You didn't fit so much in her social circles anymore after she pledged?

> E: Not at all. She would ignore me all the time, she would like be with all her friends. And me, I have a lot of friends, I would take my time away from them just to be with her, but she can't be without her friends. That didn't seem right to me, you know? She would ignore me to be with her friends, when I could have been with my friends. I don't think that would have worked. In a way it is good that we broke up. [...] My ex-girlfriend's mom had her when she was 15, you know, and she thought that I was gonna do the same thing to her daugh-

ter. Her mom she was like, "I have to talk to you." So I went over there. She was like, "I know how Latinos are." She had her daughter when she was 15, so she thought that I was gonna do the same thing to her, and I took that as a, I took that real deep inside, as an insult. Like somebody is shooting me in my back.

Latinos from the tree group manufactured their symbols of identity around that for which they were stigmatized and taunted by their African American and Cambodian peers: being Latinos. For several of them, who previously had identified themselves as White, or whose parents or teachers had advised them to do so, this was a new experience. Their new identity served both to antagonize others and to give them new power.

The niches of masculinity they cultivated were as interlocutors and spokespersons for their race in venues that were accepted by the school administration and official school culture. In these roles they underscored their affinity to the White power structure: the school, the teachers, the administrators. In the school-yard hierarchy, where they faced two large and hostile factions—African Americans and Cambodians—their strategy for proving masculinity was to reduce confrontations through diversification: BMX riding, playing football, playing an instrument, playing in a band, or engaging in activities such as theater or Art Club. This diversification scheme enabled them, ultimately, to "kick it with a lot of people" and develop wider social circles. The guys in the tree group carved out individual spaces where they could perform dominant masculinity in relation to a multiracial audience and thus, at the same time, develop individual, cross-racial friendships, which helped them to overcome their racially precarious position. Theirs was thus a dual strategy of, on the one hand, generating cohesion by organizing themselves collectively in official venues, and on the other, cultivating special skills to be performed in front of a wider audience.

In their relationships with girls, the guys in the tree group clearly distinguished themselves from Cambodians or African Americans. They never used the idioms of player or Mack Daddy and rejected the concept of using girls as vehicles for generating status with other males.

A WHITE GROUP PORTRAIT: "MISFITS" AND GENDER BENDERS

Roger and his friends were a group of about ten regulars, most of them White and all except one juniors and seniors. This group of friends had been exclusively White until the second year of my observation at RHS, when David, a second-generation Mexican American, and Paul, who was part African American, joined the group. Almost all of the students in this clique were enrolled in GROW, the gifted magnet. The labor-intensive courses in GROW left them little time for socializing outside of school, so lunch breaks and the time before and after school were critical for socializing.

Roger was the first one I met from this group. Roger was taller and bigger than the others. He often came to school in worn-out Birkenstock sandals, and with his shoulder-length hair tied in a ponytail. He changed his style frequently: once he shaved the lower part of his scalp; later he grew sideburns. Sometimes he wore bead necklaces. But clothes to him were merely a practical necessity, and shopping for clothes was a once-a-year chore he did with his mother, right before school started. Unlike some of his friends who were into grunge, his clothes were often pressed, not because he preferred it that way, but because his mother sent the family's laundry to the cleaners. Roger was a movie aficionado like his stepdad, a hobby that he developed further in a film course offered at RHS. Roger had entered a gifted program only after arriving at Roosevelt High. In elementary school and junior high he had been in regular programs that were more racially diverse than GROW.

Two of his close friends were Andrew and Sally, a long-term and affectionate, but rather quiet couple. Roger often gave them a ride to school and home. John was another friend of Roger's. Like Roger, John had long blonde hair usually tied in a ponytail. John's wardrobe was at times unusual among his classmates, particularly his favorite pair of pants, which resembled a skirt. He was a senior who was later accepted at a prestigious, all-male university, but eventually rejected this offer in favor of a less prestigious, more mainstream university where he intended to study economics. Despite a severe form of dyslexia, John conducted his own independent research project in microbiology at the local university during his senior year in high school.

Then there was April. She was very thin. Like some of her friends, she bleached her hair. April had a broad interest in art and liked to sculpt. She exhibited some of her work in a local art gallery. April lived with her mother, who suffered from a mental illness, on social security income in a poverty-stricken area downtown.

After the seniors in the group had graduated, a few younger students gradually joined the group. Among them was Miriam, a vibrant young woman whose latest hair color was pitch black, but who had dyed her hair many unconventional colors before. Miriam's distinct style—which usually involved dressing all in black, often in short skirts, net stockings, and twelve-hole Doc Martens boots—made her a visual focal point of the group. Miriam was a self-described expert on teens and drugs; she reported having been addicted to speed and said she'd spent a week in juvenile detention. Throughout her self-proclaimed involvement with drugs, the GROW counselor had helped her keep up with her classwork in the gifted program. The counselor even helped her find a job at Wendy's. Others in the group, though, such as Bruce and Anne, doubted Miriam's stories about her drug addiction, and the rumor was that much, if not all, of the information that she so eagerly volunteered about herself was made up.

Paul was the youngest in the group. He was interested in dance. For him, the GROW program did not offer much that would help him develop his interests. Paul lived with his mother, who was White. He described his father as a very wealthy African American professional who had never acknowledged him as his son. His father, he said, was the "kind of guy that would tamper with a DNA test only to not have to pay alimony." Paul was very serious. He explained that he hung out most of his life with White kids, who accepted him, although they had wondered about his curly hair and dark complexion. He now bleached his hair and was a careful, though not ostentatious dresser. Both April and Paul were gay, but Paul talked more freely about it with his friends and in interviews.

After John graduated, Bruce had become more and more a part of this group. Bruce was considered good looking by his peers and described himself as a "goth." He usually dressed in black pants and a black T-shirt. Like Roger and some others in this group, he often wore a bead necklace and was hardly ever seen without his wallet chain, which had become his trademark. Bruce was kicked out of GROW in tenth grade, after his art teacher, Mrs. Dumont, had written eleven disciplinary referrals for him in one week. Later on, the GROW counselor asked Bruce to join the gifted magnet again. By that time, however, Bruce had decided that he wanted to do more with his life than study. So he stayed in one of the mid-level academies, where he appeared to be well respected generally, but, as his electronics teacher said, was something of a "rebel without a cause."

Finally, there was Jorge. Jorge pronounced his name the Spanish way and forbade others to call him Joe. He was very active in Latino politics on and off campus, and also sometimes hung out with the Latino tree group, described earlier. Jorge lived with his gay father, after his parents divorced when he and his twin brother were six years old. His twin, Robert, attended RHS for one year, but then moved to San Jose to live with their mother. Robert told me that he could not get used to what he called the "goody-two-shoe" mentality of the GROW kids, nor could he bear the "wannabe alternatives" who were too scared to try anything new. Their father, a consultant for bilingual education at a local university, was disappointed when Robert decided to become a dentist, because, as Jorge explained, becoming a dentist was not in the family tradition of social activism. Jorge and his dad called Robert and his mother, an elementary school teacher, the hedonists of the family.

As these personal portraits show, the family backgrounds of the people in Roger's group were diverse. Some came from middle- or upper-middle-class families, but others came from poor, single-parent households. Several in the group had been in gifted programs since starting school. Others, like Roger and Jorge, had first entered a gifted program at RHS. Despite the fact that all except Bruce were in GROW, they had very few classes together, making their shared time during breaks an important part of their social lives.

Because the group was so heterogeneous, many of their activities overlapped with those of the other friendship group members. April, involved in the art scene, had connections with some of the Latinos in the tree group, as well as with Joey, a member of the Cambodian clique. Jorge, who was so outspoken on Latino politics, was another link to the Latino tree group. Bruce, after being kicked out of the gifted magnet, was the only one who had regular contact with non-White students in his classes. At times Bruce questioned the liberal airs of his friends, particularly Roger, although Roger—during his last year in school—had elected a course in business English, a class designed for the BusTech Academy, a move, as discussed earlier, that his GROW counselor found very disturbing.

The group usually met in front of Building B, next to the rally stage. This location was close to the White fraternity, the Trojans, and the Black students' hangout in front of the administration building. Their location revealed some of the most defining characteristics of their group. Roger and his friends had organized the Surrealist club, inspired by their popular English teacher and the surrealist literature they were discussing at the time they formed the club. Club members were allowed to meet in a classroom during lunch, under the supervision of a sponsoring teacher. The group chose Fridays to meet, because that was the day the weekly rallies took place on the stage right next to their hangout. Staying inside with the club allowed them to avoid the rally and the noise and crowd that came with it, a crowd that they described as consisting primarily of African American students.

The spatial location of Roger's friendship group positioned it squarely between the White fraternity on one side and cliques of African American students on the other. Their location and their formation of the club symbolized their symbolic displacement and their reclaiming of their own space. Roger and his friends described themselves as "alternative," "liberal," pro-gay, and pro-feminist.

Roger explained that what brought their group together was their common marginalization and stigmatization by others:

> I think the common tie of this clique is that at one time or another pretty much all of us have been persecuted, put down, or something, because we don't fit anywhere else. The outsiders band together instead of being just separate factions. I

guess we're just forced together. [. . .] I think all of us are pretty liberal, we're pretty much all liberal. In varying degrees. There are a few of us that aren't. [. . .] But that's fine.

Roger might have considered his own stigma to be connected to his appearance. He was heavy-set and suffered from acne. His self-image might have been reflected in a poem published in a collection with works by other RHS students. In this gripping poem he described the monster that stared back at him every morning from the bathroom mirror. Whatever his self-image, Roger had a sympathetic and gentle personality and was a sought-after knowledge bank for the women in his French class, where he was one of only two guys.

John was ostracized by peers outside his group of friends because of his friendship with April and Margie, two lesbians, and his somewhat feminine style of dressing. He was overtly non-macho, even gender-ambiguous, in his interaction with others. Bruce, expelled from GROW for lack of discipline, did not fit the mold of the nerdy GROW student, but neither, with his gothic style, did he look like his Asian, African American, or Latino classmates in the mid-level academies. For April and Margie, the group provided support for their visible difference: their short haircuts and radical hair color, which were interpreted by people outside the group as unambiguous statements of their sexual difference. And for all of them, the clique provided a refuge from what Jorge's twin brother, Robert, had called the goody-two-shoe attitude of many GROW students: the tendency to internalize uncritically the expectations and desires of their parents and teachers.

For many students in the gifted magnet, scholastic competition was the daily bread of their lives. Competition dictated who their friends were and with whom they socialized. However, in Roger's group, this competition was toned down. Instead of wearing a T-shirt with the slogan "second winner is the first loser," so popular among many GROW students, a more typical description was to call themselves "lazy," implying that even without studying hard they were able to stay in GROW, and, in some cases maintain high grade-point averages.

Emphasizing their "laziness" was just one way in which Roger's group represented a more rebellious element among the otherwise rather conservative GROW population. Roger's group also stood out from other White students for its distinct style. In the school as a whole, most of the girls wore their hair long, and boys— except Samoans and some White Rastas—wore their hair short or shaved; in Roger's group it tended to be the other way around. Most of the girls had very short hair, while the boys wore it long. Their preference for unusual hair colors such as green and purple also contrasted with the general appearance of the larger student body.

Although Newtown had a large and well-known lesbian and gay strip that stretched from downtown to the more affluent east side of town, there was little openness at RHS about homosexuality. Other school districts in the area had experimented with some protective provisions for gay and lesbian students, but not NUSD. The term faggot was so common at RHS that it had almost lost its punch. But it indicated a widespread atmosphere of hostility toward homosexuality among many students and teachers.

Protesting the dominant ideology of gender conformity was one of the defining and self-conscious characteristics of Roger's group, notwithstanding the fact that only three of them, Paul, April, and Margie, identified themselves as gay. Not only did their friends accept them, but the three also embraced and underscored the image of their sexual nonconformity as one of their trademarks. Rather than denying it, they often even deliberately encouraged the rumors that they were gay. This counteridentity worked on various fronts. It set them apart from the proper, preppy, and conservative average GROW student; it allowed them to draw a clear line between the outwardly macho posture of the Trojans and what they considered the dominant Black masculinity on campus.

Roger and his friends proved their masculinity ironically through a performance of gender ambiguity or gender reversal, which allowed them to create a space in which to perform dominance. Through this they established their own version of masculinity. While John was taking a break from some experiments in his marine biology class, I commented about his—by RHS standards—unusually long hair. John explained that some people interpreted it as meaning he was homosexual, which by the way, he assured me, did not bother him. Just the opposite; he had a lot of lesbian friends. He wondered, however, why any stranger would want to know about his sexuality.

In a conversation with Roger a couple of days after my interview with John, I hinted at the same issue, asking him about his shoulder-length hair that was so atypical for RHS. Roger explained sarcastically:

R: My hair, it's just, because . . . , someone said the way how you can tell women from men is that women have long hair and men have short hair and I think it's stupid.

ADS: Are you afraid that others might think you are gay?

R: No, I don't think so. And if people think I am homosexual, they have the right to do so, I suppose. No. I am not afraid of it. I think it is really their feeling against me, you know. It is not part of me, it is them that's being stupid, I guess.

With their long hair, John and Roger consciously challenged their peers' notions of what was gender-appropriate. But John went a lot further than that. The yearly prom—with its conspicuous protocol of gender norming—provided a unique platform for making a statement about dogmatic gender conventions. To demonstrate their critique of rigid gender roles, John and April planned to shock their fellow students by going cross-dressed: April was planning to wear a tuxedo, and John was to go in a fancy evening dress. At the last minute, however, they changed their minds. Similarly, two other girls in the group had planned to go to the prom as a same-sex couple. Both of them were suspected by many to be lesbians, bisexuals, or otherwise "weird," primarily because of their short haircuts and unconventional green or purple hair, although in reality both of them were straight. Nevertheless, they both enjoyed the idea of fueling people's imagination.

Like Roger, April described herself and her friends as "alternative." At the time of our interview, which took place while she was serving detention in the cafeteria for being late, a few Asian American guys started to call her "skinhead." She just shrugged it off, saying that Asian kids often did not know what they were talking about. During the interview, she spoke of herself and her sexuality. Men generally just made her feel uncomfortable and all of her close friends were female, except John. But whether gay or bisexual, she did not feel harassed because of her sexuality. In April's eyes, the school campus was not particularly intolerant. Her life, she felt, revolved more centrally around her art and her activities in the Unitarian Church. Paul, though also quiet, was more flamboyant in his self-description. He portrayed himself as more vulnerable to the snide remarks of his classmates and preferred to talk about his sexual identity only to his close friends.

Both April and Paul, and a few others, provided a focal point for Roger and his friends, something to protect, something obvious to rally around. Their perceived sexuality and sexual difference became the symbol of the group's identity, the diacritica itself. Thus, in some ways, Paul and April served almost as mascots for the group. But neither Paul nor April had the same enthusiasm and excitement about their difference that their support group did. Their friends used it as a symbol of identity and also turned it into an arena in which to develop distinction. Roger's friends' self-representation as gay, bisexual, or sexually ambiguous produced a point of convergence for Roger's group, enacted in the demarcation of boundaries between themselves and the homophobic and aggressive masculinity of the Trojans and between themselves and the African American students.

Roger expressed the conflict with his classmates from the Trojans in his film analysis class, an elective course open to students from all academies. This class was taught by Mr. Kubrick, a sympathetic middle-aged teacher, whose long gray hair and liberal views suggested that he might have once been in the counter-culture movement. Because Mr. Kubrick had pointed out the abundance of phallic symbols in the movie they had watched that day, the Trojans had ridiculed Mr. Kubrick and called him gay. Roger commented:

> All the people in there are into off-campus, like, fraternities and sororities. They are kind of stupid, they are kind of up in fashion. No, I just don't like them. [. . .] They are all pretty fascist. If you don't fit the mold, if they see male bonding they have to speak out against it. [They make fun of Mr. Kubrick for pointing out phallic symbols in various films and] they talk about Mr. Kubrick, mainly the boys; they reaffirm their manliness by saying "Oh he is gay."

Roger's friends shared his passionate dislike of the Trojans and their sexist and macho behavior. But while Roger and his group felt strongly about the Trojans, their biggest challengers were racial others: African Americans and sometimes Asians, who criticized the girls' unconventional styles. As Roger explained earlier, their group was based on their common experience of marginalization, and they became most cohesive in the face of aggression from outsiders, particularly students who harassed the girls in their group for looking different. Such encounters occurred periodically:

> ADS: So, it is the guys who are picking on the girls?
>
> R: Yeah, that's right. But it's not the guys from inside the group. It's the guys from outside. [. . .] Yeah, so, the girls look more different, 'cause they're lashing back at society, you know. When they, say, wear a certain type of makeup, they'll go over it and make up their face White, and it won't be the type of makeup you know men want. It's basically much more, they're fighting spirits. So, the women look different, and the men are gonna pick on everyone that looks different. [. . .] I think it is, it could be because they are women. I am not sure. It could be, keep the women in line, or keep the more freakish people in line.
>
> ADS: Are they White guys, are they Black guys, are they GROW guys?
>
> R: The ones that have spoken out are usually African American or Asian.
>
> ADS: No fights?
>
> R: Oh no. The closest we came, somewhat close, two or three years ago, just, some people were totally flaky. They were saying "Why do you look different?" But they said it in a real weird tone. Like "Why do you look different, what's your problem, you freak." [. . .] They had that really antagonizing sort of bite to it. [. . .] It's usually "You look different, we're gonna pick on you." You know, that was kind of, something different. It really comes down, like, "You look like

creeps, we put you in line," or something like that, or, "Why do you look like that?" in the sense of "Why are you different, why aren't you like us?"

The provocations Roger described provided an opportunity for the guys in the group to show their loyalty and protection of the girls when others harassed them. It was through their connection with this collective that they were provided the opportunity to engage in a performance of masculine dominance.

The perception that their African American peers were trying to "keep the women in line," as Roger described it, was also echoed in a heated debate among Bruce, Paul, and Anne about what they perceived as preposterous performances of Black masculinity. With Bruce—who had the most immediate contact with African American, Latino, and Southeast Asian students—as the driving engine, and with Paul as counterpoint, they talked about how it was usually African American guys who referred to women as bitches, tricks, or hoes. It was Black guys, Bruce emphasized, who made sure to keep "their bitches in line."

Probing them about the notions of masculinity that I encountered in Ben's group, I asked them whether they had heard about the idea of girls courting guys with lavish presents, Bruce explained:

B: I'm in regular [track], and I hear all these jokes and lines from rap songs and stuff. [. . .] My friend told me a story. They were watching a nature film. I mean a nature film has nothing to do with anything, I mean sex or women or anything. One tiger, um, jumped on the female and battered her down into the ground. [. . .] I don't know why. And, one of the guys in the back goes "Well that's keeping your bitch in check." That's a rap line. I am not saying that rap is Black, I am just saying what I see at RHS, that's how it appears to me.

P: See, I take my experiences from, like, the community. My mother dated lots of Black men, and we're involved in the African American community for a long time. [. . .] Ah, and so, I just noticed that the women are dominant, and seem to have most of the power in the society.

A: Is it they just boss the men around when they are there?

P: No, it's not that they boss them around. It's that, rather than having to do everything, like cleaning the house . . . , the men already know that's their job. And also the woman tells them that they gotta do something, and they go and do it. [. . .] [Women] are dominant, they are the ones that control things, that keep everyone in line. Rather than it being the guy. Personally I think it is like a false masculinity that some of the guys put on.

A: Ya, I was gonna say, like, doesn't that make, like, a community of overgrown kids being told what to do, by, like, mother figures, pretty much?

P: Yeah, pretty much.

B: I never see women, like, at this community at RHS, as being referred to as women. They are always tricks, bitches, thugs. [. . .] I mean that's just in rap. I mean that's what I see. I mean all the guys follow all the examples that you can watch on MTV. [. . .]

P: I also kind of think, they do that in their little guy group. But if they are around with their girlfriends, they are just pussy whipped.

B: Yeah, then they're just whipped. That's sad.

A: Isn't that just like, little kids, like talking about their moms when they aren't there, but when they are there they are all "Okay, mom." [other girl laughs]

P: Yeah, right. This is the same thing.

Bruce thought that the men in his class showed a lot of disrespect to women, whereas Paul felt that African American men treated women much more as equals than White men did. Anne, whose words seemed to carry much weight, characterized Black men as little boys rebelling against their mothers. During almost the entire hour and a half of this conversation, all of them took up issues their group had with Black men, and what they perceived as posturing, imposing, and even domineering elements of Black students' behavior. All three of them found ways to trivialize what they experienced as challenges to their group, and maybe to an internalized consciousness of White dominance outside their peer culture. In this juxtaposition of themselves with Black students, they assumed a marked status without explicitly talking about whiteness. While Bruce and Paul often assumed controversial positions, it was Anne whose opinion everyone agreed with in the end. This was in accordance with the role of Anne, April, and Margie as group emblems or mascots, or even as the raison d'être of the group in the first place.

As discussed in Chapter 3, GROW students, who were told over and over again by their teachers that they were special, were also told they needed protection. Theirs was thus a contradictory form of identity, where unmarked White dominance went hand in hand with the marked minority status of whiteness, a status in need of protection. The ambiguous White-Black relationship was most clearly expressed in Bruce's self-positioning, which shifted from loyalty to his classmates to loyalty to his closer White peers among the Surrealists.

Their discussion of the term "jocking," to which I turn now, revealed their awareness that the discourse of protection marked them as in need of shelter from the non-Whites and regular students, but it also revealed a clash with what they perceived as preposterous Black masculinity.

A marginal figure in this interview was Jenny. She was not part of Roger's group, the Surrealists, but happened to sit at the table with the other ones when I began our interview. Although she remained quiet most of the time, she finally brought up an example of what she felt was typical Black macho behavior. By revealing that she did not know what "jocking" meant, she not only showed how successfully she had been "sheltered," but she marked herself as an outsider to the group. Roger's friends, in contrast to Jenny, indicated that knowledge of such terms had currency and signaled cultural competence. Bruce, Paul, and Anne, joined by Ethan this time, admitted the importance of demonstrating familiarity with Black culture at RHS:

J: Shaquil, the other day he [. . .] got up to do his project [about how he tried to "condition" a girl not to jock him anymore]. And, he used a new term that he called "jockin," or whatever.

B: That's not new. I've been jocked for two years by Ashley Putnam. [. . .]

J: Well, he just, made a big deal about that and wrote it on the board, and, like, . . .

B: He did it because that is what Mr. Jones said.

J: Did he?

[Everybody else agrees that Mr. Jones asked him to do so.]

A: That's not new. I heard it, like, a long time ago.

P: I heard it a long time ago, but I never knew what it meant. It's like one of those words that is like, yeah, whatever.

B: I like better the way he explained it like jockstrap. 'Cause, the explanation that I heard was, she is sitting at the end of his dick. It's funny, but, it seems kind of far-fetched, it doesn't really seem to fit, like, out of that you got jocking?

In summary then, Roger and his friends performed a masculinity that was a defense against being challenged by African Americans. Their performance of masculinity took shape against the imposition of the dominant Black masculinity on campus.

Among the Surrealists, proving one's masculinity to other men in the group was not as central as defending the group against homophobic aggression. Nevertheless, playful skirmishes and mock battles between John and Roger were not uncommon. This was apparent in Mr. Joy's popular psychology class, an elective that was supposed to bring "gifted" and regular students together but was really an unofficial gifted class because almost all of the students were from the gifted program. It was also one of the few classes where Roger had a classmate from his peer group.

Many of the males in the class, particularly John and Roger, made a sport of trying to outwit each other as well as Mr. Joy through smart and daring remarks and mock questions. Mr. Joy seemed to enjoy this competition as much as his students. Girls usually stayed out of this contest. Their participation consisted more in engaging in flirtatious, charming banter with the teacher.

Their performance of masculinity as gender protest became most self-consciously mobilized when they protected the nonconforming females in their clique. In Roger's opinion, it was not the guys who created a subcultural identity, but the girls, who were more likely to express their disagreement with society in their appearance and style; and it was the girls who were regularly harassed by others for the way they looked. It was the girls' protest against traditional femininity and sexuality that outsiders interpreted as a provocation. For Roger, it was this tension from guys outside their group against their women, particularly against those considered lesbians, that made them "band together." Roger explained:

> We really don't have, like, cultural pride. [. . .] It's funny though, 'cause, every so often, somebody will come up to us, and will start something. And that happens just every year. [. . .] The only time that we band together, that's, when it's trouble on the home front, [. . .] and, it usually happens to the women. The men are usually antagonizing the women over, like . . .

Thus, while the women were the ones that were picked on for being different, the guys in their group rallied behind them and defended them. Through this defense of "their" women they created another arena in which to prove their masculinity.

As mentioned earlier, though, it was not only through their defense of queerness, but also through their performance of queerness that guys seemed to compete with each other and tried to gain acceptance. A particularly revealing demonstration of such a "staged" performance of queerness was evident in a video coproduced by John and Sally. Both served as narrators, and each assumed the gender of the opposite sex: John became "Ann" and Sally became "Bill." However, despite this gender reversal, John's voice impersonating "Ann" was clearly the dominant voice, speaking most of the time and with authority. Sally's voice impersonating Bill was rarely heard, and when she spoke it was with much less authority.

Like the narration, the content of the film bore the imprint of a more conventional masculinity that Roger's group seemed to challenge in so many other ways. For example, John told Roger about the fun he had setting up the scene in which a house was burned down, and another one in which a friend videotaped him doing a tailspin with his car, to which Roger nodded his head in approval and said:

"That's real cool." Similarly, outside of school, Roger had no problem performing conventional heterosexual masculinity. One day he told me excitedly that he had played a game in a video arcade that simulated, in 3-D, the experience of killing somebody. Playing games in this arcade all weekend, he said, half-serious half-joking, made him realize what masculinity really meant.

Their enactment of feminist masculinity and emphasis on gender reversal was also context-specific. In his creative writing class, Roger listened patiently and sympathetically to a girl's account of her sorority's initiation rite, which supposedly involved girls being asked to pretend—with a banana—that they were being raped. On another occasion, Roger mentioned that he found the girls at a neighboring high school a lot nicer looking than the girls at RHS, and jokingly suggested trading a few pretty girls from there for a few smart ones from RHS.

Roger's group assumed a largely defensive position in regard to masculinity. Their symbol of identity, being gender misfits, collapsed to a large extent with their lines of contest: their challenge of dogmatic gender norms. They proved their masculinity in the collective male arena by using the female-male theme of protection. Their gender ambiguity was a subcultural "solution" to their marginalization for not conforming to gender role expectations and was contested by African American males.

Roger's group, notwithstanding their liberal self-identity, positioned itself in relation to performances of Black masculinity as a defining foil. Finding themselves challenged by male Black students in particular, they countered the challenge by trivializing it and performing masculinity in opposition to it. This, however, also indicated their own, rather powerless position in the school-yard hierarchy. Roger and his friends were irritated by what they perceived as a presentation of Black dominance. If they had not accorded African Americans so much power, however, they would not have felt so challenged by it and would not have needed to put it down among themselves. According to Roger, the actual confrontation that developed between African American and some Asian guys over women that looked "different" indicated that some African American students took it on themselves to police even those who were not part of their peer group, thus demonstrating their dominance over Roger's group.

MASCULINITIES THROUGH RACE: CHOOSING YOUR BATTLES

Examining the idioms and performances of masculinity in the lives of different peer groups brought to light the ways in which adolescents cultivate niches of masculinity in and through the racial landscape of Roosevelt High. From the vantage point of collective positions as expressed in their idioms and performances, this analysis has illustrated how groups take deliberate stands in relation to selected others, ignoring those they deem insignificant or irrelevant.

The central idioms and performances of masculinity in Ben's clique were styling, being a pimp, and being a player. Although women appeared to be the subject of these performances, it was their male audience who validated them. Ben and his friends deliberately distanced themselves from Newtown's gang culture; they were oblivious to Latinos, whom they tended to regard as more of a nuisance than a challenge; they paid little attention to Cambodians, who claimed to be their allies; and they had few contacts with Whites. Instead, their frame of reference was the larger White society, where the icons of pimp and player were part of a discursive resource, or "signifying practice," that capitalized on the stigma of Black hypermasculinity.[66]

Adopting the roles of pimp and player enabled Ben's clique to perform a dominance that was connected to a larger urban African American culture and symbolized blackness. The personas of pimp and player turned their racial subordination in the educational hierarchy and in society at large into a performance of power and domination that defied White values and stereotypes. This repertoire of racialized masculinity was not unique to Ben's group, but was embedded in existing counterculture elements—such as rap music and hip-hop culture more generally—that created a space for challenging White domination.

The Cambodian peer group articulated a code of masculinity that looked similar but was in fact very different. Mickey's clique readily deferred to African Americans and their culture through their identification with the "Dawgs" and with black skin color, and through their self-identification as the Blacks among the Asians. By assembling their own code of masculinity from elements of an African American masculinity and emphasizing a warrior image through frequent references to gangs, Mickey and his friends engaged in a form of "blackening" and thus tapped into Black racial hegemony at the school to form a bulwark against Latinos.

At the same time, the Cambodians' use of outdated cultural resources belied their ostensible connections to Black culture. As recent immigrants, their history as a community in the United States was short. They did not have comparable cultural resources that could be tapped into. Their own conflict with Latinos made African Americans natural allies. Whites were conspicuously absent in this scenario: few of them were classmates, they did not live in the same neighborhoods, and even though they shared social space, Whites literally did not understand the Black vernacular they used.

The Latino students who gathered at the tree constituted the most well-defined group both racially and spatially. Their strong social cohesion was emphasized by their common stigmatization through Proposition 187, a process that racialized them as Latinos. This group de-essentialized race within the school-yard culture, where they internalized a code of masculinity that emphasized a regime of diversification in order to stand out: they engaged in BMX racing, painted, played in bands, or adopted subcultural styles such as those of greasers and Rastas. Their participation in these individual extra-curricular activities might seem to have emphasized their exposed and isolated status in the school yard. However, as the lowest ranking racial group in the peer culture hierarchy and the focus of racial hostility, their strategy of forming individual cross-racial alliances allowed them to extend their limited social sphere.

Finally, the White peer group's code of masculinity emphasized a gender politics of being "pro-feminist" and "pro-gay"; they cultivated an anti-macho, "oddball," and "alternative" image. The "alternative" they promoted was an alternative to the rigid heterosexual gender conformity of their peers. By wearing sexually ambiguous styles and hairstyles, they created a trademark out of their stigma. Through a deliberate performance of sexual ambiguity and their rejection of dogmatic gender conformity, this peer group defined itself in relation to other Whites and to Black students. Neither Latinos nor Asians loomed large in their sense of racial positioning.

Although most of the students in this group were from the gifted program, where they enjoyed a dominant position within the educational hierarchy, within the school-yard hierarchy they played an insignificant role. They positioned themselves in relation to Black students and what they rightly perceived to be dominant Black masculinity. Latinos or Asians did not threaten their masculinity in any way. Instead of essentializing whiteness as a source of identity, they essentialized sexual difference as the critical element of their identity. Reversing the gender order of male dominance and female subordination, they created arenas of dominance for themselves by emphasizing that which stigmatized them—"being gay." They produced a space for performing dominance that ran counter to the prevailing gender order on campus. It showed "balls" to resist the traditional gender order, even—or better, particularly—if it meant taking on a sexually ambiguous performance. However, because of their relative security and elevated status in the gifted program, their need to establish dominance in the school-yard hierarchy was not as urgent as it was for those whose educational resources were marginalized.[67]

Adolescents' making of racialized masculinities thus was an ongoing process of producing differences and contesting locations. Through their peer groups, they manufactured codes of masculinity to establish arenas of dominance within the race matrix. Using these codes or lines of contest, they formed distinctions between insiders and outsiders, and ignored those whose existence didn't affect them.

This perplexing insularity with which adolescents at RHS constructed identities has implications for how we understand and possibly improve multiracial interactions and conflicts in institutions. For example, interventions designed to increase cultural diversity and awareness are often based on the idea that getting to know people from different cultures is an important step in overcoming interracial and interethnic tensions. While such well-intentioned programs can play a role in opening up new lines of communication on an individual level, my research suggests that institutional group dynamics also plays a large role. Why do different groups adopt certain positions, and what formal and informal power issues are at stake? The answer requires walking a fine line between recognizing and understanding collective positions, and seeing where racial inequalities exist or emerge.

Perry's concept of the multiracial self also raises interesting questions in this regard. Citing James Baldwin, she writes, "Each of us, helplessly and forever, contains the other—male in female, female in male, white in black and black in white." Comparing how Whites construct their identity in majority-White versus minority-White social spaces, she argues, "Each and every perspective was integral to constructing the 'whole,' the complete mosaic of individual group identities and cultures. In this respect, whites were 'populated' by blacks, Latinos, Asians, and others. Whites carried those groups' perceptions of them around with them all the time." [68]

Looking at identity-making processes at Roosevelt High School through a collective lens, I found that the selections adolescents made in response to their assessments of the power and salience of their opponents and allies challenged the notion of identity as a complete mosaic. Rather, it suggested a view of identity as a surface that reflects or incorporates only some, but not others. In the racially and ethnically diverse context of RHS, the process of coalescing some racial groups and ignoring others was pronounced, as if focusing on many others at the same time was too difficult. The students paid attention only to those who could have a significant impact on them, either as threats or as allies.

CONCLUSION

The strength of ethnography lies in describing cultural practices as they are expressed in interactions at the local level. In contrast to large-scale quantitative studies and surveys, ethnography helps us to understand cultural practices by showing what people do and explaining why they do it. But although it emphasizes the perspective of different people, ethnography is more than a collage of individual voices. By "being there" an ethnographer also captures collective processes and patterns of interactions as they shape people's everyday lives.[1]

When I first walked across the school yard at RHS and tried to see patterns in the racial distribution on campus, they were not as obvious as I had expected them to be. I saw them only after learning what race meant at Roosevelt High. I was unable to see the racial dynamics not because it was not there, but, contrary to our common sense notion, because there is little inherently visible about race. In other words, being able to read the racial landscape requires more than recognizing skin color. It requires a familiarity with racial meanings that operate in a particular setting. Race can be a powerful axis of social organization, and not "knowing" racial meanings can be hazardous. Race is not an illusion, and it is not disappearing in its significance in this multiracial setting. But recognizing race is not something that one automatically knows how to do. It's something one learns anew in each new context. This study of Roosevelt High has shown how schools are sites where such learning about race takes place.

Roosevelt High was certainly not the worst of urban schools, and it was probably better than the average. Most of the students were taught by experienced and well-meaning teachers. Students did not usually get into fights with each other, and although confrontations occurred, they were not the norm. Moreover, the school offered a series of multicultural venues designed to create an environment of inclusion and an appreciation of difference. But its alleged racial integration also contained elements of window dressing, and its reputation for academic excellence came at a price.

This story of Roosevelt High provides one glimpse into the layers of social relationships embedded in this multiracial institution. It illustrates not only how a school was directly involved in racializing students, but also the relationships and possibilities students experienced and created at school. In looking at the relationships that constitute the social space of the school, inside and outside the classroom, this study has unmasked the power structures operating at the school. Through its structure, organization, and social relationships, the school engendered and cemented racialized identities. But the school was also a site where individuals fashioned their own identities to meet collective and sometimes strategic goals.

One of the central questions I asked in this book was how racial identities are articulated in a multiracial and multiethnic social space, particularly in the seemingly color-blind discourse of the post–civil rights movement. When more than two different racial groups are involved, race relations are more complicated than they are between a dominant and a subordinate group. Furthermore, in a city such as Newtown, with rapidly growing populations of Latinos and Asians and declining numbers of Whites, restructuring and displacements were destabilizing and reorganizing existing power relations.

CREATING A BELL CURVE

Relationality is central to understanding race, but racialized groups also share experiences in specific and local relations. Therefore it is impossible not to see a larger pattern of race operating across different domains. The most encompassing experience shared by students at Roosevelt High was the generally privileged position of Whites. While the school personnel in general employed a color-blind discourse and embraced equality and multiculturalism, the majority of students at RHS made no such claims.

As my analysis of educational structures and their relationship to students' sense of their racial identities has shown, the deepest rifts were those between Whites and non-Whites, orchestrated through the magnet program for the "gifted." Yet there was also a split between Black students and others, accomplished through the label "at risk." The labels themselves seemed as racially neutral as the programs designed for them. But programs for the "gifted" and for those "at risk" engineered differential access to educational opportunities and in the process conflated an educational label with race. This produced deeply felt experiences of racial privilege on one hand and racial disadvantage on the other.[2]

Thus, presumably well-intentioned and racially progressive programs ended up reproducing racial inequality and racial stereotypes. Other scholars have found also that even schools that are successfully desegregated can fall short of social integration.[3] This study of RHS has helped to show how segregation at the classroom level is reproduced in a way that does not challenge the image of integration: this is accomplished through the way the school communicates with different publics, and through a discourse of "protection" that functions as a racial codeword for differentiating between the White/gifted and the non-White/non-gifted. At the opposite end of the spectrum, BusTech illustrated how reform programs for "at-risk" students struggle with and contribute to the perception of Black students as failures. The benefit of an ethnographic study here is also to show how the people involved experience and respond to these conditions and how students internalize these educational structures. Although none of the teachers or school personnel uttered derogatory racial comments, within-school segregation was a physical and psychological reality that remained invisible to the outside.

The implications of such new forms of school segregation are far-reaching. Psychological harm is done to students of color when they have learned that the label "gifted" excludes them de facto, if not by definition. Schools, explicitly or implicitly, are places where identities are made, where differences are forged, where distinction is rewarded. If non-White students find themselves consistently barred from the most desirable programs, they learn to feel racially inferior. Instead of fulfilling their potential to undo racial inequality, schools have instead helped to perpetuate it.

The reputation of RHS for academic success suggested that there was no reason for outsiders to question its practices. But the implications of a racialized tracking system are extensive not only educationally and psychologically, but also financially. Students who are able to enroll in accelerated classes are more likely to take Advanced Placement courses; some receive college credit for scoring well on AP tests, and they are more competitive for college admission and college scholarships. These factors constitute both educational and financial rewards. Maybe even more important than academic preparation, being on an accelerated track helps students to develop the self-confidence to pursue careers and other interests.

At the opposite end are the students who are told that they are receiving a challenging education, but then find themselves in a holding tank without adequate college preparation. Students enrolled in low-level high school courses often need to take remedial classes when they enter college. In addition to lacking academic knowledge, they may lack the study skills and self-confidence necessary to earn a college degree. If they do go to college, they often take longer to graduate, which means that the cost of their education rises. Some will interpret their educational shortcomings as personal failure. Moreover, while programs like BusTech might help some students stay in school, they may also lock some into an environment where a culture of opposition to school values stifles the chances of more motivated students.

Racial desegregation at the building level that transfers segregation to the classroom thus merely justifies the reproduction of White privilege as the norm to the educational, psychological, and financial detriment of non-White students who lack access to the most desirable programs.

Educational labels such as "gifted" and "at risk" carry racial connotations and the prospect of becoming self-fulfilling prophecies.[4] The identification process itself is highly racially exclusive, despite decades of attempts to address this inequality.

While I have argued that "giftedness" functions primarily as a racial label, it is unlikely that this label will be abandoned in education anytime soon.[5] Thus, at a minimum, the trend of gifted programs constituting a publicly funded elite education primarily for Whites must be reversed. Greater outreach efforts are needed to recruit more "gifted" students from minority groups. Further research is also needed to assess to what extent Whites' overrepresentation in gifted programs increases with the decrease of a White population in a district. In BusTech and GROW, the existing forms of documenting school success were misleading or insufficient, and in turn enabled a racially biased distribution of resources. School success must be recorded transparently and be broken down by program. Furthermore, when such different programs exist, admission processes should be fully disclosed.

THE USES OF RACIAL FORMATION THEORY FOR ETHNOGRAPHIES OF RACE

To understand race-making in this context I used the theoretical lens of racial formation, which stresses the fluidity and continuous remaking of race through multiple racial projects. While these projects are often connected to the state and to social movements, they also occur in contexts where the state is less prominent. The concept of racial formation has been engaged more fully at the level of macrostructural processes and discourses. This study shows how it can also advance our understanding of race at the level of everyday experience.

This analysis of structure and representation as the twin forces of racial projects has demonstrated how an apparently color-blind discourse enables racialized processes, and how complex discursive machinations and organizational procedures can conceal or gloss over the contradictions of resegregation in a desegregated school. The practices of racial formation at RHS also make clear how common sense notions about race and intelligence are reinforced through education. Students sometimes resisted or challenged these notions through their perceptual insights, reflections, and even contradictory interpretations.

With its focus on the link between macro-level and micro-level forces and between state and social movements, racial formation provides a model within which to situate these dynamic processes. This has helped to show how projects such as the gifted program, or busing, are linked to a history of racial segregation, and why color-blind labels became critical instruments of racialization in the post–civil rights era.

However, the conceptual toolbox of racial formation becomes more ambiguous when applied to the school yard, where the state is not as prominent as it is in the classroom and the various programs. When considering the riot as a racial project, questions of structure and of macro-level processes in the school-yard culture moved to the background. However, examining this project's representations and interpretations revealed an even greater degree of student agency in their production of common sense and showed their selective use of racial discourses in the broader arena. The macro-structural elements of the state bureaucracy are played out here mostly indirectly, by structuring the forms of interaction among students and how they are situated within the school.

In the domain of racialized masculinities, racial formation becomes even more difficult to apply. What can be identified as a racial project here? What is structure, what is representation? Common sense, the role of the state, and with it, the question of hegemony and social movements become even more ambiguous. Considering the small scale of collective notions of racialized masculinities, the "common" sense generated by such peer groups is becoming ever more specialized, as particular racialized masculinities become more fine-tuned and nuanced than the one invoked in the race riot. Questions about common sense and hegemony are less meaningful than questions about collective processes of identity construction and boundary maintenance. Tracing the making of racialized masculinities in peer groups brought into focus some limitations of racial formation theory in explaining everyday interactions and showed the need for a more nuanced conceptual inventory with which to tackle the many articulations and links between individual and larger social structures.

For example, if, as Omi and Winant argue, contemporary society is ruled consensually through the production of "common sense," but also challenged and contested by oppositional forms of common sense, we need to clarify how common "common sense" is and how we can better conceptualize the role of agency in the production of common sense. If the state, through schools and other institutions, works toward creating and instilling a particular common sense, how do we conceptualize individual and collective agency, and how do we account for the fact that some people develop a contradictory or oppositional common sense? And finally, how do we account for actual spaces such as school yards and symbolic spaces such as masculinity projects that function in relative isolation from the state?[6]

RACE AND MASCULINITY AS MUTUALLY REINFORCING ASPECTS OF SELF

To understand the processes involved in generating and perpetuating the racial order in the school-yard relations, I made use of an identity conceptualized as relational construction and collective identification. Identity in this framework is constructed through an outside and emphasizes boundary-making and maintenance processes.[7] Such an approach to race focuses on the mechanics of race-making and on the political processes and individual agencies involved in shaping racial structures and meanings in a multiracial space.

I was originally curious about how masculinities are expressed in and influenced by a racially diverse environment and how issues of power, domination, performance, and relationality are linked. RHS students are not the only ones who interpret racial conflict primarily as conflict between males. The literature on collective identity, whether as subculture, ethnicity, or race, has traditionally been by default about men[8] and thus naturalized these collective identities as masculinized. Since the mid-1990s, however, gender studies have come to view masculinities themselves as collective identifications, generated primarily through male-male relations, and often based on domination.[9] From such a perspective, masculinity's similarity to race is overwhelming: the inherent hierarchical structure of both, and the fact that both are seen as embodied identities, raises important issues about how both identities overlap, reinforce, or at times work counter to each other. But it is only recently that the intersections between masculinities and race have been studied. In this literature, race and masculinity are seen as two facets of interrelated identities that are relational, provisional, and strategic.

While this literature has explored cultural production, few studies have shown how such "racial maleness" is lived in a multiracial context. This examination of how peer groups develop and articulate their notions of masculinity through the racial matrix at Roosevelt High has shown that masculinities, like race, are based on boundary-making and boundary maintenance work. In many instances, masculinity boundaries coincide with or are treated as racial boundaries. For example, when Cambodians distance themselves from or identify themselves with other gangs, it is often on the basis of race. They identify themselves with African Americans racially, and at the same time adopt the masculinity of the dominant Black gang. If Cambodians set themselves apart from Latino gangs, they do it by positioning themselves in relation to Latinos generally. In that regard then, race has become masculinity writ large.

Maintaining boundaries is costly and therefore must be done selectively. Each of the four peer groups portrayed here positions itself primarily in relation to one or two other groups, but never invests in maintaining boundaries with more than two groups. As a result the relations between groups are often not symmetrical. Adolescents in powerful groups might pay very little attention to the frustration they cause members of less powerful groups, as was the case with African American and Latino peer groups. While African Americans were sometimes hostile toward Latinos in class and elsewhere, the African American peer group paid no attention to them in fashioning their own sense of masculinity. They were likewise also oblivious to being courted by Cambodians. Instead, in carving out spaces for masculinity, the African American peer group positioned itself primarily in relation to Whites.

Peer groups fashioned a code of masculinity in regard to those with the same or greater power. There is little point in developing a masculinity that challenges an already weak other. In other words, the stuff of which masculinities are made is organized around who or what is considered one's greatest adversary. Masculinities, then, can be read as the sediment of previous challenges and ongoing struggles. In the case of the Surrealists, their primary challenges were the homophobia of their goody-two-shoes White peers and the homophobia prominent in the dominant Black culture on campus. By deliberately reversing gender roles, they emphasized their differences and signaled their opposition to the prevailing gender roles.

Masculinities, then, like racial identities, are strategic because they are developed to achieve some advantage or dominance over an other. Racialized culture provides a toolbox for shaping repertoires of masculinity.

But there are also limits to what can be said. The racialized masculinities at Roosevelt High School cannot be seen as blueprints for racialized masculinities elsewhere. Rather than their content, it is the means by which masculinities are generated that can be applied to other contexts. Further, although women were an integral part of this study of masculinity, its focus on primarily male peer groups does not permit us to draw conclusions about men and masculinity in relation to women. More research is needed to look at the ways women are positioned racially and in the context of urban schools, how women engage in collective identity-making processes, and to what extent they are subjected to a patriarchal culture in the school.

RACE BEYOND BLACK AND WHITE

If this story showed how a school facilitates educational structures that entail privileges for some and handicaps for others, it also showed the racializing processes between Whites, Latinos, Blacks, and Cambodians. In a majority-minority context, it is likely that the majority group will be dominant, although its members are not necessarily aware of their dominance unless something challenges this norm. In a more than biracial setting without a clear majority, the power afforded by racial identity can become more visible, and possibilities for alliances and dominations multiply. In this context, maybe too little attention has been paid to racial identity as a tool for empowerment. If race lends itself to oppression, it necessarily also lends itself to domination.

In the school-yard relations, race is a tool for political mobilization: witness how Latinos organized a tight political identity around their common opposition to Proposition 187. Resorting to the social category of race can provide a tool for strategies of empowerment. It is not surprising that ethnic groups would assume a collective panethnic or racial identity, as occurred with the categories "Latinos" and "Asian Americans." [10] At RHS, Proposition 187 was critical for Mexican Americans and other Latinos to perceive themselves and be perceived by others as "Latinos" or "Mexicans." But it is surprising when one group adopts another racial identity, as the Cambodians did when they described themselves as the Blacks of the Asians, and when they identified with Blacks as "ethnic mens" against Mexicans and Whites. By organizing a collective identity around blackness, Cambodians distanced themselves from other Asians, and at the same time fashioned alliances with an established political force in the school yard.

This suggests that increasingly diverse settings do not necessarily produce multiple identities, but rather fuse racial and ethnic identities along established lines, as collective experiences of oppression, domination, or political expediency require. Such a forging of new racial identities can engender new political mobilization and new social movements that challenge or disrupt the prevailing racial order.

There is, however, also the possibility that groups that strategically identify themselves on the basis of race also discriminate against others on the basis of race. Some have argued that this is not racist, but a form of "strategic essentialism" because groups that are racially disempowered cannot in effect be racist and because racial essentializing alone is not sufficient to produce racist outcomes. [11]

The Cambodians' identification with blackness does not easily fit this model of power and oppression. Certainly blackness was stigmatized in the school curriculum and in society at large, but in the school yard, African Americans exerted a dominant influence over their peers. Thus when Cambodians identified themselves as Blacks, they were tapping into a local power structure where African Americans were at the top. Claiming blackness here was a form of essentializing. It was also strategic because it enabled a degree of empowerment and a means to unite against an adversary. African Americans' and Cambodians' frequent discrimination against Latinos was substantial, and although the former were powerful only in the school yard and in the neighborhood, and disempowered and discriminated against in most other aspects of their lives, they were not above the charge of racism in the context of the school.

Scholars have called for breaking out of the bipolar mold of conceptualizing race exclusively as a Black-White issue. This is what I set out to do by studying the multiracial Roosevelt High School in Newtown. However, one important finding of this study was that a bipolar racial order did exist. I conclude, then, that Black–White relations retain a formative function in fashioning a racially more complex future. Even though we need to be sensitive to the different ways in which collective identities are created and to the new possibilities of a multiracial order and cross-racial alliances, any emerging racial order will be affected by previous struggles. For example, the civil rights struggle was originally an African American struggle for equality, but it paved the way for the subsequent political struggles of other disenfranchised minorities.[12]

Similarly, Black culture as an expression of a struggle for racial equality might then also provide a pathway for other groups' struggles against oppression, so that in fact the Black-White dichotomy remains the master narrative for other racial struggles. The contagious nature of Black popular culture, from blues to hip-hop, and its popularity around the world, could be interpreted as such a development. Thus African American culture might provide not only political but also cultural pathways for racial struggles.

That racial identity is relationally constructed was one premise of this study. That it is also contextually constructed was another. Roosevelt High is a site where different contexts, each with its own racial hierarchy and racial order, are superimposed and interconnected. Although these domains operate separately, they do not operate entirely independently. Sometimes these different contexts reinforce each other, as in the case of Proposition 187, and sometimes they counteract each other, as in the case of the educational hierarchy versus the school-yard hierarchy. Contradictions about race become understandable when race-making is seen as a complex process that takes place in different domains, such as urban space, school programs, or the school yard. Such a perspective derives from the concept of racial formation, which understands race as the sum of multiple racial projects operating at every level of society.

As the discussion of Proposition 187 has shown, it became the focal point for White–Latino hostilities in the urban context, and in the context of the school it became a strategic resource for African Americans and Asians against Latinos. When the focus is on isolated individuals, stripped of the social contexts in which they live their lives, the relational aspects that are so fundamental for shaping identities are ignored. But people inhabit different kinds of social space simultaneously, each space with its own dynamic. The same person can be at the top of a racial hierarchy in one context and at the bottom of a racial hierarchy in another. The lesson here is that the focus should be on the relations that constitute the person, not on the person in isolation. This is often lost in studies of identity, which see the locus of racial identity in the person, not in the relations in which this person is constituted.

To the extent that Roosevelt High is representative of other urban areas and their institutions with similar racial, ethnic, and socioeconomic demographics, greater ethnic and racial diversity does not necessarily mean that race plays a smaller role or that there is automatically greater interracial contact. Rather, despite or because of the increasing ethnic and racial diversity of many urban areas, race is more likely to come to the fore as a social category, although how this category is delimited is in constant flux.

REFERENCES

Almaguer, Tomás. 1994. *Racial Fault Lines: The Historical Origins of White Supremacy in California*. Berkeley: University of California Press.

Anderson, Elijah. 1990. *Streetwise: Race, Class, and Change in an Urban Community*. Chicago: University of Chicago Press.

Baldwin, James. 1998. "Going to Meet the Man." In *Black on White*, edited by David Roediger, pp. 255–73. New York: Schocken Books.

Barnes, Julian E. 1997. "Segregation Now." In *U.S. News and World Report*, September 22, pp. 22–27.

Barth, Frederik. 1994. "Enduring and Emerging Issues in the Analysis of Ethnicity." In *Anthropology of Ethnicity: Beyond Ethnic Groups and Boundaries*, edited by Hans Vermeulen and Cora Govers, pp. 11–32. Amsterdam: Het Spinhuis.

———. ed. 1969. *Ethnic Groups and Boundaries*. Boston: Little, Brown.

Bederman, Gail. 1995. *Manliness and Civilization*. Chicago: University of Chicago Press.

Bell, Derrick. 1992. *Faces at the Bottom of the Well: The Permanence of Racism*. New York: Basic Books.

Berbrier, Mitch. 2000. "The Victim Ideology of White Supremacists and White Separatists in the United States." *Sociological Focus* 33 (2): 175–91.

———. 1998. "White Supremacists and the (Pan) Ethnic Imperative: On 'European-Americans' and 'White Student Unions.'" *Sociological Inquiry* 68 (4): 498–516.

Bhabha, Homi K. 1992. "Postcolonial Authority and Postmodern Guilt." In *Cultural Studies*, edited by Lawrence Grossberg, Cary Nelson, and Paul A. Treichler, pp. 56–68. New York: Routledge.

Blau, Judith. 2003. *Race in the Schools*. Boulder, Colo.: Lynne Rienner.

Bonilla-Silva, Eduardo. 2003. *Racism without Racists: Color-Blind Racism and the Persistence of Inequality in the United States*. Lanham, Md.: Rowman and Littlefield.

Bourdieu, Pierre. 2001. *Masculine Domination*. Stanford, Calif.: Stanford University Press.

———. 1996. *The State Nobility*. Stanford, Calif.: Stanford University Press.

———. 1986. "The Forms of Capital." In *The Handbook of Theory and Research for the Sociology of Education*, edited by John G. Richardson, pp. 241–60. Westport, Conn.: Greenwood Press.

Bourdieu, Pierre, and Jean Claude Passeron. 1977. *Reproduction in Education, Society and Culture*. Beverly Hills, Calif.: Sage.

Bourgois, Philippe. 1996. *In Search of Respect: Selling Crack in El Barrio*. Cambridge, UK: Cambridge University Press.

Bradburd, Dan. 1998. *Being There: The Necessity of Fieldwork*. Smithsonian Series in Ethnographic Inquiry. Washington, D.C.: Smithsonian Institution Press.

Brodkin, Karen. 1999. *How Jews Became White Folks and What That Says about Race in America*. New Brunswick, N.J.: Rutgers University Press.

Brown, Claude. 1965. *Manchild in the Promised Land*. New York: Macmillan.

Brown, Michael K. 2003. *Whitewashing Race: The Myth of a Color-Blind Society*. Berkeley: University of California Press.

Burawoy, Michael, ed. 1991. *Ethnography Unbound: Power and Resistance in the Modern Metropolis*. Berkeley: University of California Press.

Bush, Melanie. 2004. *Breaking the Code of Good Intentions: Everyday Forms of Whiteness*. Lanham, Md.: Rowman and Littlefield.

Butler, Judith. 1993. *Bodies That Matter: On the Discursive Limits of "Sex."* New York: Routledge.

California Department of Education. 2001. "California Safe Schools Assessment: 1999–2000 Results." http://www.cde.ca.gov/spbranch/safety/.

———. 1995a. *Gifted and Talented Education: Ethnic Data*. Sacramento.

———. 1995b. *High School Performance Report 1994–1995. Research, Evaluation, and Technology*. Sacramento.

California Partnership Academies. 2000. *The Law*. Section 54690b. http://www.cde.ca.gov/partacad/law.html.

Carter, Prudence. 2005 *Keepin' It Real: School Success beyond Black and White*. Oxford: Oxford University Press.

Cayton, Horace. 1965. *Long Old Road*. New York: Trident.

Chan, Jachinson. 2001. *Chinese American Masculinities: From Fu Manchu to Bruce Lee*. New York: Routledge.

Chandler, David P. 1983. *A History of Cambodia*. Boulder, Colo.: Westview Press.

Chesney-Lind, Meda, and John Hagedorn, eds. 1999. *Female Gangs in America: Essays on Girls, Gangs, and Gender*. Chicago: Lake View Press.

Conchas, Gilberto Q. 2001 "Structuring Failure and Success: Understanding the Variability in Latino School Engagement." *Harvard Educational Review* 71 (3): 475–504.

Connell, Robert W. 2002. *Gender*. Oxford, UK: Polity Press.

———. 2000. *The Men and the Boys*. Berkeley: University of California Press.

———. 1995. *Masculinities*. Berkeley: University of California Press.

Cross, Tracy L. 2003. "Examining Priorities in Education—Leaving No Gifted

Child Behind: Breaking Our Educational System of Privilege." *Roeper Review* 25 (3): 101–02.

Cuban, Larry. 1989. "The 'At Risk' Label and the Problem of School Reform." *Phi Delta Kappan*: 780–801.

Daniel, Reginald. 2002. *More Than Black? Multiracial Identity and the New Racial Order*. Philadelphia: Temple University Press.

Davidson, Ann Locke. 1996. *Making and Molding Identity in Schools: Student Narratives on Race, Gender and Academic Engagement*. Albany: State University of New York Press.

Davis, Mike. 2000. *Magical Urbanism*. 2000. New York: Verso.

———. 1990. *City of Quartz*. New York: Verso.

Dayton, Charles, Marilyn Raby, David Stern, and Alan Weisberg. 1992. "The California Partnership Academies: Remembering the 'Forgotten Half.'" *Phi Delta Kappan* 73 (7): 539–45.

Denzin, Norman K. 2003. "The Call to Performance." *Symbolic Interaction* 26 (1): 87–207.

———. 2001. "Symbolic Interactionism, Poststructuralism, and the Racial Subject." *Symbolic Interaction* 24 (2): 243–49.

———. 1992. *Symbolic Interactionism and Cultural Studies*. Oxford: Blackwell.

Devine, John. 1996. *Maximum Security: The Culture of Violence in Inner-City Schools*. Chicago: University of Chicago Press.

Doane, Ashley, and Eduardo Bonilla-Silva, eds. 2003. *White Out: The Continuing Significance of Racism*. New York: Routledge.

Dolby, Nadine. 2000. "Changing Selves: Multicultural Education and the Challenge of New Identities." *Teachers College Record* 102 (5): 898–912.

Dominguez, Virginia. 1994. "A Taste of 'the Other': Intellectual Complicity in Racializing Practices." *Current Anthropology* 35 (4): 333–48.

Donovan, M. Suzanne, and Christopher T. Cross, eds. 2002. *Minority Students in Special and Gifted Education*. Washington, D.C.: National Academy Press.

Downey, Douglas B., and James W. Ainsworth-Darnell. 2002. "The Search for Oppositional Culture among Black Students." *American Sociological Review* 67 (1): 156–64.

D'Souza, Dinesh. 1995. *The End of Racism*. New York: Free Press.

DuBois, W. E. B. 1989. *The Souls of Black Folk*. New York: Bantam Books.

Dunn, Rita, and Shirley Griggs. 1998. *Multiculturalism and Learning Style*. Westport, Conn.: Praeger.

Duras, Marguerite. 1985. *Lover*. New York: Pantheon Books.

Durkheim, Emile. 1956. *Education and Sociology*. Glencoe, Ill.: Free Press.

Eaton, Susan. 1996. "Slipping toward Segregation." In *Dismantling Desegrega-*

tion—*The Quiet Reversal of Brown v. Board of Education*, edited by Gary Orfield, Susan Eaton, and the Harvard Project on School Desegregation, pp. 207–40. New York: The New Press.

Eder, Donna, Catherine Colleen Evans, and Stephen Parker. 1995. *School Talk*. New Brunswick, N.J.: Rutgers University Press.

Eng, David. 2001. *Racial Castration*. Durham, N.C.: Duke University Press.

Erikson, Erik H. 1968. *Identity, Youth, and Crisis*. New York: W. W. Norton.

Ewing, Norma J., and Fung Lan Yong. 1992. "A Comparative Study of the Learning-Style Preferences among Gifted African-American, Mexican-American and American Born Chinese Middle-Grade Students." *Roeper Review* 14 (3): 120–23.

Fab 5 Freddy. 1992. *Fresh Fly Flavor: Words and Phrases of the Hip-Hop Generation*. Stamford, Conn.: Longmeadow Press.

Farkas, George, Christy Lleras, and Steve Maczuga. 2002. "Does Oppositional Culture Exist in Minority and Poverty Peer Groups?" *American Sociological Review* 67 (1): 148–55.

Feagin, Joe R. 2000. *Racist America: Roots, Current Realities, and Future Reparations*. New York: Routledge.

Feagin, Joe R., Vera Hernan, and Pinar Batur. 2001. *White Racism*. New York: Routledge.

Ferguson, Ann Arnett. 2001. *Bad Boys: Public Schools in the Making of Black Masculinity*. Ann Arbor: University of Michigan.

Ferguson, Ronald F. 2001. "Test Score Trends along Racial Lines, 1971–1996: Popular Culture and Community Academic Standards." In *America Becoming: Racial Trends and Their Consequences*, edited by Neil Smelser, William Julius Wilson, and Faith Mitchell, pp. 348–90. Washington, D.C.: National Academy Press.

Fine, Michelle. 1997. "Witnessing Whiteness." In *Off White: Readings on Race, Power, and Society*, edited by Michelle Fine et al., pp. 57–65. New York: Routledge.

———. 1991. *Framing Dropouts*. Albany: State University of New York Press.

Fine, Michelle, and Lois Weis. 2003. *Silenced Voices and Extraordinary Conversations: Re-Imagining Schools*. New York: Teachers College Press.

Fine, Michelle, L. Powell, and Lois Weis. 1997. "Communities of Difference: A Critical Look at Desegregated Spaces Created for and by Youth." *Harvard Educational Review* 67: 247–84.

Fine, Michelle, Lois Weis, Linda C. Powell, and L. Mun Wong, eds. 1997. *Off White: Readings on Race, Power, and Society*. New York: Routledge.

Folb, Edith A. 1980. *Runnin' Down Some Lines: The Language and Culture of Black Teenagers*. Cambridge, Mass.: Harvard University Press.

Foley, Douglas. 1991. "Reconsidering Anthropological Explanations of Ethnic School Failure." *Anthropology and Education Quarterly* 22: 60–86.

———. 1990. *Learning Capitalist Culture: Deep in the Heart of Tejas.* Philadelphia: University of Pennsylvania Press.

Ford, Donna Y. 1995. "Desegregating Gifted Education." *Journal of Negro Education* 64 (1): 51–63.

Ford, Donna Y., and Tarek C. Grantham. 1998. "A Case Study of the Social Needs of Danisha: An Underachieving Gifted African-American Female." *Roeper Review* 21 (2): 96–101.

Ford, Donna Y., J. John Harris III, Cynthia A. Tyson, and Michelle Frazier Trotman. 2002. "Beyond Deficit Thinking: Providing Access for Gifted African-American Students." *Roeper Review* 24 (2): 52–28.

Fordham, Signithia. 1996. *Blacked Out.* Chicago: University of Chicago Press.

Fordham, Signithia, and John U. Ogbu. 1988. "Black Students' School Success and Coping with the Burden of 'Acting White.'" *Urban Review* 18 (3): 176–206.

Foucault, Michel. 1977. *Discipline and Punish.* New York: Pantheon Books.

Frankenberg, Ruth. 1993. *White Women, Race Matters: The Social Construction of Whiteness.* Minneapolis: University of Minnesota Press.

Friedman, Jonathan. 1994. *Cultural Identity and Global Process.* London: Sage.

Gallagher, Charles. 2004. "Racial Redistricting: Expanding the Boundaries of Whiteness." In Heather M. Dalmage, ed., *The Politics of Multiracialism: Challenging Racial Thinking*, pp. 59–76. Albany: State University Press of New York Press.

———. 2003. "Miscounting Race: Explaining Whites' Misperceptions of Racial Group Size." *Sociological Perspectives* 46 (3): 381–96.

———. 1995. "White Reconstruction in the University." *Socialist Review* 94 (1-2): 165–87.

Gallup Poll Social Audit. 2001. *Black-White Relations in the United States, 2001 Update.* Washington, D.C.: Gallup Organization.

Garbarino, James. 1999. *Lost Boys.* New York: Free Press.

Garoutte, Eva Marie. 2001. "The Racial Formation of American Indians." *American Indian Quarterly* 25 (2): 224–39.

Gates, Henry Louis. 1987. *Figures in Black.* New York: Oxford University Press.

Gibson, Margaret. 1988. *Accommodation without Assimilation.* Ithaca, N.Y.: Cornell University Press.

"Giftedness and the Gifted: What's It All About?" 1990. *Eric Digest* 476. Reston, Va.: Council for Exceptional Children.

Gilmore, David. 1991. *Manhood in the Making.* New Haven, Conn.: Yale University Press.

Goffman, Erving. 1961. *Asylums*. Garden City, N.Y.: Anchor Books.

Gracia, Jorge J. E., and Pablo De Greiff, eds. 2000. *Hispanics/Latinos in the United States: Ethnicity, Race, and Rights*. New York: Routledge.

Gregory, Steven. 1998. *Black Corona*. Princeton, N.J.: Princeton University Press.

Gutmann, Matthew. 1996. *The Meanings of Macho*. Berkeley: University of California.

Hall, Stuart. 1996. "Who Needs 'Identity?'" In *Questions of Cultural Identity*, edited by Stuart Hall and Paul Du Gay, pp. 1–17. London: Sage.

———. 1992. "What Is This 'Black' in Black Popular Culture?" In *Black Popular Culture*, edited by Gina Dent, pp. 21–33. Seattle: Bay Press.

Hall, Stuart, and Paul Du Gay, eds. 1996. *Questions of Cultural Identity*. Thousand Oaks, Calif.: Sage.

Hall, Stuart, and Tony Jefferson. 1976. *Resistance through Rituals*. Cambridge, UK: Harper Collins Academic.

Harris, Cheryl I. 1993. "Whiteness as Property." *Harvard Law Review* 106 (8): 1709–91.

Harris, John H., and Donna Y. Ford. 1999. "Hope Deferred Again; Minority Students Underrepresented in Gifted Programs." *Education and Urban Society* 31 (2): 225–37.

Hartigan, John. 1999. *Racial Situations: Class Predicaments of Whiteness in Detroit*. Princeton, N.J.: Princeton University Press.

Heard, Nathan C. 1968. *Howard Street*. New York: Dial Press.

Hebdige, Dick. 1969. *The Meaning of Style*. London: New York.

Henze, Rosemary, Anne Katz, Edmundo Norte, and Susan Sather. 2002. *Leading for Diversity: How School Leaders Promote Interethnic Relations*. Thousand Oaks, Calif.: Corwin Press.

Herrnstein, Richard J., and Charles Murray. 1994. *The Bell Curve: Intelligence and Class Structure in American Life*. New York: Free Press.

Herzfeld, Michael. 1985. *Poetics of Manhood*. Princeton, N.J.: Princeton University Press.

Hewitt, Roger. 1986. *White Talk, Black Talk*. Cambridge, UK: Cambridge University Press.

Holstein, James A., and Gale Miller. 1990. "Rethinking Victimization: An Interactional Approach to Victimology." *Symbolic Interaction* 13: 103–22.

Hwang, David H. 1989. *M Butterfly*. New York: Plume Books.

Iceberg Slim. 1987. *Pimp*. Los Angeles: Holloway House.

Ignatiev, Noel. 1995. *How the Irish Became White*. New York: Routledge.

Jencks, Christopher, and Meredith Phillips. 1998. *The Black-White Test Score Gap*. Washington, D.C.: Brookings Institution Press.

Kaiser Family Foundation. 1995. *The Four Americas: Government and Social Policy through the Eyes of America's Multi-Racial and Multi-Ethnic Society.* Menlo Park, Calif.: Kaiser Family Foundation.

kelley, robin d. g. 1997. *Yo Mama's Disfunktional!: Fighting the Culture Wars in Urban America.* Boston: Beacon Press.

Kemple, James J., and Jason C. Snipes. 2000. "Career Academies: Impacts on Students' Engagement and Performance in High School," Manpower Research Corporation, New York. http://www.mdrc.org/publications/41/execsum.htm [accessed 6/09/06].

Kenny, Lorraine Delia. 2000. *Daughters of Suburbia: Growing up White, Middle Class, and Female.* New Brunswick, N.J.: Rutgers University Press.

Kim, Elaine. 1982. *Asian-American Literature.* Philadelphia: Temple University Press.

Kimmel, Michael. 2003. "I Am Not Insane; I Am Angry." In *Adolescents at School*, edited by Michael Sadowski, pp. 69–78. Cambridge, Mass.: Harvard Education Press.

———. 1996. *Manhood in America.* New York: Free Press.

———. 1987. *Changing Men.* Newbury Park, Calif.: Sage.

Kimmel, Michael S., and Abby L. Ferber. 2003. *Privilege: A Reader.* Boulder, Colo.: Westview Press.

Kochman, Thomas. 1972. *Rappin' and Stylin' Out: Communication in Urban Black America.* Urbana: University of Illinois Press.

———. 1969. "Rapping in the 'Black Ghetto.'" *Trans Actions* (February): 26–34.

Kozol, Jonathan. 1991. *Savage Inequalities: Children in America's Schools.* New York: Crown.

Labov, William, Paul Cohen, Clarence Robins, and John Lewis. 1981. "Toasts." In *Mother Wit from the Laughing Barrel*, edited by Alan Dundes, pp. 329–26. New York: Garland.

Laclau, Ernesto. 1990. *New Reflections on the Revolutions of Our Time.* London: Verso.

Lareau, Annette, and Erin McNamara Horvat. 1999. "Moments of Social Inclusion and Exclusion: Race, Class, and Cultural Capital in Family-School Relationships." *Sociology of Education* 72 (1): 37–53.

Leblanc, Lauraine. 1999. *Pretty in Punk.* New Brunswick, N.J.: Rutgers University Press.

Ledgerwood, Judy, May M. Ebihara, and Carol A. Mortland, eds. 1994. *Cambodian Culture since 1975: Homeland and Exile.* Ithaca, N.Y.: Cornell University Press.

Lévi-Strauss, Claude. 1963. *Totemism.* Boston: Beacon Press.

Lewis, Amanda. 2003. *Race in the School Yard*. New Brunswick, N.J.: Rutgers University Press.

Liebow, Elliot. 1967. *Tally's Corner: A Study of Negro Streetcorner Men*. Boston: Little, Brown.

Lipman, Pauline. 1998. *Race, Class, and Power in School Restructuring*. Albany: State University of New York Press.

Lipsitz, George. 1998. *The Possessive Investment in Whiteness: How White People Profit from Identity Politics*. Philadelphia: Temple University Press.

Logan, John R. 2004. *Resegregation in American Public Schools? Not in the 1990s*. http://mumford.albany.edu /schoolsegregation /reports /noresegregation /no resegregation_report.pdf.

———. 2001. *Ethnic Diversity Grows, Neighborhood Integration Is at a Standstill*. Report by the Lewis Mumford Center for Comparative Urban and Regional Research, April 3, 2001. Metropolitan Racial and Ethnic Change – Census 2000. http://mumford1.dyndns.org/cen2000/ WholePop/ WPreport /page1 .html [accesssed 7/18/01].

Logan, John R., Deirdre Oakley, Jacob Stowell, and Brian Stults. 2004. *The Continuing Legacy of the Brown Decision: Court Action and School Segregation, 1960–2000*. http://mumford.cas.albany.edu /schoolsegregation /reports/ brown01.htm [accessed 8/31/04].

———. 2001. *Living Separately: Segregation Rises for Children*. Report by the Lewis Mumford Center for Comparative Urban and Regional Research, May 6, 2001. Metropolitan Racial and Ethnic Change – Census 2000. http:// mumford1.dyndns.org/cen2000/Under18Pop/U18Preport /U18Ppage1.html. [accessed 7/18/01].

Lopez, David, and Yen Espiritu. 1990. "Panethnicity in the United States: A Theoretical Framework." *Ethnic and Racial Studies* 13 (2): 198–211.

Losen, Daniel J., and Gary Orfield. 2002. *Racial Inequity in Special Education*. Cambridge, Mass.: Harvard Education Press.

Louie, Vivian S. 2004. *Compelled to Excel: Immigration, Education, and Opportunity among Chinese Americans*. Stanford, Calif.: Stanford University Press.

Lucas, Samuel R., and Mark Berends. 2002. "Sociodemographic Diversity, Correlated Achievement, and de Facto Tracking." *Sociology of Education* 75 (4): 328–48.

Mac An Ghaill, Máirtín. 1996. *Understanding Masculinities*. Philadelphia: Open University Press.

———. 1994. *The Making of Men: Masculinities, Sexualities, and Schooling*. Philadelphia: Open University Press.

MacLeod, Jay. 1995. *Ain't No Makin' It: Aspirations and Attainment in a Low-Income Neighborhood*. Boulder, Colo.: Westview Press.

Mahoney, Martha R. 1995. "Segregation, Whiteness, and Transformation." *University of Pennsylvania Law Review* 143 (5): 1659–84.

Major, Clarence, ed. 1994. *Juba to Jive*. New York: Penguin.

Majors, Richard, and Janet Mancini Billson. 1992. *Cool Pose: The Dilemmas of Black Manhood in America*. New York: Touchstone Books, Simon and Schuster.

Malcolm X and Alex Haley. 1999. *The Autobiography of Malcolm X*. New York: Ballantine Books.

Mancini, Janet. 1981. *Strategic Styles: Coping in the Inner City*. Hanover, N.H.: University Press of New England.

Margolin, Leslie. 1994. *Goodness Personified*. New York: Aldine de Gruyter.

Massey, Douglas S. 2000. "Residential Segregation and Neighborhood Conditions in U.S. Metropolitan Areas." In *America Becoming: Racial Trends and Their Consequences*, edited by Neil Smelser, William Julius Wilson, and Faith Mitchell, pp. 391–434. Washington, D.C.: National Academy Press.

Massey, Douglas, and Nancy Denton. 1993. *American Apartheid: Segregation and the Making of the Underclass*. Cambridge, Mass.: Harvard University Press.

McAdam, Doug. 1988. *Freedom Summer*. New York: Oxford University Press.

McIntosh, Peggy. 1990. "White Privilege: Unpacking the Invisible Knapsack." *Independent School* 49 (2): 31–36.

McNamara Horvat, Erin, and Kristine S. Lewis. 2003. "Reassessing the 'Burden of "Acting White"': The Importance of Peer Groups in Managing Academic Success." *Sociology of Education* 76 (4): 256–81.

Messerschmidt, James W. 2000. *Nine Lives*. Boulder, Colo.: Westview Press.

———. 1993. *Masculinities and Crime*. Lanham, Md.: Rowman and Littlefield.

Messner, Michael A., and Donald F. Sabo. 1994. *Sex, Violence and Power in Sports*. Freedom, Calif.: Crossing Press.

Metz, Mary Haywood. 2003. *Different by Design*. New York: Teachers College Press.

Mirande, Alfredo. 1997. *Hombres Y Machos: Masculinity and Latino Culture*. Boulder, Colo.: Westview Press.

Morgan, Stephen. 2003. *On the Edge of Commitment: Educational Attainment and Race in the United States*. Stanford, Calif.: Stanford University Press.

Mosse, George. 1985. *Nationalism and Sexuality*. New York: Howard Fertig.

National Center for Education Statistics. 2001. *Digest of Educational Statistics*. Washington, D.C. http://nces.ed.gov/pubs2001/digest/ch4.html [accessed 5/17/01].

Nightingale, Carl Husemoller. 1992. *On the Edge: A History of Poor Black Children and Their American Dream*. New York: Basic Books.

Oakes, Jeannie. 1985. *Keeping Track: How Schools Structure Inequality*. New Haven, Conn.: Yale University Press.

Oakes, Jeannie, Amy Stuart Wells, and Makeba Jones. 1997. "Detracking: The Social Construction of Ability, Cultural Politics, and Resistance to Reform." *Teachers College Record* 98 (3): 482–510.

Oakes, Jeannie, Karen Hunger Quartz, Steve Ryan, and Martin Lipton. 2000. *Becoming Good American Schools: The Struggle for Civic Virtue in Education Reform*. San Francisco: Jossey-Bass Publishers.

Ogbu, John. 1994 "Racial Stratification and Education in the United States: Why Inequality Persists." *Teachers College Record* 96 (2): 264–98.

———. 1991. "Immigrant and Involuntary Minorities in Comparative Perspective." In *Minority Status and Schooling: A Comparative Study of Immigrant and Involuntary Minorities*, edited by Margaret Gibson and John Ogbu, pp. 3–33. New York: Garland.

———. 1990. "Minority Education in Comparative Perspective." *Journal of Negro Education Quarterly* 59 (1): 45–57.

———. 1987. "Variability in Minority School Performance: A Problem in Search of an Explanation." *Anthropology and Education Quarterly* 18: 312–34.

———. 1985. "Cultural-Ecological Influences on Minority School Learning." *Language Arts* 68 (8): 860–69.

———. 1978. *Minority Education and Caste*. New York: Academic Press.

———. 1974. *The Next Generation : An Ethnography of Education in an Urban Neighborhood*. New York: Academic Press.

Ogbu, John U., and Herbert D. Simons. 1998. "Voluntary and Involuntary Minorities: A Cultural-Ecological Theory of School Performance with Some Implications for Education." *Anthropology and Education Quarterly* 29 (2): 155–88.

Oliver, Melvin L., and Thomas M. Shapiro. 1995. *Black Wealth / White Wealth*. New York: Routledge.

Omi, Michael, and Howard Winant. 1994. *Racial Formation in the United States*. New York: Routledge.

Ong, Aihwa. 2003. *Buddha Is Hiding: Refugees, Citizenship, the New America*. Berkeley: University of California Press.

———. 1996. "Cultural Citizenship as Subject-Making: Immigrants Negotiate Racial and Cultural Boundaries in the United States." *Current Anthropology* 37 (5): 737–62.

Orfield, Gary, and Chungmei Lee. 2004. *Brown at 50: King's Dream or Plessy's Nightmare?* Harvard Civil Rights Project. http://www.civilrightsproject.harvard.edu/research/reseg04/resegregation04.php [accessed 8/16/04].

Orfield, Gary, and Susan E. Eaton. 1996. *Dismantling Desegregation: The Quiet Reversal of Brown v. Board of Education*. New York: New Press.

Orfield, Gary, and Nora Gordon. 2001. *Schools More Separate: Consequences of a Decade of Resegregation*. Harvard Civil Rights Project. http://www.law.harvard.edu/civilrights/publications/pressseg.html [accessed 7/29/01].

Patterson, Orlando. 1997. *The Ordeal of Integration: Progress and Resentments in America's Racial Crisis*. Washington, D.C.: National Academy Press.

Perry, Pamela. 2002. *Shades of White*. Durham, N.C.: Duke University Press.

———. 2001. "'White Means Never Having to Say You're Ethnic': White Youth and the Construction of 'Cultureless' Identities." *Journal of Contemporary Ethnography* 30 (1): 56–91.

Perry, Theresa, Claude Steele, and Asa G. Hilliard III. 2003. *Young, Gifted, and Black*. Boston: Beacon Press.

Persell, Caroline Hodges. 1977. *Education and Inequality*. New York: Free Press.

Peterson, J. S., and L. Margolin. 1997. "Naming Gifted Children: An Example of Unintended 'Reproduction.'" *Journal for the Education of the Gifted* 21 (1):82–100.

Phillips, Susan. 1999. *Wallbanging: Graffiti and Gangs in L.A.* Chicago: University of Chicago Press.

Pizarro, Marcos. 2005. *Chicanas and Chicanos in School: Racial Profiling, Identity Battles, and Empowerment*. Austin: University of Texas Press.

Pollock, Mica. 2004. "Race Wrestling: Struggling Strategically with Race in Educational Practice and Research." *American Journal of Education* 111 (1): 25–67.

Popkewitz, T. S. 1995. "Policy, Knowledge, and Power: Some Issues for the Study of Educational Reform." In *Transforming Schools*, edited by Peter W. Cookson and Barbara L. Schneider, pp. 413–56. New York: Garland.

Pratt, Mary Louise. 1987. "Linguistic Utopias." In *The Linguistics of Writing*, edited by Nigel Falb, pp. 48–66. New York: Methuen.

Robinson, Ann. 1998. "Giftedness: An Exceptionality Examined." *Annual Review of Psychology* 49: 117–41.

Rodriguez, Clara. 2000. *Changing Race: Latinos, the Census, and the History of Ethnicity in the United States*. New York: New York University Press.

Roediger, David R. 2002. *Colored White: Transcending the Racial Past*. Berkeley: University of California Press.

———. 1991. *Wages of Whiteness*. London: Verso.

Rossell, Christine. 1990. *The Carrot or the Stick for School Desegregation Policy*. Philadelphia: Temple University Press.

Rothenberg, Paula. 2002. *White Privilege: Essential Readings on the Other Side of Racism*. New York: Worth.

Sanchez, George J. 1993. *Becoming Mexican American*. New York: Oxford University Press.

Sandefur, Gary D., Molly Martin, Jennifer Eggerling-Boeck, Susan E. Mannon, and Ann M. Meier. 2001. "An Overview of Racial and Ethnic Demographic Trends." In *America Becoming: Racial Trends and Their Consequences*, edited by Neil J. Smelser, William Julius Wilson, and Faith Mitchell, pp. 40–102. Washington, D.C.: National Academy Press.

Sanjek, Roger. 2000. *The Future of Us All*. Ithaca, N.Y.: Cornell University Press.

Sapon-Shevin, Mara. 1994. *Playing Favorites: Gifted Education and the Disruption of Community*. Albany: State University of New York.

———. 1993. "Gifted Education and the Protection of Privilege: Breaking the Silence, Opening the Discourse." In *Beyond Silenced Voices*, edited by Michelle Fine and Lois Weis, pp. 25–44. Albany: State University of New York Press.

Scherzer, Teresa, and Howard L. Pinderhughes. 2002. "Violence and Gender: Reports from an Urban High School." *Violence and Victims* 17 (1): 57–72.

Schofield, Janet Ward. 1989. *Black and White in School*. New York: Teachers College Press.

Shipler, D. 1998. *A Country of Strangers: Black and Whites in America*. New York: Vintage Books.

Sinha, Mrinalini. 1995. *Colonial Masculinity: The 'Manly Englishman' and the 'Effeminate Bengali' in the Late Nineteenth Century*. Manchester, UK: Manchester University Press.

Slaughter-Defoe, Diana T. 1990. "Toward Cultural-Ecological Perspectives on Schooling and Achievement in African- and Asian-American Children." *Child Development* 61: 363–83.

Solomon, R. Patrick. 1992. *Black Resistance in High School: Forging a Separatist Culture*. New York: State University of New York Press.

Spackman, Barbara. 1996. *Fascist Virilities: Rhetoric, Ideology, and Social Fantasy in Italy*. Minneapolis: University of Minnesota Press.

Spiegler, Marc. 1996. "Marketing Street Culture: Bringing Hip-Hop Style to the Mainstream." *American Demographics* 18 (11): 28–35.

Spindler, George, and Louise Spindler. 1983. "Roger Harker and Schoenhausen: From the Familiar to the Strange and Back Again." In George Spindler, ed., *Doing the Ethnography of Schooling*, pp. 20–47. Prospect Heights, Ill.: Waveland Press.

Staiger, Annegret. 2005a. "Recreating Blackness-as-Failure through Educational Reform? A Case Study of a California Partnership Academy." *Equity & Excellence in Education* 38 (1): 35–48.

———. 2005b. "'Hoes can be hoed out, players can be played out, but pimp is for life'—The Pimp as Strategy of Identity Formation." *Symbolic Interaction* 28 (3): 407–28.

———. 2005c. "School Walls as Battle Grounds: Technologies of Power, Space, and Identity." *Paedagogica Historica* 41 (4/5): 555–69.

———. 2004. "Whiteness as Giftedness: Racial Formation at an Urban High School." *Social Problems* 51 (2): 161–81.

Steele, Claude. 1997. "A Threat in the Air." *American Psychologist* 52 (6): 613–29.

Stephens, Kristen R., and Frances Karnes. 2000. "State Definitions for the Gifted and Talented Revisited." *Exceptional Children* 66 (2): 219–38.

Stoler, Ann L. 1989. "Making Empire Respectable: The Politics of Race and Sexual Morality in 20th Century Colonial Cultures." *American Ethnologist* 16 (4): 635–60.

Swadener, Beth Blue. 2005. "Children and Families 'at Promise': Deconstructing the Discourse of Risk." In *Children and Families "at Promise": Deconstructing the Discourse of Risk,* Beth Blue Swadener and Sally Lubeck, eds., pp. 17–49. Albany: State University Press of New York.

Swadener, Beth Blue, and Sally Lubeck, eds. 1995. *Children and Families "at Promise": Deconstructing the Discourse of Risk.* Albany: State University of New York Press.

Tuan, Mia. 1998. *Forever Foreigners or Honorary Whites? The Asian Ethnic Experience Today.* New Brunswick, N.J.: Rutgers University Press.

Tyson, Karolyn, William Darity Jr., and Domini Castellino. 2003. "Breeding Animosity: The 'Burden Of Acting White' and Other Problems of Status Group Hierarchies in Schools." Unpublished paper, University of North Carolina, Chapel Hill.

U.S. Surgeon General. 1985. *Youth Violence: A Report of the Surgeon General.* http://www.surgeongeneral.gov/library/youthviolence/report.html.

Van Ausdale, Debra, and Joe R. Feagin. 2001. *The First R: How Children Learn Race and Racism.* Lanham, Md.: Rowman and Littlefield.

Wagner-Pacifici, Robin. 1994. *Discourse and Destruction.* Chicago: University of Chicago Press.

Wallace, Maurice. 2002. *Constructing the Black Masculine.* Durham, N.C.: Duke University Press.

Wallace, Michele. 1979. *Black Macho and the Myth of the Superwoman.* New York: Dial Press.

Waters, Mary. 2001. *Black Identities: West Indian Immigrant Dreams and American Realities.* Cambridge, Mass.: Harvard University Press.

———. 1990. *Ethnic Options.* Berkeley: University of California Press.

Weis, Lois, and Michelle Fine, eds. 2000. *Construction Sites: Excavating Race, Class, and Gender among Urban Youth*. New York: Teachers College Press.

Wells, Amy Stuart, and Irene Serna. 1996. "The Politics of Culture: Understanding Local and Political Resistance to Detracking in Racially Mixed Schools." *Harvard Educational Review* 66 (1): 93–118.

West, Kimberley C. 1994. "A Desegregation Tool That Backfired: Magnet Schools and Class Room Segregation." *Yale Law Journal* 103 (8): 2567–92.

White, Shane, and Graham White. 1998. *Stylin': African American Expressive Culture from Its Beginnings to the Zoot Suit*. Ithaca, N.Y.: Cornell University Press.

William T. Grant Foundation. 1988. *The Forgotten Half: Pathways to Success for America's Youth and Young Families*. Youth and America's Future. Washington, D.C.: William T. Grant Foundation Commission on Work, Family, and Citizenship.

Willis, Paul. 1977. *Learning to Labor: How Working Class Boys Get Working Class Jobs*. New York: Columbia University Press.

Wilson, William J. 1986. *The Truly Disadvantaged: The Inner City, the Underclass, and Public Policy*. Chicago: University of Chicago Press.

———. 1978. *The Declining Significance of Race*. Chicago: University of Chicago Press.

Winant, Howard. 2004. *The New Politics of Race: Globalism, Difference, Justice*. Minneapolis: University of Minnesota Press.

———. 2002. *The World Is a Ghetto*. New York: Basic Books.

———. 2001. "White Racial Projects." In *The Making and Unmaking of Whiteness*, edited by Brander Rasmussen et al., pp. 97–112. Durham, N.C.: Duke University Press.

———. 1994. *Racial Conditions: Politics, Theory, Comparisons*. Minneapolis: University of Minnesota Press.

Wolf, Eric, and Sydel Silberman. 2001. *Pathways of Power: Building an Anthropology of the Modern World*. Berkeley: University of California Press.

Wong, Daniel. 1999. *Race, Ethnicity, and Nationality in the United States: Toward the Twenty-first Century*. Boulder, Colo.: Westview Press.

Yon, Daniel. 2000. *Elusive Culture*. Albany: State University of New York Press.

Yong, Fung Lan, and Norma J. Ewing. 1992. "A Comparative Study of the Learning-Style Preferences among Gifted African-American, Mexican-American and American Born Chinese Middle-Grade Students." *Roeper Review* 14 (3): 120–23.

Zou, Yali, and Enrique T. Trueba. 1998. *Ethnic Identity and Power*. Albany: State University of New York Press.

CHAPTER 1

1. Chapter 3 combines two articles published earlier: "Whiteness as Giftedness—Racial Formation at an Urban High School," *Social Problems* 51 (2) and "Recreating Blackness-as-Failure through Educational Reform? A Case Study of a California Partnership Academy," *Equity & Excellence in Education* 38 (1). A portion of the ethnographic data used in Chapter 4 I also used in "'Hoes can be hoed out, players can be played out, but pimp is for life'—The Pimp as Strategy of Identity Formation," *Symbolic Interaction* 28 (3). A small portion of the descriptive data in Chapter 2 was used in "School Walls as Battle Grounds: Technologies of Power, Space, and Identity," *Paedagogica Historica* 41 (4/5).

2. To protect the anonymity of people, institutions, and locations, all names used in this book are pseudonyms.

3. In this book I treat Latino, Asian, Black, and White as racial categories. Because Asian and Latino are capitalized both as nouns and as adjectives, I also capitalize all similar occurrences of the racial signifiers Black and White, except when referring to established concepts (i.e., "acting white" hypothesis).

4. Using the term "racialized" foregrounds the notion that racial boundaries between groups of people are not natural or intrinsic, but are made. Racialization is a process accomplished through institutions, discourses, ideologies, and interactions (Dominguez 1994), and increasingly is a process to which Whites are also subjected (Hartigan 1999). See also Omi and Winant (1994) for a discussion of racialization.

5. See Bonilla-Silva (2003); and Fine, Weis, and Powell (1997).

6. See D'Souza (1995); and Wilson (1986, 1978).

7. See Kaiser Family Foundation (1995); Shipler (1998); Bush (2004).

8. See Gallagher (2004); Bonilla-Silva (2003); M. Brown (2003).

9. The most influential work on cultural explanations for student failure is that of John Ogbu and his collaborators, which has had a very large impact in schools of education as well as in anthropology (Ogbu 1994, 1987, 1985, 1974; Ogbu and Simons 1998). A more detailed discussion of John Ogbu's position is presented in Chapter 3. For the literature on learning styles, see Yong and Ewing (1992) and Dunn and Griggs (1998).

10. On discipline regimes, see A. Ferguson (2001); on course assignment, see Oakes (1985) and Oakes, Wells, and Jones (1997); on institutional neglect, see Metz (2003), A. Ferguson (2001), Lewis (2003), and Blau (2003).

11. Feagin, Hernan, and Batur (2001) define "sincere fictions" as whites' negative beliefs about others and positive beliefs about themselves: "The key to understanding white racism is to be found not only in what whites think of African Americans and other people of color but also in what whites think of themselves. It is on these fictions that white privilege is constructed as a taken-for-granted base of U.S. society" (p. 5).

12. California's Proposition 54 of 2003, the so-called racial privacy proposition, which was defeated on the 2003 ballot, would have pushed this agenda further. By barring state institutions from collecting racial data, it would have made it more difficult to document racial inequality.

13. See Gallagher (1995); Berbrier (1998, 2000); Brown (2003); and Bonilla-Silva (2003).

14. Orfield and Eaton (1996).

15. See, for example, the work by Ogbu and his colleagues: Ogbu (1991, 1994); Ogbu and Simons (1998); Gibson (1988); and A. Ferguson (2001).

16. See Perry (2002).

17. See, for example, Yon (2000); Lewis (2003); and Perry (2001, 2002).

18. As Eric Wolf put it: "There is too much talk about agency and resistance and too little attention to how groups mobilize, shape, and reshape cultural repertoires and are shaped by them in turn; how groups shape and reshape their self-images to elicit participation and commitment and are themselves shaped by these representations; how groups mobilize and deploy resources but do not do this 'just as they please,' either in the course of mobilization or in the wake of the effects they so create" (Wolf and Silberman 2001, pp. 410–11).

19. Lévi-Strauss coined the expression "good to think" in regard to totems, when he wrote: "We can understand, too, that natural species are chosen [as totems] not because they are 'good to eat' but because they are 'good to think'" (Lévi-Strauss 1963, p. 89).

20. See Bourdieu (1986).

21. Sandefur et al. (2001); Logan (2001).

22. On Irish immigrants identifying themslves as White, see Brodkin (1999) and Ignatiev (1995); on West Indians identifying themselves as Black, see Waters (2001).

23. On honorary Whites, see Tuan (1998); on Asians seeing themselves as White, see Gallagher (2004).

24. Erikson (1968); Davidson (1996).

25. Bourdieu and Passeron (1977); Bourdieu (1996, 1986); Willis (1977); Foley (1990).

26. See Orfield and Lee (2004).

27. See Fine and Weis (2003).

28. See, for example, Pizarro (2005); A. Ferguson (2001); Fordham (1996); Ogbu and Simons (1998); Louie (2004); Solomon (1992); Vigil (1997); Foley (1990); Schofield (1989).

29. For similar arguments see Almaguer (1994); Van Ausdale and Feagin (2000); Yon (2000); Sanjek (2000); Zou and Trueba (1998).

30. For research on whiteness and White privilege, see Gallagher (2004); Bonilla-Silva (2003); Doane and Bonilla-Silva (2003); Brown (2003); Fine and Weis (2003); Lewis (2003); Rothenberg (2002); Roediger (2002, 1991); Perry (2001, 2002); Lipsitz (1998); Hartigan (1999); Fine (1997); Mahoney (1995); Harris (1993); Frankenberg (1993).

31. Both Feagin (2001) and Ong (2003) argue that established patterns of relations between Blacks and Whites remain at the root of ethnoracial classifications evolving in the multiracial context.

32. See, for example, Mac An Ghaill (1996, 1994); Hall and Jefferson (1976); Schofield (1989); Yon (2000); Lewis (2003).

33. See Kozol (1991).

34. See Kimmel (2003).

35. See Staiger (2005c).

36. See Foucault (1977).

37. See Hartigan (1999); Perry (2002, 2001).

38. See Hall (1996).

39. See Lewis (2003, p. 188).

40. See Omi and Winant (1994).

41. See, for example, Almaguer (1994); Daniel (2002); Omi and Winant (1994); Winant (1994, 2001); Wong (1999).

42. See Hartigan (1999); Frankenberg (1993); Gregory (1998); Sanjek (2000).

43. See Omi and Winant (1994).

44. Bourdieu (1996).

45. Winant (2004).

46. See Barth (1994, 1969); Hall (1996).

47. Winant (2004).

48. See Hall (1996).

49. Ibid. The concept of discourse employed here follows Frankenberg (1993), who understands discourses as "historically constituted bodies of ideas providing conceptual frameworks for individuals, made material in the design

and creation of institutions and shaping daily practices, interpersonal interactions, and social relations" (p. 265).

50. See Perry (2002).

51. See, for example, Oliver and Shapiro (1995) for a discussion of generational wealth accumulation.

52. Connell (1995, p. 42).

53. Bhabha (1992); Butler (1993).

54. See Mac An Ghaill (1994); Connell (1995, 2000).

55. Herzfeld (1985).

56. Willis (1977).

57. Barth (1994, 1969).

58. See A. Ferguson (2001).

59. Connell (2000).

60. Bourgois (1996).

61. Fordham (1996).

CHAPTER 2

1. See Massey and Denton (1993); Logan (2001); Logan et al. (2004); Orfield and Eaton (1996); Logan (2004).

2. See Orfield and Eaton (1996); Wells (1996). While Orfield and Lee (2004) see a pattern of increasing resegregation since the 1990s, due to the retreat of the courts from desegregation rulings, Logan (2004) sees the main reason for the continued levels of segregation in the rates of immigration of Latinos and Asians, and in the natural growth of Latino, Asian, and Black populations, which are outpacing the White population.

3. See Massey and Denton (1993).

4. Davis (1990).

5. See Sanchez (1993).

6. See Ledgerwood, Ebihara, and Mortland (1994).

7. Ong (1996, 2003) has argued that through their structural position as dependent refugees and failure to demonstrate an "entrepreneurial self" that would signal their status as "worthy citizens," Cambodians have become increasingly racialized as Black in the bipolar racial mold of ethno-racial classifications in the United States.

8. Omi and Winant (1994) explain: "By 'trajectory' we mean the pattern of conflict and accommodation which takes shape over time between racially based social movements and the policies and programs of the state" (p.78).

9. See Goffman (1961).

10. This description of RHS is similar to and forms the basis of an article (Staiger 2005c) in which I explore the subject of school colors and their dynamic relationship to graffiti.

CHAPTER 3

1. GROW is a pseudonym for this magnet program.

2. See Losen and Orfield (2002); R. Ferguson (2001); Barnes (1997); Oakes, Wells, and Jones (1997); Solomon (1992); Oakes (1985).

3. Some administrators attributed this to the strong presence of Southeast Asians and the ongoing conflicts between Latinos and Southeast Asians. There were many more Southeast Asians than Latinos at Roosevelt High, and the school's representation of Latinos was skewed toward a middle-class background. These Latino students thus were less likely to be identified as gang members.

4. Omi and Winant (1994, p. 56, italics in original).

5. See, for example, Herrnstein and Murray's bestseller *The Bell Curve* (1994) and the work of its critics Jencks and Phillips (1998).

6. See Omi and Winant (1994).

7. Statistics on the racial makeup of NUSD (Newtown Unified School District) are based on "Racial and Ethnic Background of NUSD Students, Grades K–12," for 1966, 1970, 1980, 1992, 1996, and 2001, Newtown Unified School District (pseudonym).

8. This information was confirmed in a telephone interview on September 25, 2003, with the public relations officer for NUSD.

9. See Rossell (1990).

10. Margolin (1994); Peterson and Margolin (1997); Sapon-Shevin (1993, 1994); Stephens and Karnes (2000: 219ff).

11. On these problems, see Wells and Serna (1996); Sapon-Shevin (1993); and Lareau and McNamara Horvat (1999).

12. Bourdieu (1986) considers cultural capital to be different from economic and social capital. Cultural capital consists of knowledge (capital's "embodied state"), cultural goods (capital's "objectified state"), and educational credentials (capital's "institutionalized state") that can be converted into status and economic capital and is validated in schools.

13. Oakes (1985); Peterson and Margolin (1997).

14. According to "Racial and Ethnic Survey of Employees, 1993," Newtown Unified School District.

15. Margolin (1994); Oakes (1985); Persell (1977); Lucas and Berends (2002).

16. Oakes, Wells, and Jones (1997); Wells and Serna (1996).

17. Omi and Winant (1994, p. 60).

18. Fine (1997); Frankenberg (1993); Harris (1993); Hartigan (1999).

19. McIntosh (1990).

20. Berbrier (1998); Waters (1990).

21. For an exploration of racialization among Whites, see, for example, Hartigan (1999) and Kenny (2000).

22. Margolin (1994, p. 109).

23. See Tuan (1999).

24. See Margolin (1994).

25. Omi and Winant (1994, p. 123).

26. Berbrier (2000).

27. Perry (2001, p. 73).

28. Ibid. (p. 69).

29. Margolin (1994).

30. Perry (2001, p. 85).

31. See Rodriguez (2000); and Gracia and De Greiff (2000).

32. Waters (1990).

33. Feagin, Hernan, and Batur (2001).

34. Steele (1997).

35. The "riot" was a physical confrontation between Latino, African American, and Cambodian students and is described in detail in the following chapter.

36. Personal communication with the district's coordinator for grants and funding, Feb. 22, 1999.

37. Dayton et al. (1992, pp. 539–40).

38. California Partnership Academies, 1995/96 Evaluation Report, p. i.

39. See Popkewitz (1995).

40. Swadener and Lubeck (1995); Fine (1997); Cuban (1989).

41. Swadener (1995, p. 21).

42. See CAPA 1995/96 Evaluation Report, p. 1. In 1995 the program guidelines were revised to waive the requirement that one-third of the newly admitted students be at risk.

43. Kemple and Snipes (2000).

44. Personal communication with the district's coordinator for grants and funding, Feb. 22, 1999.

45. Hall and Jefferson (1976) write: "Negotiation, resistance, struggle: the relations between a subordinate and a dominant culture, wherever they fall within this spectrum, are always intensely active, always oppositional, in a structural sense. [. . .] Their outcome is not given but made. The subordinate class brings to

this 'theatre of struggle' a repertoire of strategies and responses—ways of coping as well as of resisting" (p. 44). See also Fordham (1996).

46. See Willis (1977).

47. Ogbu (1974, 1991); Fordham and Ogbu (1988); Fordham (1996). John Ogbu, one of the most widely influential anthropologists of education, explicitly addressed the role of schools on student outcomes in his early work (1974). However, by focusing on students' home culture and their culture's terms of incorporation as voluntary versus involuntary, he helped to channel the debate of racial inequality away from structural approaches.

48. Fordham writes: "In the dominant community, resistance as avoidance is defined by the larger society as failure or incompetence, the inability to acquire and display culturally appropriate skills. [. . .] Within the African American community, avoidance is constructed as willful rejection of whatever will validate the negative claims of the larger society regarding Black people's academic abilities. Thus constructed, avoidance enables its adherents to retain a sense of power and agency" (1996, p. 39).

49. Perry, Steel, and Hilliard (2003); Kozol (1991). Compare, for example, the work of Farkas, Lleras, and Maczuga (2002), who support the "acting white" hypothesis with that of Downey and Ainsworth-Darnell (2002) and A. Ferguson (2001), who find no support for this thesis.

50. See, for example, Foley (1991) and Slaughter-Defoe (1990).

51. Pollock (2004).

52. Tyson, Darity, and Castellino (2003) argue that those "high school enrollment patterns are to some extent predetermined by elementary school placement though. AG [academically and intellectually gifted] placement is an important gateway to placement/enrollment in rigorous courses at the middle and high school levels. [. . .] AG participation in the early grades builds the confidence and competence that better prepares students to succeed in upper-level classes" (p. 34). See also McNamara Horvat and Lewis (2003).

53. Gates (1987, p. 236).

54. Kochman (1969, p. 32).

55. Fordham (1996, p. 39).

56. Ibid. (pp. 235–36).

57. See Omi and Winant (1994, p. 60).

58. See Sapon-Shevin (1994).

59. See Omi and Winant (1994, pp. 78–79).

60. Ford et al. (2002); Margolin (1994).

61. Omi and Winant (1994, p. 86).

62. Rossell (1990).

63. Dayton et al. (1992).

CHAPTER 4

1. See Winant (1994).

2. See California Department of Education (2001). The accuracy of these data has been questioned because the schools and principals collecting these statistics have not always applied the criteria consistently.

3. See Phillips (1999).

4. See Staiger (2005c).

5. See Foley (1990).

6. See Gallagher (2003).

7. Hebdige's (1969) seminal work on subculture, which describes the rise of different youth cultures in postwar England, does not specifically address gender but is based on the understanding that subcultural style is primarily a male endeavor. Women might or might not be involved, but the men set the tone. For innovative work on women in male-dominated subcultures, see Leblanc (1999).

8. "I's" is a contraction of "it is."

9. See Fordham (1996).

10. See Staiger (2005b).

11. Laclau (1990, p. 33).

12. See Waters (1990).

13. Roediger (1991); Bell (1992); Harris (1993); Frankenberg (1993); Fine (1997); Mahoney (1995).

14. Later I found swastikas scratched on my car. I never found out whether my car was an arbitrary canvas for a White supremacist logo or a target because I was German.

15. See Lewis (2003); Blau (2003).

16. Henze et al. (2002).

17. It is also interesting to compare the racial consequences of Proposition 187 with the rise in hate crimes after Germany's reunification, which profoundly reorganized German identities. While West Germans often treated East Germans as second-class citizens, the victims of reunification were Turks and others, such as asylum-seekers from Africa, who did not fit the phenotypical image of a German.

18. Omi and Winant (1994, p. 59).

CHAPTER 5

1. Did girls get involved in fights more easily because they were *less* likely to be in gangs, and thus were also less fearful of retaliation and large-scale ramifications? Were they freer to lash out on their own because they did not need to wait for orders from someone higher up in the hierarchy? Or were girls just more "noticeable" when they fought because they are usually considered less aggressive than boys?

2. Although men are more likely to perpetrate violence than women, conclusive evidence about gender and violence in school does not exist since school crime statistics are not broken down by gender; and gender is never the explicit focus of school violence (Henze et al. 2002; California Department of Education 2001; U.S. Surgeon General 2003).

3. Garbarino (1999).

4. Messerschmidt (2000, 1993). The implicit assumption of RHS's administration was that violence was committed mainly by boys, with girls possibly being instigators but not political players or architects of racial conflict. The school's take is echoed in the research on adolescents and gender violence, which portrays girls primarily as victims of male sexual objectification (see, for example Eder, Evans, and Parker 1995), but rarely as agents of aggressions (Devine 1996). Similarly, in research on gangs, girls are often portrayed as pale imitations of or auxiliaries to male gangs (Chesney-Lind and Hagedorn 1999), although new evidence from Newtown suggests that girl gangs are becoming more prominent and girls are now leading in arrests for gang-related crimes. But in the way adolescents narrated and conceptualized race and racial conflict, the role of girls in instigating and perpetrating violence was not a subject of their analysis.

5. Connell (2000).

6. Gilmore (1991), for example, describes the performance of masculinity in relation to women as "inseminator, provider, and protector"; and Kimmel, in his earlier years argued that "one cannot understand the social construction of either masculinity or femininity without reference to the other" (Kimmel 1987, p. 12).

7. Kimmel (1996, p. 7).

8. Kimmel (2003); see also Foley (1990); Eder (1993).

9. Connell (1995, p. 37).

10. See also Connell (2000); Butler (1993). The relationship of masculinity to collective identity is also evident in Mosse's (1985) analysis of German fascism, where he shows the link between German nationalism and its glorification of Aryan masculinity and vilification of Jewish sexuality; and in Spackman's (1996) analysis of Italian fascism, where she argues, "virility is not simply one of many

fascist qualities, but rather the cults of youth, of duty, of sacrifice and heroic virtues, of strength and stamina, of obedience and authority, and of physical strength and sexual potency that characterize fascism are all inflections of that master term, virility"(p. xii). In the colonial context, Sinha (1995) argues that British colonial administrators produced the concept of Bengali men as "effeminate," and that the concept of the "manly Englishman" himself was a product of Britain's colonization of Bengalis.

11. Herzfeld (1985, pp. 10–11).
12. Eng (2001).
13. See Duras (1985).
14. Kim (1982).
15. Hwang (1989, p. 83), cited in Eng (2001, p. 1). See also note 10, above.
16. Gutmann (1996).
17. Chan (2001).
18. Gutmann (1996), Kimmel (1996), Connell (1995, 2000, 2002).
19. Butler (1993).
20. Kimmel and Ferber (2003).
21. See Bedermann (1995).
22. Omi and Winant (1994, p. 68).
23. Barth (1994, 1969).
24. Hall (1996).
25. Winant argues for an analysis of the meso-level processes to better understand the bidirectional links between micro- and macro-level phenomena of racial formation. He writes: "Here civil society and state institutions interact; here collective forms of agency operate; here movements and states shape each other" (Winant 2004, p. 202). This captures what happens on a previously neglected level at which racial formation occurs, but still considers the state to be a more critical variable than school-yard masculinities seem to warrant.
26. Barth (1994, p. 17).
27. Ibid. (p. 16).
28. Herzfeld (1985).
29. Willis (1977).
30. For oppositional identity see A. Ferguson (2001) and Fordham (1996); for subcultures as solutions to conflicts see Hall and Jefferson (1976).
31. See, for example, Hall (1996).
32. Barth (1994).
33. Barth (1994, p. 16).
34. Herzfeld (1985).
35. See Pratt (1987).

36. See Barth (1994); Connell (1995).

37. See Frankenberg (1993). See also discussion of discourse on page 1 and in note 49 to Chapter 1.

38. Pratt (1987, p. 60), cited in Wagner-Pacifici (1994, pp. 2–3).

39. See, for example, Hartigan (1999).

40. Choosing what some might consider a "hegemonic" Black group such as Ben's peer group to compare with the "marginalized" White peers of the surrealists could seem to be a skewed selection likely to reproduce stereotypes about "predatory" Black masculinity, hegemonic White masculinity, and the "softer" masculinity of Asians and Latinos, as one anonymous reviewer suggested. One might ask whether the Trojans, the mostly White fraternity, would not make a better comparison with Ben's clique and thus provide a more balanced representation of racialized masculinities.

As mentioned earlier, my choice of peer groups was representative of the racial distribution among the educational tiers. The Trojans, for example, were far less concentrated in the gifted program than in the next lower tier, a much more racially integrated program. Many students were disgusted with the Trojans, and officially, the school did not allow fraternities. Seen in this context, it is hard to regard them as a more representative or hegemonic version of White masculinity. In contrast, although the White peer group I chose identified themselves as outsiders or outcasts, they were much more similar to their peers in the gifted program than the Trojans. In regard to Ben's clique, it is equally wrong to regard them as a more mainstream group of African Americans. Ben's clique was not into sports, they did not particularly care for rap music, and they distanced themselves entirely from gangs, to name just three characteristics commonly associated with Black masculinity. Yet their discourse of racialized masculinity reflects a familiarity with and use of African American folklore that operates at the interface of Black-White relations (see Staiger 2005b).

41. See Kochman (1972), White and White (1998), and Folb (1980) for analyses of style and styling in African American cultures.

42. See Spiegler (1996) about the marketing strategy of Tommy Hilfiger. To gain entrance to a wide suburban consumer market, Hilfiger first marketed his products to rappers and "hip" inner-city youth, on the assumption that this would give his style urban authenticity and thus make it more desirable to affluent White suburban consumers.

43. California Department of Education (1995b).

44. See White and White (1998), who argue that styling is a form of Black resistance going back to slavery.

45. Based on this research and overlapping with this chapter in regard to the

pimp persona, I have developed the idea of the pimp as a strategy of racial identity formation (see Staiger 2005b).

46. Pimp, player, and hustler are idioms associated with verbal traditions in urban Black folklore (Kochman 1972; Folb 1980) and are also frequently used in rap. Both pimp and player have as their core dynamic a discourse of an exploitative, heterosexual relationship, which has been described for several urban settings (Major 1994; Anderson 1990; Labov et al. 1981; Folb 1980; Liebow 1967). "Both men and women brag about how they are exploiting the other sex. Men not only in terms of sex, but also in terms of money" (Liebow 1967, p. 116). According to Folb (1980), and Major (1994), pimp and player have multiple meanings and are linked to a larger set of related terms. Both stand for exploiting a relationship for material resources.

47. "Playing on somebody" and "pimping" in this sense are considered identical (Folb 1980; Nightingale 1993). Labov et al. (1981) report the ubiquity of the personas of pimp and hustler in toasts, a verbal art form characteristic of urban Philadelphia, Oakland, and Harlem, and provide an extensive bibliography on the persona of the pimp (including Iceberg Slim 1987; Heard 1968; Cayton 1965; C. Brown 1965). For an analysis of how my selective focus on "girls" rather than "parents" as financiers of Ben's life style at the beginning of this interview set the stage for his subsequent presentation of self, see Staiger 2005b.

48. "Mack" could be derived from "mack," which Fab 5 Freddy (1992) traces back to British dandies called macaronies, a term and posture that was picked up by Black pimps in the 1950s. It connotes someone with a flamboyant lifestyle supported by women, or generally, someone who is in control of a situation with his wits as the chief tool. Folb explains mack as "seductive, manipulative talk aimed at winning favor with a member of the opposite sex" (Folb 1980, p. 245).

49. On men using women as status symbols, see Kimmel: "Women themselves often serve as a kind of currency that men use to improve their ranking with other men" Kimmel (1996, p. 7). Nightingale (1993, p. 162) describes how a rapper was ridiculed by women for admitting that he gave his girlfriend a lot of expensive gifts.

50. Majors and Billson (1992, p. 70).

51. Mancini (1981, p. 23), cited in Majors and Billson (1992, pp. 71–72).

52. White and White (1998).

53. Majors and Billson (1992, p. 71). robin d. g. kelley makes a similar argument about the meaning of style in regard to the zoot suit during World War II: "Seeing oneself and others 'dressed up' was enormously important in terms of constructing a collective identity based on something other than wage work, presenting a public challenge to the dominant stereotypes of the Black body, and reinforcing a sense of dignity that was perpetually being assaulted" (1997, p. 238).

54. See Iceberg Slim (1987); kelley (1996); Ice T (1994); Quinn (2000); Staiger (2005b).

55. White and White (1998).

56. See Staiger (2005b).

57. A "road dog" is a close friend or buddy. The image of the dog is a widespread icon for males in the inner city. The term road dog also identifies the domain of the street as one's legitimate territory. The rap artist Snoop Dogg plays on this word in a myriad of ways in his lyrics to the CD "Doggy Style."

58. Names such as Babe G and Li'l Monster indicate an association with gangs. Note also the references to being small in Cambodian gang names.

59. See Hewitt (1986).

60. Incidentally, the emphasis on nonviolent Buddhism on the one hand and soldiering and warfare on the other was widespread among Mickey and his friends. Mickey and many of his friends wore gold necklaces with jade Buddhas as protection, particularly in their confrontations with Mexicans.

61. Ledgerwood et al. (1994) and Chandler (1983) have noted that among Cambodians vertical patron-client relations have more social power than horizontal relations between equals. This might play a role in the racial politics between African Americans and Cambodians here as well.

62. Two-tone skinheads are skinheads who are antiracist.

63. CLA stands for Coalition of Latin Americans and is also a pseudonym.

64. OG stands for Old Gangster.

65. "Being from somewhere" means being from a gang.

66. Staiger (2005b).

67. This discussion of the different groups' codes of masculinity, of being good at being a man, illustrates how in order to create spaces to perform dominance, peer groups collectively negotiate their locations in the educational and peer culture racial hierarchies. Because different peer groups within a racial group often share similar social locations, the masculinity codes these peer groups developed were often not limited to their own cliques. Race, then, is a critical element in a peer group's formation of masculine ethos, but race does not determine which masculine ethos a peer group will embrace.

68. Perry (2002, pp. 129, 186).

CONCLUSION

1. Bradburd (1998); Buroway (1991).

2. See Staiger (2004).

3. Schofield (1989); Fine (1997); Lipman (1998); Metz (2003); Lewis (2003).

4. Steele (1997).

5. See Cross (2003); Donovan and Cross (2002); and Harris and Ford (1999).

6. Winant (2004) has deferred the micro-structural aspects of racial forma-tion to symbolic interactionist frameworks and concepts. Seeking to explain some of the identity strategies described in Chapter 5, I have argued for moving from a symbolic interactionist framework to the broader and more inclusive conceptualization offered by Denzin (2003, 2001) and Hall (1996), because these allow for taking into account the collective imaginings and histories, transgres-sive identities, and discursive memories that are part of how collective identities are formed and expressed. See Staiger (2005b).

7. Hall (1996); see also Barth (1994, 1969).

8. See, e.g., Hall and Jefferson (1976); Barth (1969); MacLeod (1995).

9. Connell (1995, 2000); Kimmel (1996).

10. Lopez and Espiritu (1990).

11. Omi and Winant argue, "Members of subordinate racial groups, when faced with racist practices such as exclusion or discrimination, are frequently forced to band together in order to defend their interests. [. . .] Such 'strategic es-sentialism' should not, however, be simply equated with the essentialism prac-ticed by dominant groups, nor should it prevent the interrogation of internal group differences" (Omi and Winant 1994, p. 72).

12. McAdam (1988).

ABI (Agriculture, Business, and Industry)
Academy, 36, 63, 101, 104
academies, 36, 37, 56, 59, 62, 87; racial
breakdown of, 36. *See also* California
Partnership Academies (CAPA)
"acting white," 69–71, 72–74, 75, 77–78,
95, 203n49. *See also* Fordham, Signithia
adolescence: identity formation and, 9; socialization and, 9; studies of, 9
affirmative action, 5, 49, 50, 61, 114
African American peer group (Ben's
group), 119–133; and African American
culture, 132; composition of, 119–120;
on love, 130; and male-male relations,
132; and masculinity, 119–133; performance of dominance, 132, 170; pimp,
meaning of, 123; pimping, 123–133; racial boundary, style as 132; representa-
tiveness of, 207n40; selection of, 118;
and styling, 119–122, 124, 132, 134;
Whites, positioning towards, 133. *See
also* Ben; Jorge; Latasha; Ryan; Steve;
Sylvie
African Americans, 1–2, 15, 16, 22, *23fig*,
25–26, 28–29, 38, 39–40, 49–51, 58,
59, 62–81, 91–95, 119–133, 136, 137,
142, 145, 154, 157, 159, 161, 163–169,
170, 179, 181, 203n48; and affirmative
action, 50; and Dawgs, 94; as dominant,
91–92; and gangs, 2, 94; and gender segregation, 92; myth of, as intellectually
inferior, 24; pimp and player, role of,
133; and Proposition 187, 87, 88, 108,
109, 151; and sports, 50; and style, 91–
95, 119–122

African Americans and gifted program(s):
distribution of, in 44, 47–48; gifted, 48;
about giftedness, 60; about GROW, 58;
GROW students sheltered from, 52; percentage of, in gifted programs in Newtown, *42fig*; and testing for giftedness, 40
African Americans and BusTech, 62–81;
and "acting white," 70, 72–74, 95; as "at
risk" students, 39, 78; and "Black fictive
kinship," 15, 69, 74; as high achievers,
74–78; as low achievers, 74–78; overrepresented in CAPA, 64, 66; and resistance, 74; and signifying, 71–72. *See also*
Fordham, Signithia
African Americans and interracial relations: about Asians, 93–95; compared to
Cambodians, 28; discrimination of, 25;
dominance over Latinos, 94; history of,
in School District, 39–41; Latinos,
about, 88; location in school yard, 34,
91; in Newtown, 29; perceptions of
about racial groups, 55; and racial
boundaries, 92, 95; and racial conflict,
30; racist leaflet against, 31; residential
segregation of, 25–26, 29, 35; tensions
among Latinos, and Cambodians, 2; relations between Whites and, 31–32
African Americans and RHS: and educational programs, 38; distribution of, in
GROW, RHS, and district, 44; numbers
of, overestimated, 91; population of, 22;
position in school yard hierarchy, 91;
about RHS, 59; teachers' views of, 92;
underrepresented in top tier programs,
38

154, 155; and non-violence, 155; and personal space, 155; on race, 155; on romance, 156; on Samoans, 155; and style, 155; and self-defense, 155; on social network, 153; and tree group, 153; on Whites, 155

"ethnic mens," 1, 2, 97, 98, 136, 138, 180

ethnography, 3, 15–17, 173; and collective processes, 173; of Crete Villagers, 113 ; at RHS, 15–17. *See also* fieldwork; Herzfeld, Michael

ethos of masculinity, 19, 127, 209n67. *See also* masculinity, ethos of

Eva (Latino peer group), 146, 147, 148; and style, 147, 149; and Alpha Girls (sorority), 147

Feagin, Joe, 198n11

fieldnotes, 8–10, 36, 62–63, 68

fieldwork, 15–17

Fordham, Signithia, "acting white" hypothesis of, 70, 75, 203n48

Gallagher, Charles, 91

gangs, 2; African American, 85, 89, 94, 95; Cambodian, 86, 96, 133–142, 144; and crime statistics, 85; Dawgs, 85, 94; and fraternities, 86; and graffiti, 85–86; and hand signs, 86; identification of, 85; Islanders (Samoan), 150–151; Locos, 89, 138; Latino, 85, 89, 94; Mexican, 85, 89, 96, 138, 140; Mob, 94, 135; in Newtown, 85–86; paraphernalia, 85; at RHS, 84–86; and Samoans, 86; school, 95; and school administrators, 85; and school police, 85; and taggers, 85–86; White Supremacists, 85. *See also* Asian Deuces; Asian Posse; Dawgs; race and gangs

Gary (African American student): about GROW, 58

Gender and violence, 205n4

graffiti, 85–86; and school painter, 85–86

"gifted", 4, 18

gifted label, 37–61; and admission criteria for GROW, 41

giftedness, 36–61; and Advanced Placement (AP) exams, 42–43; African Americans, and knowledge about, 40; and capital, cultural, 40–41; and GROW web page, 42; identification of, 176; and immigrants, 40; Latinos, and knowledge about, 40; and maturity, 51; and minority groups, 176; in Newtown, historically, 39–41, 42 *fig.*; racial label, functioning as, 176; and SAT Scores, 43, 43t; and teachers' referrals, 40; testing for, 40, 50; and victimization, 50

giftedness and whiteness (*see also*), 36–61: "naturalized whiteness", 50; and entitlements, 40–41. *See also* whiteness as giftedness

gifted program (*see* GROW)

gifted programs in NUSD, 41: White students in, 42fig; Black students in, 42fig; Hispanic students in, 42fig; Asian students in, 42fig

girls and racial violence at RHS, 111

graffiti, 85–86; and school painter, 85–86

GROW and desegregation: racial breakdown of, 36–37, 44fig; tool, for 37

GROW Program, 36–61; and admission criteria, 41; and affirmative action, 50; and Asians, 50; and class, 55–56; classrooms of, 37; counselor, 48; director of, 37, 50; and discipline, 52–53; as entitlement, 53; and Filipinos, 50; and Latinos, 50; and Mexican Americans, 50; parents 47; and "protection," 47–49, 52; public image of, 37, 48, as racial project, 38–61; students, 36–61; teachers, critical of,

administration, supported by, 149; and school yard hierarchy, 157; selection criteria for, 118; and self-defense, 152; spokesperson for, 147, 148, 149, 150, 152, 157; and style, 146–7, 148; and superiority, moral, 152, 154; and "tree pride", 149; and undocumented immigrants, 147; and Whites, 146, 157; and women, 156. *See also* Enrique; Eva; Marco; Jorge (White peer group); Pablo

"learning styles," 4

Lewis, Amanda, 10

Li'l Monster (Cambodian peer group): 97, 133, 136; on girlfriend, 144; on male honor, 138; on "putting in work," 140; on race war, 138; on skin color, 97–98; on tattoos, 136

"lines of contest," 172; in peer groups, 117; style as, 122; White peer groups', 169

Mack Daddy, 134, 134, 142, 143, 144, 145, 157, 208n48; Babe G as, 134, 143–144; Mickey on, 143

magnet program. *See* GROW; gifted program

Malcolm X, 36

Marco (Latino peer group), 146, 147, 149: on African Americans, 150; and class, 147; and diversification, 154; as Latino spokesperson, 147, 150; parents, connection to 150; politics, insights into, 150; and Proposition 187, 149–150; on riot, 149; and style, 146, 147; and Surrealists, 154; and Trojans, 147, 149; and Whites, 147

masculinity, 8, 12, 14–15, 19; "arenas of convergence," 116; and "being good at being a man", 14, 116, 117; and boundary formation, 115–116; and boxing match, 114–115; code of, 15; and collective identity, 205n10; and common sense notions of race, 115; competition over, 15, 114; as dominance, performance of, 13, 14–15, 19, 117, 133, 154, 162, 165, 170, 171, 209n67; as eghoismos, 113; ethos of, 19, 113, as homosocial enactment, 112; and identity, collective, 115; making of, 117, 118; "market place of," 15; niches of, 15, 114–115, 117; and playing the dozens, 116; as poetry, improvised, 116; as power and domination, 114; and race, 14–15; racialized culture as toolbox for, 179; and racial formation, 14, 112,115; and racial others, 117; and racial project, 115; and schools, 112; as strategic identities, 179; studies of, 14; and state, 115; subordinate, 116; talk about, 118; and White privilege, 114; and women, 179; and Yemeni men, 116. *See also* "arenas of convergence"; "axis of masculinity"; code of masculinity; Connell, Robert; ethos of masculinity; "good at being a man"; Herzfeld, Michael; racialized masculinity

Max (African American student), on style, 92

Mr. McAuley, 68, 71–73, 75, 119, 120, 121, 122, 123, 127, 131, 134

mediation meeting/sessions, 86

Mexican Americans, 1, 2, 20, 21, 23, 26, 28; experience of, 28; Mexican American community, 26. *See also* Latinos

Mexicans. *See* Latinos

Mexican American. *See* Latinos

methodology, 15–17; ethnography, 173; peer groups, selection of, 118–119, 207n40; and representation, 117–119

Mickey (Cambodian peer group), 1, 75, 97, 209n60; and Asian Posse, 134, 139; and Ben's clique 134; BusTech, role in, 133–

race: as axis of power, 19; code words for, 4; common sense notions of, 3; consciousness, 5; and domination, 180; empowerment, as tool for, 180; and gangs, 84–86; geography of, 22; and intelligence, 39; and "looks", 9; and masculinity, 19,178–180; and oppression, 180; and political mobilization, 180; "race riot," 18; and relationality, 174; and white privilege, 174

race making, 6, 19; as agency, individual, 178; collective, 82–110; domains of, 181; 10; as political process, 178; mechanics of, 4,8; in schools, 10. *See also* Lewis, Amanda

race and masculinity, 178–180; as boundary maintenance, 178; as collective identifications, 178; in multiracial context, 178; as relational constructions, 178; similarities of, 178

race matrix, 117–172

race politics, 82–110

"race riot" at RHS, 82–84; and gender, 111; and girls, 83, 111; interpretation of, 111; Latinas, role of, in, 83; as male affair, 111; and masculinity, 111

racial categories, 2, 3, 36–37

racial classification system: of school district, 84; of students, 84

racial conflict, 2, 3, 8; between Cambodians and Latinos, 82–83; and gender, 83, 111; and Latinos, 82–83; between Latinos and African Americans, 82–83; and masculinity, 111; solutions to, 107

racial differences, learning of, 3–6

racial discourse, 84

racial distribution, pattern of, 173

racial diversity, 40

racial equity, 7

racial exclusion, 4

racial formation, x, 7, 11–12, 14, 17, 22, 29–30, 38–39; 176–178, 182; and agency, 177; and BusTech, 62–81; and common sense, 46; definition of, 38; and experiences, everyday, 176; and GROW, 60–61; limitations of, 177–178; and racialized masculinities, 177; and riot, 177; and state, 177. *See also* racial project

racial geography, 8–10, 18

racial hierarchy, 83–84, 182

racial identity, 2, 6, 15; and educational programs, 174–175; forging of, 180; and identifying racial others, 108; and multiracial settings, 180; and political mobilization, 180; as political strategy, 108; as scale specific, 108; and Proposition 187, 181

racial inequality 4, 7, 18, 29, 38, 61, 64, 175

racial integration, alleged, 174

racialization, 3, 5, 110, 197n4; and post-civil-rights era 177; spatial, 22; of Whites, 202n21

racialized masculinity, 113–115; African American peer group's, 119–133; Asians as "castrated race," 113; Cambodian peer group's, 133–146; and common sense notions of race, 115; and dominance, performance of, 170–171; and frame of reference, 170–171; idioms and performances, 170; Latino peer group's, 145–157; and lines of contest, 117, 148, 169, 171; and male-collective arena, 113, 152, 154, 165, 169, 172, 205n10; male-female arena, 113, 169; male-male arena, 113, 122, 123, 127, 142, 154, 155; in popular culture, 113; stereotypes about, 113; symbol(s) of identity, 117, 122, 130, 135, 157, 163, 169; White peer group's, 157–169. *See also* African American peer